MAPPING THE
TRAIL OF A CRIME

MAPPING THE TRAIL OF A CRIME

How experts use geographic profiling to solve the world's most notorious cases

GORDON KERR

The Reader's Digest Association, Inc.
New York/Montreal/Sydney/London/Singapore/Mumbai

Produced by Amber Books Ltd
Bradley's Close
74–77 White Lion Street
London, N1 9PF
United Kingdom
www.amberbooks.co.uk

FOR AMBER BOOKS
Project Editor Michael Spilling
Design Joe Conneally
Design Manager Mark Batley
Picture Research Terry Forshaw

FOR READER'S DIGEST
U.S. Project Editor Siobhan Sullivan
Canadian Project Manager Pamela Johnson
Australian Project Editor Annette Sayers
Project Designer Jennifer Tokarski
Senior Art Director George McKeon
Executive Editor, Trade Publishing Dolores York
Associate Publisher, Trade Publishing Rosanne McManus
President and Publisher, Trade Publishing Harold Clarke

Library of Congress Cataloging in Publication Data

Kerr, Gordon.
  Mapping the trial of a crime : how experts use geographic profiling to solve
the world's most notorious cases / Gordon Kerr.
      p. cm.
  ISBN 978-1-60652-328-5
  1. Geographical offender profiling. 2. Criminal
investigation--Psychological aspects. I. Title

HV8073.5.K47 2011
363.25--dc22

                      2011012275

We are committed to both the quality of our products and the service we provide to our customers.
We value your comments, so please feel free to contact us:
          The Reader's Digest Association, Inc.
          Adult Trade Publishing
          44 S. Broadway
          White Plains, NY 10601

For more Reader's Digest products and information,
visit our website:
              www.rd.com (in the United States)
              www.readersdigest.ca (in Canada)
              www.readersdigest.co.uk (in the UK)
              www.rdasia.com (in Asia)
              www.readersdigest.com.au (in Australia)
              www.readersdigest.com.nz (in New Zealand)

Printed in Singapore

1 3 5 7 9 10 8 6 4 2

CONTENTS

Introduction

Getting away with murder is a little more difficult these days than it used to be. Investigators today are armed with an astonishing array of sophisticated tools, from the most basic forensic method of fingerprinting to DNA sampling and highly scientific, analytical methods that harness the processing power of computers and involve specially developed software programs.

Analyzing the geography of a crime has always been an important step in an investigation. Geographic profiling was developed from research carried out in 1989 at Simon Fraser University's School of Criminology in Vancouver, British Columbia, and it is the science of this analysis. Prioritizing information from investigations involving an astonishing amount of data, geographic profiling uses the locations of an apparently connected series of crimes to estimate the likeliest location of an offender's

Kenneth Bianchi, one of the Hillside Stranglers, testifies in court against his cousin and accomplice Angelo Buono, Jr.

residence or base. Most often used in cases of murder or rape, it helps investigators to analyze the locations of a series of crimes and to apprehend the perpetrator.

Mental Maps

Kenneth Bianchi and Angelo Buono, Jr.—the duo collectively known as the Hillside Strangler—murdered 10 women in the Los Angeles and Bellingham, Washington, areas between October 1977 and January 1979. Little did they know that each time they claimed a victim and dumped the body, they were creating a pattern, a pattern that pointed to Buono's upholstery store as the most likely location in which the victims had died.

In our daily lives we follow patterns. Using experience and familiarity with the locations of the things we need for our daily lives, we create mental maps of our surroundings, maps that provide us with information about our individual access routes to things we need such as food, school, work, and transport.

A killer's mental map will take into account the things he needs—convenience and ease of access and escape for a murder or body-dump site, for example. A criminal's primary residence is usually integral to his mental map. As we take the easiest routes to and from the places where the things we need are located, we establish patterns. It was the recognition of such a pattern that contributed to the conviction of Bianchi and Buono.

> "The secret of geographical profiling is to go beyond the dots on the map to understand the significance of the places the offender is choosing and the meaning to him of the journey he is making."
> —DAVID CANTER, *MAPPING MURDER: THE SECRETS OF GEOGRAPHIC PROFILING*

The Geographic Profile

To create a useable geographic profile, a number of elements have to be taken into consideration. The distance an offender is prepared to travel to commit his crimes is critical and, of course, this means that the method of transportation to the crime scene is also important. The less freedom an offender has—the need to travel by public transport, for instance—the more restricted his area of operation will be. Attractiveness of an area or a road must also be taken into account. It could be that a particular road is, for instance, more isolated. Or, remarkable though it sounds, it might even be that one road just looks prettier to the offender than others. This is, of course, entirely subjective and dependent upon individual cases and offenders.

Familiarity with roads is crucial, however, and will lead to an offender traveling greater distances to kill or to dispose of his victims' bodies. Needless to say, the greater the distance, the more difficult the investigation will prove for detectives. As has already been said, the ease of flight from a murder or burial site is also a vital element of the analysis; as noted criminologists Holmes and Holmes have pointed out, "the existence of multiple routes of travel will enhance the capability of the offender to find and flee desirable locations."

The Geography of Crime

The important role that geography plays in the psychology of the criminal has long been known to investigators. In days gone by, as we have often seen on television or in movies, detectives would use thumbtacks pinned in a wall map of a city or an area to record the pattern of a particular series of crimes.

> "By establishing the probability of the offender residing in various areas and displaying those results on a map, police efforts to apprehend criminals can be assisted. This ... allows police departments to focus their investigative efforts [and] geographically prioritize suspects...."
>
> —DR. KIM ROSSMO

Over the last 30 years, however, computer technology has allowed profilers to develop complex methodologies that now help police forces around the world to understand the movements of criminals and analyze their behavior.

The first police department to apply the techniques of geographic profiling to its investigative methods was the Vancouver Police Department, led by Dr. Kim Rossmo, in 1995. The method is now widely used, helping to solve crimes in other parts of Canada, the United

Dr. Kim Rossmo: The "Hound of the Data Points"

In the late 1980s, Dr. Rossmo was a Canadian police detective with the Vancouver Police Department. He was working toward a Ph.D in criminology, studying under respected professors, Paul and Patricia Brantingham, at Simon Fraser University's School of Criminology. The Brantinghams had recently developed a theory of crime prevention that would predict where crimes were likely to occur. Dr. Rossmo adapted their theory, turning it on its head by using the locations of a crime to discover where an offender might actually live. He calculated that behind the apparently random locations of crimes, there was often a pattern. After all, he reasoned, each of our lives follows a pattern. We each spend the majority of our time in a particular geographical area, making the same journeys, walking the same streets, and always following the shortest routes home. He applied such thinking to criminals, reasoning that they were more likely to want to operate in the areas they knew best, where they did not look out of place, and importantly, where they knew the escape routes. He came up with a mathematical equation that expressed this theory and from that developed a software program known as Rigel.

Dr. Rossmo's theory and its supporting data would prove to be one of the most important developments in crime solving in recent times. His theory would help law enforcement agencies around the world, including Scotland Yard, the FBI, and the Bureau of Alcohol, Tobacco, Firearms and Explosives (ATF). Since the 1990s, Dr. Rossmo has been involved in investigating more than 200 cases of serial crime around the world, amounting to some 3,000 individual crimes.

As well as bringing his expertise to the investigation of criminal cases, Dr. Rossmo now heads the Texas Center for Geospatial Intelligence and Investigation (GII). There he uses his methodology in projects that now range from border control to counter-terrorism. By analyzing locations where people illegally cross from Mexico into the United States, he is able to predict other likely locations, allowing authorities to deploy resources more effectively. The GII project also analyzes the geospatial relationships among the locations of terrorist cells, safe houses, weapon stores, and pay phones in order to establish patterns to enable predictions of other likely sites.

Dr. Kim Rossmo, the former Vancouver policeman who developed geographic profiling into a useable theory.

States, the United Kingdom, as well as in many other countries.

Now there are several different types of specialized computer programs that enable specially trained police officers to apply the principles of geographic profiling to the cases they are investigating. Among these are Dr. Rossmo's Rigel software, the spatial statistics program, CrimeStat, developed by Ned Levine, and the geographic prioritization software package, DRAGNET, created by British investigative psychologist David Canter.

Into these systems are fed crime location addresses, murder sites, and burial sites. After analyzing this information, the system outputs what is known as a jeopardy surface—a three-dimensional probability pattern—that contains height and color probability codes. When superimposed on a map of an area in which a series of crimes have been committed, the jeopardy surface gives an indication of the areas in which an offender is most likely to live and, therefore, the areas in which investigators should focus their efforts. The savings in time, cost, and resources are considerable.

Dr. Rossmo, a pioneer of geographic profiling who studied under Canadian environmental criminologists Patricia and Paul Brantingham, has said: "By establishing the probability of the offender residing in various areas and displaying those results on a map, police efforts to apprehend criminals can be assisted. This information allows police departments to focus their investigative efforts, geographically prioritize suspects, and concentrate patrol efforts in those zones where the criminal predator is likely to be

Rigel software presents information in a 2-D and 3-D result value map, showing the most probable locations of criminal activity.

active." The approach offers practical assistance that can be invaluable during an investigation.

Those Who Chase the Hunters

It was the intriguing case of the Beltway Sniper that first brought geographic profiling to the attention of the media and the public. The authorities were baffled by a series of apparently random sniper incidents in the Washington, D.C., area that claimed the lives of 10 people and, with their investigation floundering, they enlisted Dr. Rossmo to apply his geographic profiling techniques in the investigation. His work did not lead to the ultimate location of the perpetrators—an eagle-eyed truck driver at a rest stop on Interstate 70, north of Washington, did that— but, as Montgomery County, Maryland, Assistant Police Chief Deirdre Walker, was quick to point out, "the joint task force found geographic profiling a helpful and useful tool in strategically prioritizing information in this investigation." So, as well as helping to catch perpetrators,

Witness for the prosecution Christine Goodwin points to a diagram of the crime scenes as she testifies during the trial of John Allen Muhammad in a Virginia courtroom, 2003.

Dr. Rossmo's Formula

Dr. Rossmo devised a mathematical algorithm based upon observations about criminal behavior that estimates where a criminal lives. In considering the formula, it is essential to bear in mind first that a serial criminal will have a buffer zone near his home in which he will not commit a crime. Second, beyond that zone, the frequency of crime locations decreases as the distance from the criminal's residence increases.

The diagram shows a number of streets in an anonymous town. Overlaid on top of it is a grid whose origin lies at the bottom left-hand corner. Similar crimes have been committed at

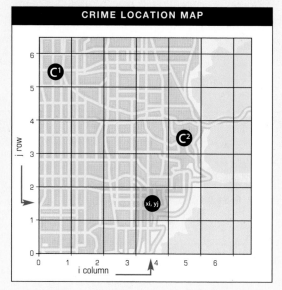

locations marked on the grid as C1, which has the coordinates on the grid of 1.6, and C2, which has the coordinates 5.4. Dr. Rossmo's formula calculates the probability that the criminal lives in the square that is shaded blue and has the coordinates xi, yj. The part of the formula that measures the distance of the target square from the site of the crime is as follows:

$$([x_i - x_n] + [y_j - y_n]\ldots(1)$$

Dr. Rossmo's formula attempts to predict not where a criminal might offend, but in which quadrant a criminal is most likely to live. The farther a quadrant is from the offender's home, the lower the probability. This also applies to the buffer zone around the criminal's home, where the offender is unlikely to commit a crime. Outside the buffer zone, therefore, the probabilities should decrease with distance from home but increase in the vicinity of a crime site.

Interestingly scientists have also found that Dr. Rossmo's formula works for certain types of predatory animals. When the theory was applied to a series of shark attacks against seals, results demonstrated that the sharks actually waited in one specific area, stalking their prey prior to the attacks.

geographic profiling can provide strategic benefits to police forces involved in complex investigations.

The Beltway Sniper case may not have been solved by Dr. Rossmo's methods, but many other cases have been. Not that it has been easy to convince others of the effectiveness of his Rigel software. In order to provide evidence of how Rigel can work, in his doctoral dissertation, *Geographic Profiling: Target Patterns of Serial Murderers,* he applied the methodology to a number of notorious cases, including the Boston Strangler (Albert DeSalvo), Jeffrey Dahmer, Joel Rifkin, and Aileen Wuornos.

His theories were effectively demonstrated by the jeopardy surface maps produced by his computers. In every case, the location of the residence of the killer was scientifically predicted by Rigel. Since then, geographic profiling has been developed into a powerful investigative tool.

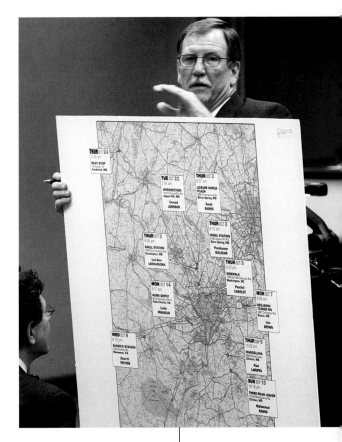

Prince William County Attorney Richard Conway holds a map of the Washington, D.C., area marked with locations of the shootings during the trial of John Allen Muhammad in Virginia Beach Circuit Court, November 10, 2003.

Learning from Crime

The cases in this book include a range of different types of serial criminals, mostly murderers. The book explores the geography of the murderers' actions, examining the decision making that went into the selection of a place to commit a crime or dispose of a victim. The book also looks at the investigative methods used by police to understand perpetrators' choices and actions, which often helped them prioritize their efforts, resulting in a more focused investigation and a better use of resources. Today geographic profiling is an invaluable weapon in the increasingly sophisticated fight against crime.

Deadly Visitors

Terrorizing people in their own homes, they are the most feared of killers, creating terror in communities because of the apparently random nature of their attacks. No one knows where or when they are going to strike next, a lack of certainty that adds endless complexity to any police investigation. Some, such as Albert DeSalvo, the Boston Strangler, charmed their way into women's homes. Others, such as Richard "the Night Stalker" Ramirez, arrived uninvited through a loose window or a carelessly unlocked door.

- Albert DeSalvo
- Wayne Clifford Boden
- Richard Trenton Chase
- Richard Ramirez

Richard Ramirez, found guilty of the deaths of 13 people, sneers during a court appearance.

Albert DeSalvo: The Boston Strangler

No one has ever stood trial for the 13 murders that terrorized the city of Boston between June 1962 and January 1964, but at least 11 of them were popularly attributed to the character described in the media as "the Boston Strangler." The police, however, were less sure that the killings were, in fact, the work of one individual. In October 1964, a serial sex offender in police custody, Albert DeSalvo, confessed to the 13 murders, but there is debate to this day as to whether he actually was the man they called "the Boston Strangler."

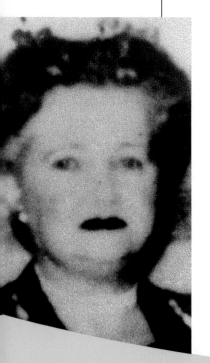

This police file photo shows one of the Boston Strangler's early victims, Jane Sullivan (67), who was murdered on August 20, 1962.

Knock, Knock, Who's There?

The Boston Strangler was a poacher, a killer who commuted into Boston and cruised seedy areas, searching for buildings that were home to students, transients, or the elderly. These areas were familiar to him because he had traveled to them when he had been employed as a maintenance man for a construction company. They were also far enough away from where he lived in Malden, north of Boston, to make it more difficult for investigators to catch him.

His first victim was 55-year-old church-going divorcée Anna Slesers, at her home in Back Bay. A blow to her head with a blunt instrument had disabled her. Her legs were spread grotesquely before the Strangler sexually assaulted her with an unknown object. He left her with the belt of her bathrobe, which he had used to strangle her, tied in an elaborate bow around her neck. The apartment had been ransacked, and detectives surmised that she had interrupted a burglar who had become aroused when he saw her in her bathrobe and had then killed her to prevent her from identifying him. They ignored the fact, however, that nothing had been stolen.

Two weeks later he knocked on the door of 85-year-old Mary Mullen's apartment, telling her that he had been sent to carry out

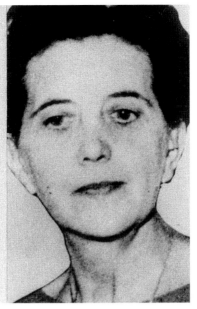

Other poor victims of the Boston Strangler included (from left) Sophie Clark (21), strangled with her own nylon stockings and found on December 5, 1962; and Anna E. Slesers (55), who was killed with the belt of her bathrobe and found on June 14, 1962.

some repairs. When he wrapped his arm around her throat to strangle her, she suddenly died, probably of heart failure. Until he confessed this after his arrest, it was thought she had died of natural causes.

Another Slaying

On June 30, 1962 he killed again. Nina Nichols, 68, was on the phone with a friend in her apartment in Boston's Brighton area when her doorbell rang. She hung up, first promising she would call back. She never did. She was found in the same position as Anna Slesers. She had been sexually assaulted with a wine bottle and strangled with her nylon stockings, which were tied in a fancy bow around her neck. Again her apartment had been ransacked.

The Strangler then traveled to the suburb of Lynn, 15 miles (24 km) north of Boston, and sometime between 8:00 P.M. and 10:00 P.M., he strangled 65-year-old Helen Blake, a retired nurse. She was found two days later, face down on her bed, strangled and—like the others—sexually assaulted with an object, her stockings and bra tied around her neck.

A City Held Hostage

Police leave was canceled as panic began to grip the city. Women living alone were warned not to open their doors. In each of the three cases so far, there had been no visible sign of forced entry, and it appeared that the victims had willingly opened their doors to the assailant. They either knew the man, or he provided a sufficiently plausible reason for them to open their doors to him.

The warnings failed to get through to everyone though. Ida Irga, 75, was found strangled on August 21, having been killed two days earlier. She wore a delicately knotted pillowcase around her neck, and her legs had been balanced on two chairs, grotesquely exposing her private parts. Sixty-seven-year-old Jane Sullivan had been dead for 10 days by the time she was discovered, kneeling in her bathtub, the customary bow tied at her neck.

Newsmen and photographers gather in front of the entrance to the third-floor apartment in Boston where Mary A. Sullivan (19) was found strangled to death on January 4, 1964.

A Couple of Younger Victims

An interval of three months allowed people to dare hope that it was all over, but on December 5, he killed again. This time, however, he changed tactics. His victim was a younger woman, 21-year-old African-American student Sophie Clark, who lived in Back Bay. Police found semen, which made this attack different from the others. She had not been raped, but her slip had been tied around her neck.

While questioning neighbors, the police learned that a woman had opened her door to a man who had knocked earlier that afternoon, claiming to have been sent to paint her apartment. When she mentioned that her husband was asleep in the next room, the man took off. She provided a description. He was between 25 and 30 years old, of average height, and with honey-colored hair. The building superintendent confirmed that he had not sent anyone to paint her apartment. She had spoken to the Boston Strangler.

Patricia Bissette, 23, failed to turn up for work on December 31. Her boss found her in bed in her Back Bay apartment. Her stockings were arrayed around her neck, and she had been raped.

In March 1963 the Strangler reverted to killing older women, traveling 25 miles (40 km) north of Boston to Lawrence where he beat and strangled 68-year-old Mary Brown. Two months later on May 8, 23-year-old Beverly Samans failed to turn up for choir practice. She had been killed not by strangulation but by four stab wounds to the throat. She had the Boston Strangler trademark bow around her neck but had not been sexually assaulted. There was no semen found in the apartment.

Three months passed before the Boston Strangler killed again. On September 8 Evelyn Corbin, 58, was found in Salem, strangled with her stockings. Semen-stained tissues were scattered around the room. Joanne Graf, age 23, was also brutally raped and strangled on November 23. Several people spoke of someone sneaking around in the building's corridors that day.

The next murder was particularly brutal. Nineteen-year-old Mary Sullivan was found with semen dripping from her mouth and a broom-handle rammed into her vagina. She was the Boston Strangler's last victim.

DeSalvo was recaptured following his escape from the Bridgewater State Hospital, Massachusetts, in February 1967. His escape with fellow inmates triggered a massive manhunt.

The Measuring Man

Albert DeSalvo had been in trouble with the police before. In March 1961 he was arrested for breaking into a house but confessed while in custody to being a sex attacker known as "the Measuring Man."

He would introduce himself to attractive young women at their doors as a representative of a modeling agency. Telling them they could earn $40 an hour as models, he would ask if he could take their measurements. He would then take out a tape measure and record their measurements. He was sentenced to 18 months in prison but was released just two months before the Boston Strangler tied his first bow.

The Green Man

When the Boston Strangler stopped killing, another criminal emerged. "The Green Man," so-called because he wore green trousers, raped about 300 women across a vast area that took in Massachusetts, Connecticut, New Hampshire, and Rhode Island. He seemed everywhere: on one day he raped four women. He gained entry using a strip of plastic in the door lock and threatened his victims with a knife. He stripped them, caressed their bodies, and, if he judged that they "wanted him to," he raped them. Police were baffled until a detective, hearing a description of the Green Man, thought that he sounded just like the Measuring Man—Albert DeSalvo. DeSalvo was arrested on November 5, 1964, and committed to Bridgewater State Hospital.

It was there that he began to boast to another inmate, George Nassar, that he was the Boston Strangler. But he would never be brought before a court on those charges. Instead DeSalvo was convicted of the Green Man rapes and sentenced to permanent detention in Walpole State Prison where he was to receive psychiatric help.

On November 26, 1973, Albert DeSalvo was found dead in his cell, stabbed in the heart. No one was ever charged with his murder, and the motive remains unknown.

> "You're putting together so many different patterns that it's inconceivable behaviorally that all these could fit one individual."
>
> —FBI PROFILER ROBERT RESSLER ON THE BOSTON STRANGLER CASE

Was Albert DeSalvo the "Boston Strangler"?

No one was ever convicted of the murders and many suspect that Albert DeSalvo was not the perpetrator. For a start, the women killed by the Strangler were of varying ages and ethnic groups. Furthermore, the modus operandi often changed from murder to murder. Several experts have suggested that the killings were, in fact, the work of several people. Noted former FBI profiler, Robert Ressler, argues that, "you're putting together so many different patterns that it's inconceivable behaviorally that all these could fit one individual."

There were also a number of inconsistencies between DeSalvo's confessions and the crime scenes and circumstances of the murders. For example, he claimed to have strangled Mary Sullivan, the last victim, manually, but she was, in fact, strangled with a ligature. Most curious of all, however, is the fact that DeSalvo confessed to sexually assaulting Sullivan: Later DNA testing in 2001 showed the semenlike traces on her body did not match Albert DeSalvo's DNA.

Many have looked with suspicion upon George Nassar, the fellow inmate to whom DeSalvo initially confessed. Nassar is considered to be a misogynistic, psychopathic killer, a description never ascribed to DeSalvo. It has been suggested that Nassar provided DeSalvo with details of the murders so that DeSalvo could gain the notoriety he needed to be able to earn money to support his family while he was in prison. Nassar remains in prison maintaining that he had nothing to do with it. "I'm convicted under the table," he has said, "behind the scenes."

George Nassar (center) as he arrived for his arraignment on a charge of murdering Irvin Hilton in Andover, Massachussetts, September 29,1964.

Mapping the Crime

As the Boston Strangler, Albert DeSalvo was a killer who commuted from his home in Malden, to the north of Boston, to the areas where he murdered. As is often the case with serial criminals, he committed his crimes in places he knew, places his work as a construction company maintenance man had brought him on many occasions.

Case History: Albert DeSalvo

▶ **June 14, 1962** Anna Slesers (55) is strangled to death with a belt from her bathrobe.

▶ **June 28** Mary Mullen (85) dies from a heat attack after being attacked by DeSalvo.

▶ **June 30** Nina Nichols (68) is sexually molested and strangled to death with her own nylon stockings.

▶ **June 30** Helen Blake (65) is also molested and strangled to death with her own nylon stockings.

▶ **August 19** Ida Irga (75) is molested and strangled to death.

▶ **August 20** Jane Sullivan (67) is sexually molested and strangled to death with her own nylon stockings.

▶ **December 5** Sophie Clark (21) is strangled to death.

▶ **December 31** Patricia Bissette (23) is strangled to death with her own nylon stockings.

▶ **March 9, 1963** Mary Brown (68) is stabbed, strangled, and beaten to death.

▶ **May 6** Beverly Samans (23) is stabbed to death.

▶ **September 8** Evelyn Corbin (58) is sexually assaulted and strangled with her own nylon stockings.

▶ **November 23** Joanne Graf (23) is sexually assaulted and strangled.

▶ **January 4** Mary Sullivan (19) is sexually assaulted and strangled to

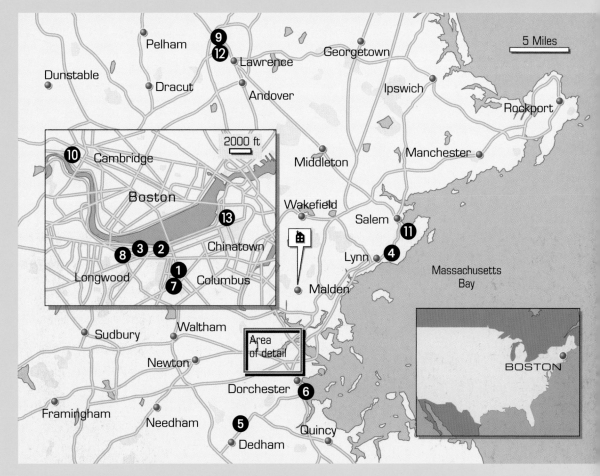

Locations of the Murders

1 **Back Bay**—Anna Slesers murdered, June 1962

2 **Back Bay**—Mary Mullen murdered, June 1962

3 **Greater Boston**—Nina Nichols murdered, June 1962

4 **Lynn**—Helen Blake murdered, June 1962

5 **West End**—Ida Irga murdered, August 1962

6 **Dorchester**—Jane Sullivan murdered, August 1962

7 **Back Bay**—Sophie Clark murdered, December 1962

8 **Back Bay**—Patricia Bissette murdered, December 1962

9 **Lawrence**—Mary Brown murdered, March 1963

10 **Cambridge**—Beverly Samans murdered, May 1963

11 **Salem**—Evelyn Corbin murdered, September 1963

12 **Lawrence**—Joanne Graf murdered, November 1963

13 **West End**—Mary Sullivan murdered, January 1964

Wayne Clifford Boden: Vampire Rapist

Like American serial killer Ted Bundy, Canadian killer Wayne Boden transported his murderous habits from one place to another. Bundy killed in several states, and Boden killed while he lived in Montreal, Quebec, and then also murdered after he had moved to Calgary, a city 2,500 miles (4,000 km) away in Alberta. His conviction also shared a similarity with that of Bundy. Both their trials featured vital odontological evidence in the form of bite marks that they left on their victims. This evidence was key in convincing jurors of their guilt.

From Male Model to Murderer

He was a good-looking man—a former male model, now working as a salesman—who seemed to have little trouble attracting women. He was also a sexual sadist, however, who savagely killed four women.

The first body was found on October 3, 1969. Twenty-year-old Shirley Audette had been raped and strangled, and her assailant had left savage bite marks on her breasts. Shirley had been treated for some time at the Douglas Hospital in Montreal for mental health problems and had moved into an apartment on Dorchester Boulevard in the center of the city with her boyfriend. In October 1969 her boyfriend was working the nightshift, and Shirley, now five months pregnant, was lonely and anxious about being left on her own overnight. In spite of this, she would sometimes sit outside the building on a fire escape in the early morning hours.

A Fatal Encounter. On one of those early mornings, Wayne Boden, living at the time in a nearby apartment, found Shirley sitting there. He talked to her, soothing her nerves a little, and at 3:00 A.M., she called her boyfriend and told him about the stranger she had met. However, when her boyfriend called back a couple of hours later to check on how she was, there was no answer. Shirley's body was found at the foot of the fire escape. She had been raped, but her body was fully dressed, and the absence of any blood or skin under her fingernails suggested that there had not been much of a struggle.

One sign of abuse that caught investigators' attention and would prove to be a lead worth noting—fierce-looking bite marks on her breasts.

"Getting Into Something Dangerous." One of Shirley's former boyfriends later told police that he believed she had become involved with a domineering, attractive man. Her friend said that he had gotten the impression from her that she may have been afraid of "getting into something dangerous." This phrasing, taken with some of the things that other women later said about Wayne Boden, caused investigators to speculate that the killer may have had a way with women through his good looks, charm, and assertive manner.

A Killer Named "Bill"

Five weeks later, on November 23, 1969, Boden met a young woman outside her place of work—the Charbonneau jewelry store in Place Ville Marie in Montreal. The two had made each other's acquaintance at one of the city's clubs, and 20-year-old Marielle Archambault was immediately attracted to the well-dressed, good-looking young man whom she introduced as "Bill" to her coworkers. They later told investigators that she seemed happy and somewhat smitten by this handsome stranger.

This police file **photograph** from 1972 shows a handcuffed Wayne Boden in custody in Montreal.

Another Victim. The next morning, Marielle failed to turn up for work, and as the morning wore on and she did not call in sick, her coworkers began to worry. Her boss eventually decided to go to her apartment at 3688 Ontario to see if she was OK. When there was no answer at her door, he alerted her landlady, and the two found her fully-clothed body on the couch in her living room. She had been asphyxiated. Like Shirley Audette, she had been raped, and on her breasts there were savage bite marks. There was some excitement when a crumpled photograph was discovered in the apartment. Marielle's colleagues thought that the man shown in the photo closely resembled "Bill." It was released to the media, but hopes of a major lead were dashed when it turned out that the man was actually Marielle's father.

The "Vampire Rapist" is Born. Again, strangely, there was no sign of a struggle. The room was neat, and Marielle was even reported to have looked serene. Investigators had to conclude that these victims had been happy in the company of their killer before he turned nasty. The media put it another way, claiming that he somehow entranced them, as a vampire did before sucking the blood of his victims. This, coupled with the bite marks, inevitably led to the murderer being dubbed the "Vampire Rapist."

The Final Victim in Montreal

At 8:15 P.M. on January 16, 1970, 24-year-old Jean Way's boyfriend, stockbroker Brian Caulfield, arrived at her apartment on Lincoln Avenue in downtown Montreal to pick her up for a date. When there was no answer to his knocks at her door, he went to a nearby bar before returning at 9:30 P.M. This time, there was still no answer to his knocking, but he discovered that her door was unlocked. Pushing the door open, he went in and found her naked on the bed, apparently asleep. When he tried to wake her, however, he realized that she was, in fact, dead. A gray-blue woolen belt, wrapped tightly around her neck, had been used to strangle her. With a shudder, he later realized that the killer had in all likelihood been in the apartment with her when he had first called.

A Desperate Struggle. Reports differ as to whether or not police found the customary bite marks, but this time they found fibers on her left hand, indicating that she had put up a desperate struggle. Even with this evidence, however, police were no closer to finding the "Vampire Rapist."

This latest killing created even more fear among the women of Montreal. Unknown to them, however, Jean Way would be Wayne Boden's final victim in their city. By 1971, he had moved to Calgary, where he would claim his fourth and final victim.

On to Calgary

Thirty-three-year-old Calgary high school teacher Elizabeth Porteous was reported missing from work on May 18, 1971. After her apartment manager

Forensic Odontology

Like fingerprints, our teeth possess many unique and identifying features. Most often, forensic dentists use these features to identify victims of accidents or violent crimes when the body is left unrecognizable in any other way. In the Boden case, bite marks on the dead women's bodies were the biggest clues that investigators had to work with in trying to identify the killer. After Boden's arrest in Calgary, investigators turned to a local orthodontist, Gordon Swann, to see if he could help them match Boden to the bite marks on the body of Elizabeth Porteous.

This subject was entirely new to Canadian forensic science, however, and there was little literature on the subject. Swann got in touch with the FBI in the United States, believing they were his best chance of getting some advice. Swann received a letter from then-FBI director J. Edgar Hoover, who put him in touch with a British orthodontist who had worked on 30 cases where bite marks had been vital evidence. Swann returned with the necessary information and identified no fewer than 29 points of similarity between a cast of Boden's teeth and the bite marks on the body of Elizabeth Porteous. After this evidence proved conclusive enough to convict Boden of Elizabeth's murder, he was also convicted of the three murders he had committed in Montreal.

was called, her body was discovered on the floor of her bedroom, the evidence of a violent struggle strewn around her. She had been raped and strangled, and her breasts were peppered with bite marks. Officers found a man's cufflink under her body.

The Return of "Bill." Investigations revealed that a couple of Elizabeth Porteous's colleagues recalled seeing her in a car, a blue Mercedes, with a young man on the night she died. Furthermore, they remembered that in one of the vehicle's windows there had been a distinctive bull-shaped decal, advertising beef. A friend of the dead woman informed police that Elizabeth had recently started dating a new boyfriend. He was described as a flashy dresser with neat, short hair. His name? "Bill."

The next day, a couple of patrol officers found the blue Mercedes and arrested its owner, Wayne Clifford Boden, as he was about to get into the car. He told investigators that he had been dating Porteous and that he had indeed been with her on the night she was killed. He also confirmed that a cufflink they had found under her body belonged to him, but he insisted that she had been fine when he had left her.

Forensic Dentistry Enters the Case. The cufflink was important, but, of course, the main pieces of evidence in this case were the bite marks found on the bodies of the dead women. A scientific analysis of the bite marks determined that they matched key features of Boden's teeth. This evidence, based on the application of forensic dentistry, also called forensic odontology, was sufficient to convince a jury of Boden's guilt in the rape and murder of Elizabeth Porteous.

Charges and Conviction in Montreal

Following his 1971 conviction and sentencing to life imprisonment in Calgary, and faced with similar forensic evidence, Boden confessed to the rapes and murders of the three women whose bodies had been found in Montreal in 1969 and 1970. In 1972, Boden was sentenced to three additional terms of life in prison. Similarities between the deaths of the three women killed in 1969–1970 and a 1968 killing—that of 21-year-old teacher Norma Vaillancourt—led many to believe that Boden must have been involved in that murder as well. But Boden denied any involvement in that killing, and in 1994 another man was convicted.

Escape and Death

Remarkably, Wayne Boden managed to escape, however briefly, from prison. In 1977, five years into his sentence, he applied for and succeeded in being granted an American Express credit card. While on a day pass from prison in Laval, Quebec, he managed to get away from his escorts and disappear through a door in a restroom. He was recaptured 36 hours later as he enjoyed lunch at the upscale Mount Royal Hotel in downtown Montreal. It is said that during his 36 hours of freedom, he hung out at least one bar, where he met and chatted with several young women. Boden's life sentence ended at Kingston Regional Hospital in Ontario on March 27, 2006, where he died of skin cancer.

Case History: Wayne Clifford Boden

▶ **October 3, 1969** Pregnant Shirley Audette (20) is raped and strangled on the fire escape outside her apartment complex on Dorchester Boulevard, Montreal.

▶ **November 23, 1969** Jewelry store worker Marielle Archambault (20) is raped and asphyxiated in her apartment on Ontario Street, Montreal.

▶ **January 16, 1970** After putting up a desperate struggle, Jean Way (24) is raped and strangled in her Lincoln Avenue apartment, Montreal.

▶ **May 18, 1971** Calgary high school teacher Elizabeth Porteous (33) is found raped and strangled with bite marks on her breast.

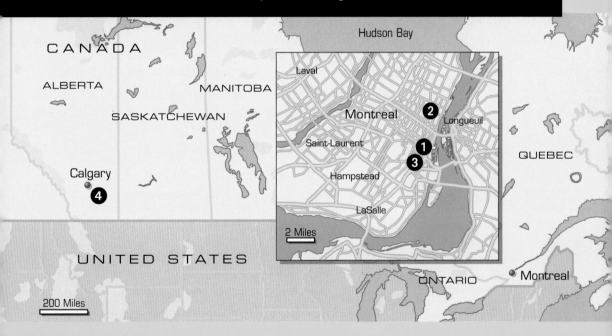

Locations of the Murders

❶ **Dorchester Boulevard, Montreal**—Shirley Audette killed, October 1969

❷ **Ontario Street, Montreal**—Marielle Archambault killed, November 1969

❸ **Lincoln Avenue, Montreal**—Jean Way killed, January 1970

❹ **Calgary**—Elizabeth Porteous killed, January 1971

Richard Trenton Chase:
The Vampire Killer

Former FBI criminologist and pioneer of criminal-profiling techniques, Robert Ressler coined the term *serial killer*. The police called him in after a seemingly motiveless murder in Sacramento, California, on January 23, 1978. The profile he provided of the probable killer was uncannily accurate. It led to the arrest of one of the scariest of all American serial killers, Richard Trenton Chase, "the Vampire Killer."

Birth of a Vampire

Born in 1950, Richard Trenton Chase displayed symptoms of the Macdonald Triad, the three behavioral characteristics associated with sociopathic behavior, as a child. He wet the bed, was a pyromaniac, and liked to torture animals. Chase claimed to have been beaten by his father and abused by his mother as a child. He was a heavy drinker and drug user, especially of the hallucinogen LSD.

Chase developed bizarre ideas, visiting a hospital on one occasion to complain that someone had stolen his pulmonary artery. He was also convinced that his blood was turning to powder and that he needed the blood of others to refresh it. To satisfy his grotesque need for blood, he killed six people in just one month—between December 26, 1977 and January 26, 1978.

Injected Himself with the Blood of a Rabbit

Chase had experimented with animals first. On one occasion he was admitted to the hospital with blood poisoning. Doctors found that he had injected himself with rabbit's blood. Following that incident, he was admitted to a mental hospital. There he drank the blood of birds that he had caught. He even drained blood from the therapy dog, an animal that was brought into the hospital to give comfort and affection to patients. He checked himself out of the hospital after just 72 hours and moved into

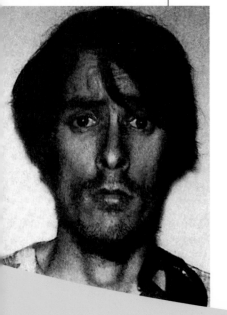

Richard Trenton Chase in one of the few existing police file photographs. His undernourished, unkempt, slovenly appearance fits well with Ressler's preliminary profile.

an apartment. In the privacy of his own place, he began eating animals raw, often putting their organs into a blender and mixing them with Coca-Cola. Before long, he was locked up again, diagnosed as schizophrenic, and given antipsychotic drugs.

Released into the custody of his mother in 1976, he was soon back in his own apartment, indulging in his old habits. Ominously, he was also buying guns and practicing with them.

Stuck in Sand. On August 3, 1977, police officers found his Ford Ranchero stuck in sand near Pyramid Lake in Nevada. Rifles lay on the seat, and blood was smeared on the inside of the vehicle's cab. In the back, they were startled to find a bucket of blood in which floated what looked like a liver. In the distance, they saw a figure. When they trained their binoculars on him, they discovered that Chase was naked. He tried to flee, but the police caught up with him. The liver, it turned out, was from a cow.

Police first encountered Chase at Pyramid Lake, Nevada, naked and with his abandoned car smeared with what turned out to be cow's blood.

Random Shots. Back in California, Chase graduated to more serious acts of violence. On December 27, 1977, he randomly fired a shot into the kitchen of a woman who lived just a few blocks away from him. Then on December 29, as he unloaded groceries from his car, Ambrose Griffin, 51, collapsed to the ground, dead. At first his wife thought that Griffin must have had a heart attack, but he had been shot. The next day, shell casings were found not far away. A 12-year-old boy also reported that a man had shot at him from a brown Pontiac TransAm that drove past him as he rode his bike. He described the shooter as being in his mid-20s with brown hair.

Madman on the Loose

On January 11, 1978, a tall, young man with unkempt hair walked up the path of Jeanne Layton's house. He tried her patio door, which was locked, and then attempted to open her windows, which were also firmly bolted shut. He stood staring at her, expressionless, before turning and walking off. Later that day, when Robert and Barbara Edwards started to bring their shopping bags into the house from their car, they were startled to see a figure jump out of their back window. Someone had broken in, ransacked their house, urinated in their bureau drawers, and defecated on one of their children's beds. It turned out to have been Richard Chase.

Mutilated and Drained of Blood

On January 21, truck driver David Wallin came home from work and was surprised to find his house in darkness. He was troubled by what appeared to be oil stains on the carpet and a bag of garbage lying on the floor. In the bedroom he found his wife.

Twenty-two-year-old Teresa Wallin, three months pregnant, lay on the bed, her breasts exposed and her trousers and underwear around her ankles. She had been shot three times, her left nipple had been sliced off, and her body had been cut open below the sternum, her spleen and intestines torn out, and other organs sliced and stabbed. Her kidneys had been cut out and then replaced. A yogurt carton stood beside her body, ringed with what appeared to be drying blood. The killer had drunk her blood from it.

> "...before this man had murdered, he had probably committed fetish burglaries in the area, and once he was caught, we'd be able to trace his crimes and difficulties back to his childhood."
>
> —FBI PROFILER ROBERT RESSLER'S PREDICTION ON THE VAMPIRE KILLER CASE

Profile of a Maniac

FBI criminologist and profiler Robert Ressler was called and delivered a profile that was uncannily fitting. He described a "white male, aged 25–27 years; thin, undernourished appearance . . ." He added that the killer's house would be a mess and that he would have a history of mental illness and drug use. He also described his car as "a wreck, with fast-food wrappers in the back, rust throughout." He concluded that the

Robert Ressler

Robert Ressler is the man who coined the term "serial killer" to describe a series of three or more murders committed over a period of more than 30 days by one person without a "cooling off" period between each murder; a serial killer has no other motive for murdering other than psychological gratification.

Ressler worked in the Federal Bureau of Investigation's Behavioral Sciences Unit at Quantico alongside John E. Douglas, interviewing serial killers in order to better understand their methods and motives. He was instrumental in establishing the Violent Criminal Apprehension Program (VI-CAP), that consists of a centralized, computerized database of unsolved murders that can be accessed by law enforcement agencies across the country to try to find similarities among crimes. This system was a response to the growing phenomenon of nomadic killers.

Ressler worked on many famous cases including that of Jeffrey Dahmer. His profile of Richard Chase, killer of six people between 1977 and 1978, was instrumental in

helping investigators catch and convict him. He accurately predicted not only personal character traits of the unsub in the case of the seemingly random brutal murders in East Sacramento, but also established that the killer undoubtedly lived locally.

FBI agent Robert Ressler was one of the earliest practitioners of psychological profiling of violent offenders.

killer lived nearby, reasoning that he would be too disorganized to drive a distance to commit such a crime and then get home again.

Ressler was accurately pointing out that the killer lived in the neighborhood. This critical description also fit an FBI axiom that the first of a series of crimes is almost always committed close to the perpetrator's home.

Vampire and Cannibal

Three days later, three bodies were discovered just 1 mile (1.6 km) away from the house of David and Teresa Wallin. Evelyn Miroth, her son Jason, and her friend Dan Meredith had all been shot dead. Like Teresa, Evelyn's body had been horribly mutilated; Beside her lay Jason, who had been shot twice from point-blank range. The killer had drunk Evelyn's blood.

Worse still, her 20-month-old nephew David, whom she had been babysitting, was missing. Chase had mutilated the child's body in the bathroom and had then taken it home with him. There, he cut off its head and ate some of its internal organs and parts of its brain.

The Bloodletting Ends

Chase was caught after a woman who had been to school with him ten years earlier became suspicious after bumping into him. She had been shocked at his appearance and informed police officers about him. When they picked him up, they found the gun used in the shootings and a wallet belonging to one of his victims.

As Robert Ressler had predicted, his car and house were a mess. The fridge contained body parts, and the food blender was streaked with blood and gore. A calendar on the wall was marked with "Today" on the dates of the killings. Chillingly, 44 other dates throughout the year were similarly marked.

Richard Trenton Chase was found guilty of six counts of murder and sentenced to die in the gas chamber at San Quentin State Prison in California. On December 26, 1980, he was found dead in his cell. He had committed suicide, using the antipsychotic pills that he had hoarded.

Case History: Richard Trenton Chase

▶ **August 3, 1977**   Police find Chase in the Nevada desert with a bucket of blood and a cow's liver.

▶ **December 27, 1977**   Chase fires shots into kitchen in East Sacramento.

▶ **December 29, 1977**   He shoots Ambrose Griffin (51) and kills him.

▶ **December 29, 1977**   He shoots at a boy (12) on a bike and misses as he drives past him.

▶ **January 21, 1978**   Chase kills and mutilates Teresa Wallin (22).

▶ **January 26, 1978**   He murders Dan Meredith (51), Jason Miroth (6), and Evelyn Miroth (38). He kills Evelyn's nephew David (20 months), takes him home, and eats parts of his body.

▶ **May 8, 1979**   Chase is found guilty of murder and sentenced to die.

▶ **December 26, 1980**   Prison guard finds Chase dead.

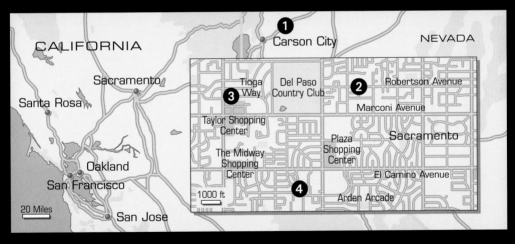

Locations of the Attacks

❶ Pyramid Lake, Nevada
—Found in desert, August 1977

❷ East Sacramento—Shoots Ambrose Griffin dead outside his house at 3734 Robertson Avenue and shoots, but misses, a 12-year-old boy, December 1977

❸ Sacramento—Kills and mutilates Teresa Wallin at 2630 Tioga Way, January 1978

❹ Sacramento—Kills four members of the Merdith family at 3207 Merrywood Drive, January 1978

Richard Ramirez: The Night Stalker

Throughout the summer of 1985, Californians slept with their windows firmly locked, despite the oppressive heat. They lived in fear of being awakened by a tall, thin Hispanic man with wavy, oily hair and halitosis, as a survivor of one of his attacks had described him. He raped and killed without mercy. Men, women, children—none were safe when the Night Stalker was on the prowl.

The Killer Who Loved Satan

The crimes committed by the Night Stalker seemed to be entirely random, although they most often took place close to freeway ramps. Strangely the houses where they took place all seemed to be single-story structures painted in light, pastel shades, especially yellow. Crucially, as geographic profiler Dr. Kim Rossmo later calculated, most of the murders were clustered close to the attacker's apartment in Los Angeles. He struck mostly to the northeast, although he did also kill in San Francisco. The attacker's methodology was usually the same, although the motive was often unclear. Sometimes he would rob the occupants, and sometimes he would leave empty-handed. He broke into houses, shot the male of the house in the head, and then he would beat and rape the female occupants, sometimes shooting them. He sometimes sexually assaulted male children. Obsessed with Satanism from an early age, he often made his victims tell him that they loved Satan. It seemed that he sought simply to terrify his victims and demonstrate his power over them.

His Satanic Majesty Requests

Richard Ramirez had been born Ricardo Leyva in El Paso in 1960. He developed into a loner, set apart by the epileptic seizures from which he suffered and a slim, girlish appearance for which he was bullied. He could not get out of Texas fast enough, and by 1978 he was living in Los Angeles. Little is known about his first few years there apart from a couple of run-ins with the police for drug possession and car theft. At some point he started housebreaking and, soon after, rape and murder.

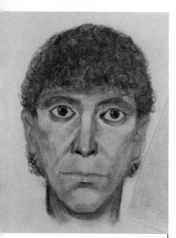

A police drawing of the murder suspect issued in 1985 bears a good likeness to Ramirez. A surviving victim, Lillian Doi, gave police the description on which this illustration was based.

His first victim was Jennie Vincow, murdered on June 28, 1984. After a night spent snorting cocaine, he removed a window screen and entered the 79-year-old's house in Glassell Park, Los Angeles, where he sexually assaulted her, stabbed her repeatedly, and slashed her throat, almost decapitating her. His horrific campaign of mayhem was underway. The following March he wounded a woman as she parked at her condo in Rosemead, Los Angeles, and shot dead another inside the building. Nearby, police found a baseball cap bearing the name of the rock band AC/DC. Ramirez was fixated with one of their songs, "Night Prowler." "Was that a noise outside your window? / What's that shadow on the blind? / As you lie there naked like a body in a tomb / suspended animation as I slip into your room…." That same night, Ramirez also shot 30-year-old Tsian-Lian Yu near her car.

Ramping Up the Horror

Ramirez's next murders a week later took him to a new level of barbarity. A 64-year-old pizzeria proprietor, Vincent Zazarra, was killed by a single shot to the head. His 44-year-old wife, Maxine, was stabbed repeatedly and shot. Ramirez had also horrifically gouged out her eyes, but thankfully after she was dead.

On May 14, 1985, he attacked William Doi, 66, and his wife, Lillian, 63, in their Monterey Park home in Los Angeles County. Ramirez shot William in the face and beat him into unconsciousness, then handcuffed and raped Lillian. William Doi lived long enough, however, to crawl to the phone and dial 911. He died en route to the hospital, but Lillian survived her ordeal and was able to provide police with a description.

In May, Ramirez attacked three women, killing two. He allowed one, Ruth Wilson, 41, to live, after she told him as he raped her that he must have had "a very unhappy life." He bludgeoned the other two, 83-year-old Malvia Keller and her invalid 80-year-old sister, Blanche Wolfe, to death with a hammer at their home in Monrovia in Los Angeles County. An inverted pentagram was drawn on Malvia's thigh, and one was sketched on the wall above Blanche's bed.

Ramirez as photographed at the San Quentin State Prison following his conviction.

More Killings. The attacks became increasingly frequent. Ramirez attacked Patty Higgins and cut her throat in Arcadia on June 27. On July 2, he returned to the same town in Los Angeles County to brutally kill 75-year-old Louise Cannon. Whitney Bennett, 16, survived a beating with a crowbar three days later, but on July 7, Ramirez beat 61-year-old Joyce Nelson to death in Monterey Park. That same night, he attacked Sophie Dickman, 63, in her home, raping her. Maxson Kneiding and his wife, Lela, both age 66, were shot and then mutilated with a machete in Glendale on July 20. The same night, he killed 31-year-old Chitat Assawahem and forced Assawahem's 29-year-old fiancée to perform oral sex on him. He also sexually assaulted the couple's 8-year-old son. On August 8, he killed Ahmed Zia, 35, and subjected his 28-year-old wife, Suu Kyi, to a sustained sexual assault.

Richard Ramirez flashes his left palm showing a pentagram, a symbol of satanic worship, while appearing in court. Ramirez pleaded not guilty to 68 counts of felony, including 13 murder charges.

A Change of Scenery

It is possible that the precautions people were taking in Los Angeles were frightening him off. His next attack took place in a San Francisco suburb where Peter and Barbara Pan were found in their blood-soaked bedroom. Peter had been shot, and Barbara had been raped, although she survived. A pentagram had been scrawled in lipstick on a wall as well as the words "Jack the Knife," which were taken from a song called "The Ripper" by British heavy metal band Judas Priest. The bullets recovered from Peter's body matched those used by the Night Stalker in Los Angeles, giving critical information to the police.

While the San Francisco Police Department threw its resources at solving the crime and preventing another, Ramirez struck in Los Angeles again. On August 24, he shot 29-year-old Bill Carns as he slept and then raped his fiancée at Mission Viejo, 50 miles (80 km) south of the city. However, she saw him drive off in an orange Toyota and memorized the license plate. The Toyota was found in a parking lot in the Los Angeles Rampart district. Police lifted a set of fingerprints and ran them through the Police

Mapping the Night Stalker

Apart from his excursion to San Francisco, where he killed Peter Pan and raped his wife on August 17, 1985, Ramirez's crimes can be seen from this graphic (created by criminologist Dr. Kim Rossmo several years after Ramirez was caught). It shows that the crimes were committed very close to home, in an arc mainly to the north of where Ramirez was living at the time. It was an area with which he was very familiar, a familiarity that would have enabled him to make a rapid escape if necessary. Short traveling time also afforded less opportunity for him to be apprehended as he made his way home from the scene of that night's crime. Had geographic profiling been as advanced then as it is today, would Ramirez have been apprehended earlier?

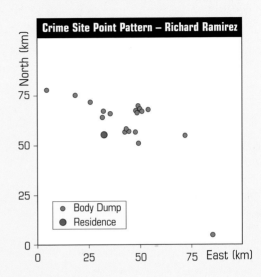

Department's newly installed, computerized fingerprint database system. A match was found—petty thief and burglar, Richard Ramirez.

In Hell with Satan

Ramirez's mug shot appeared in newspapers and on the television news, but he had been out of town and was unaware that he had at last been identified as the Night Stalker. Spotted in a store, he was forced to flee. Then, as he tried to steal a car to make his getaway, he was again identified. He was captured by Manuel Torres, husband of the car's owner, and a mob that had joined in the chase.

Following a circus of a trial in which Ramirez ranted at the courtroom, he was given 19 death sentences. "Dying doesn't scare me," he said. "I'll be in hell, with Satan." Until then, he will be incarcerated at San Quentin State Prison, California.

Case History: Richard Ramirez

▶ **June 28, 1984**   Ramirez slashes the throat of widow Jennie Vincow (79) in Glassell Park.

▶ **March 17, 1985**   He shoots Dayle Okazaki (34) dead in Rosemead but Maria Hernandez (20) survives.

▶ **March 17, 1985**   He drags Tsian-Lian Yu (30) from her car in Monterey Park and shoots her. She dies at the scene.

▶ **March 27, 1985**   He murders Vincent Zazzara (64) and his wife Maxine (44) in Whittier.

▶ **May 14, 1985**   William Doi (66) of Monterey Park is shot and later dies. Lillian Doi (63) is raped but survives.

▶ **May 29, 1985**   Ramirez bludgeons Malvia Keller and her sister Blanche Wolfe, both in their 80s, to death and scrawls satanic symbols in various places.

▶ **May 30, 1985**   Ruth Wilson (41) is raped, but she and her son are spared.

▶ **June 27, 1985**   Patty Higgins (32) is found with her throat slit.

▶ **July 2, 1985**   Mary Louise Cannon (75) is beaten in Arcadia and her throat slashed.

▶ **July 5, 1985**   Whitney Bennett (16) survives a beating with a tire iron in Sierra Madre.

▶ **July 7, 1985**   Ramirez beats Joyce Lucille Nelson (61) to death in Monterey Park.

▶ **July 7, 1985**   Sophie Dickman (63) is raped in Monterey Park but survives.

▶ **July 20, 1985**   Max and Lela Kneiding (both 66) of Glendale, are shot dead and mutilated with a machete. Ramirez murders Chitat Assawahem and forces his fiancée to perform oral sex.

▶ **August 8, 1985**   He murders Ahmed Zia (35) and rapes his wife Suu Kyi (28)

▶ **August 17, 1985**   Peter Pan (66) is shot dead in San Francisco; Barbara Pan (64) is left disabled.

▶ **August 24, 1985**   Ramirez shoots Bill Carns (29) dead and sexually assaults his 27-year-old fiancée.

▶ **September 20, 1989**   Ramírez is found guilty on multiple charges of murder, attempted murder, sexual assaults, and burglary.

Locations of the Attacks

1 **Glassell Park**—Jennie Vincow killed, June 1984

2 **Rosemead**—Dayle Okazaki shot dead, March 1985

3 **Monterey Park**—Tsian-Lian Yu shot dead, March 1985

4 **Whittier**—Vincent and Maxine Zazzara murdered, March 1985

5 **Monterey Park**—William Doi shot, May 1985

6 **Monrovia**—Malvia Keller and her sister Blanche Wolfe bludgeoned to death, May 1985

7 **Burbank**—Ruth Wilson raped, May 1985

8 **Arcadia**—Patty Higgins murdered, June 1985

9 **Arcadia**—Mary Louise Cannon murdered, July 1985

10 **Sierra Madre**—Whitney Bennett beaten but survived, July 1985

11 **Monterey Park**—Joyce Lucille Nelson beaten to death, July 1985

12 **Monterey Park**—Sophie Dickman raped but survived, July 1985

13 **Glendale**—Max and Lela Kneiding shot dead, Chitat Assawahem murdered, July 1985

14 **Diamond Bar**—Murders Ahmed Zia, August 1985

15 **Lake Merced**—Peter and Barbara Pan killed, August 1985

16 **Mission Viejo**—Shoots Bill Cairn, August 1985

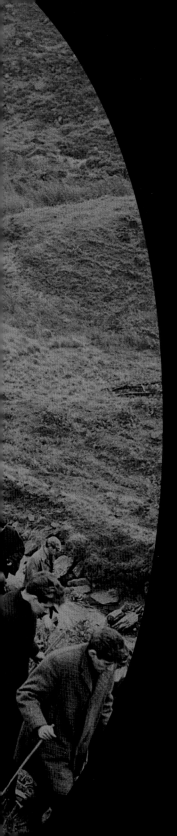

Home
and Away

For some killers—men such as Fred West, Jerry Brudos, and Paul Bernardo—home was merely a place that provided the opportunity to act out their most depraved fantasies far from the gaze of a shocked world.

- Ian Brady and Myra Hindley
- Jerry Brudos
- Fred and Rosemary West
- Kenneth Bianchi and Angelo Buono, Jr.
- Arthur Gary Bishop
- Jeffrey Dahmer
- Paul Bernardo and Karla Homolka
- Michael Fourniret
- Marc Dutroux

Volunteers search Saddleworth Moor for the remains of victims of Ian Brady and Myra Hindley, October 1965.

Ian Brady and Myra Hindley:
The Moors Murderers

Sometimes murderers' names become synonymous with a place. None have become more closely identified with the scene of their crimes than those of Ian Brady and Myra Hindley with Saddleworth Moor, the brooding stretch of South Pennine moorland that divides Oldham and Kirklees in the north of England. Situated close to where the pair lived at the time, Saddleworth Moor became notorious as the burial site of some of the victims of this serial-killing couple. When their horrific crimes were made public, the pair became the most hated people in Britain.

Police and volunteers scour an area of Saddleworth Moor, near Greenfield, UK, in October 1965, after reports that there were bodies buried on the moor. They are helped by an 11-year-old neighbor of Hindley and Brady, Pat Hodges, whom the couple had often taken onto the moor.

A Sullen, Aggressive Loner

In January 1961, Ian Brady was 21 years old and working as a stock clerk at Millwards, a chemical company in Manchester, England. It was something of a miracle that he was able to hold down a job at all, since his life had been a troubled one. Born in the rough Gorbals area of Glasgow, Scotland, he had been given up for adoption. He became an angry child, given to vicious tantrums during which he was known to bang his head on the floor in frustration. Other children at school avoided him as a result of his behavior, and he became a sullen, aggressive loner.

Between the ages of 13 and 16, Brady was often in trouble with the police, being arrested

three times for burglary. Finally, a judge, fed up with his criminal activities, presented him with a stark choice: Live with his birth mother in Manchester or face some form of imprisonment.

Brady chose Manchester, and, with the help of his stepfather, found work. Trouble was never far away, however, and he was sent to a young offenders' institution for two years for stealing from his employers. On his release, he received a job at Milwards Merchandising, and it was there that he attracted the attention of a young employee by the name of Myra Hindley.

A Good Girl

Hindley had been born in Gorton, an area in Manchester, and was brought up by her grandmother. She was a girl her grandmother could be proud of, one who could always be relied upon as a babysitter. Leaving school at the age of 15, she started working as a clerk at an electrical engineering firm. She was bored, however, and even called off an engagement when she was 17 because she balked at the dull married life that seemed to stretch in front of her. By 1961, when she started at Millwards, she was 21 and looking for excitement. She thought she had found it in the edgy and moody Ian Brady.

Taking an Interest in Nazism. The pair began to date, and Brady gradually inducted her into his world, which consisted mainly of a fascination for Adolf Hitler and Nazi Germany. He encouraged her to read Hitler's *Mein Kampf* and began to turn her into his ideal woman,

One of the many photographs of Myra Hindley taken by Ian Brady on Saddleworth Moor. Some photos show her with her dog, Puppet. In certain pictures, the dog is a puppy. Police had the dog examined to determine its age so that they could date the photographs in which he featured.

persuading her to bleach her hair blonde and wear leather skirts and high boots. He took pictures of them having sex and introduced her to sadomasochism. Before long, he had moved into the house she shared with her bedridden grandmother. Hindley would have done anything for Brady—and before long, she proved it.

Murder on the Moor

On the night of July 12, 1963, 16-year-old Pauline Reade was on her way to a dance in Manchester when she was approached by Hindley, who told her that she needed help finding an expensive glove she had lost on Saddleworth Moor. Pauline agreed to help, but as they started to look, Brady arrived on his motorcycle. He took the girl off to look for the glove, but instead raped her and then cut her throat. Brady and Hindley buried Pauline on the moor. A huge police hunt for Pauline was launched, but no trace of the girl or of the crime committed against her was found.

> "I have had enough. I want nothing, my objective is to die and release myself from this once and for all.... I'm eager to leave this cesspit in a coffin."
>
> —IAN BRADY'S REQUEST TO BE ALLOWED TO STARVE TO DEATH WAS DENIED IN 1999

More Murders. On November 23, Brady and Hindley struck again. Twelve-year-old John Kilbride had gone to the movies in the town of Ashton-under-Lyne with a friend and afterward had stayed at the market when his friend went home. There was sometimes money to be earned helping store owners clean up.

A short while later, Brady asked John to help him load his van, and he was never seen again. After sexually assaulting the boy and slitting his throat, Brady strangled him. Once again a massive police search failed to find any trace of him.

In June of the following year, 12-year-old Keith Bennett failed to arrive at his grandmother's house. She took care of Keith every Tuesday night while his mother went to play bingo. His grandmother thought that his mother had probably just decided to stay home and thought no more of it until the next morning, when her daughter arrived at her door to pick up Keith. Another huge and ultimately fruitless police search was launched for the boy, who by then had been strangled and buried on the moor.

New Depths of Depravity

On Boxing Day (a holiday celebrated in the United Kingdom on the day after Christmas), 1964, 10-year-old Lesley Ann Downey accompanied her brothers and some friends to the local fair. Soon, their money gone, her brothers left for home, but Lesley Ann decided to stay a little while longer. She was last seen by a school friend, standing by one of the rides. Thousands were questioned, exhaustive door-to-door inquiries were made, and posters and leaflets distributed, but again a child had vanished without a trace.

Recording the Horror. Brady and Hindley had, in fact, taken the frightened little girl home with them and in one of their bedrooms carried out unspeakable acts of cruelty before finally killing her. They stripped her, tied her up, and tortured her, recording her screams and photographing her. On the tapes, Brady can be heard threatening her.

A New Recruit

Brady now tried to draw Hindley's 17-year-old brother-in-law, David Smith, into his sick world. On the night of October 6, 1965, Smith came home with Hindley. As he stood in the kitchen, he heard a scream come from the living room. Hindley called for him, and he went into the living room to find Brady holding what Smith at first believed to be a life-sized doll. It was, however, the body of a young man, Edward Evans, a 17-year-old homosexual youth whom Brady had picked up in a Manchester pub earlier that evening.

A break in the case. Brady let Evans fall to the floor and then straddled him with an axe in his hand that he proceeded to bring down sickeningly

Ann Downey watches police search for her missing daughter, Lesley Ann, who had been tortured and murdered by Brady and Hindley. Ann Downey, who died in 1999, would later become a leading figure in the campaign to ensure that Hindley would never be released from prison.

on the young man's head several times. He then put a cord around Evans' neck, and muttering "You f**king dirty bastard," he pulled it tight until Evans's stopped moving and groaning.

Smith was horrified, while Brady and Hindley joked about what had just happened. They made him help them clean up the mess and tie up the body to be disposed of. After a sleepless night, Smith walked into a police station early the next morning and told the authorities what had happened.

Exposed by a Luggage Ticket

On October 7, Brady was arrested and confessed to Evans's murder. Hindley was arrested on October 11 as an accessory to the murder. Brady claimed that Evans had died during an argument. The police, however, found a luggage ticket, left between the pages of Myra Hindley's prayer book, that led them to a locker at a Manchester train station. There, they discovered a treasure trove of pornographic books and magazines. There were also pictures of Lesley Ann Downey, naked and gagged, as well as the audiotape of her torture. Throughout their trial, the pair said nothing, showing no remorse as the atrocities they had perpetrated were disclosed to a horrified courtroom and nation.

Ian Brady pictured with his dog at home.

On May 6, 1966, Brady and Hindley were found guilty and were sentenced to life imprisonment. They spent the first seven years writing to each other before Hindley suddenly stopped.

Partners No More. Hindley began to help police locate the victims' bodies, perhaps hoping that it would help her win an eventual release. Brady, however, constantly frustrated any progress she made in her case by revealing more details of her involvement in the murders. When Myra Hindley died at the age of 60 in 2002, 20 undertakers refused to handle her funeral.

CATCHEM

In the 1960s, which is when Brady and Hindley were committing their terrible crimes, computer technology and its value in police work were little more than a futuristic fantasy. One information-gathering-and-collating system that might have helped find the child killers sooner was developed in the mid-1980s by the police force in Derbyshire, England. Called the Centralized Analytical Team Collating Homicide Expertise and Management, it is better known by the acronym CATCHEM.

CATCHEM collates all available information on child homicide, stretching back to the 1960s. It was established in 1986 as part of the UK's national police effort to catch the child killer Robert Black. According to criminologist David Canter, CATCHEM has great potential both as a means of helping to solve crimes and as a research tool in understanding murder and why people commit murder.

Although CATCHEM is, of course, limited because it deals only with offenses committed against children, it innovatively records not just information about a current investigation, but also information from other investigations, including cases that have already been solved. As with all these systems, however, much of the decision making still has to be done by humans, whether in deciding which characteristics of a crime the authorities need to look at or in analyzing the results.

Despite these and other "human" components, the CATCHEM system has been useful in helping to find Robert Black and other child killers.

Frustrated Efforts to End it All. Ian Brady remains in Ashworth Psychiatric Hospital, the longest-serving prisoner in England and Wales. He went on a hunger strike in 1999, and when he was force-fed, he asked for a judicial review—a kind of appeal that would put an end to his being force-fed—saying, "I have had enough. I want nothing, my objective is to die and release myself from this once and for all.... I'm eager to leave this cesspit in a coffin." His request to be allowed to starve himself to death was denied, and he continues to be force-fed while serving his sentence.

Meanwhile, 46 years after Keith Bennett set out for his grandmother's house, his body still remains undiscovered in a shallow grave on Saddleworth Moor.

Mapping the Crime

Location was everything for Ian Brady and Myra Hindley. Saddleworth Moor was within an easy drive of their house at 16 Wardle Brook Avenue, southeast of the city of Manchester, and their first three victims were killed and buried there. Their bodies were found not far from each other on either side of the main A635 road that ran east from Ashton-under-Lyne across the moor. The convenience of this route can be seen in the case of John Kirkbride, abducted at Ashton-under-Lyne and assaulted and killed in the wilderness just a few miles up the road.

Case History: Ian Brady & Myra Hindley

▶ **July 12, 1963**
Pauline Reade (16) disappears on her way to a dance in Manchester. She is raped, murdered, and buried on Saddleworth Moor.

▶ **November 23, 1963**
John Kilbride (12) is abducted after Brady asks him to carry some boxes for him at the market in Ashton-under-Lyne. Brady sexually assaults him, cuts his throat, and then strangles him, possibly with a shoelace.

▶ **June 16, 1964**
Keith Bennett (12) disappears en route to his grandmother's house. He is sexually assaulted, strangled, and buried on the moor.

▶ **December 26, 1964**
Lesley Ann Downey (10) is abducted from a fairground and taken home by Brady and Hindley, where she is tortured and sexually assaulted before being strangled with a piece of string. She is buried on Saddleworth Moor.

▶ **October 6, 1965**
Edward Evans (17) is beaten with an axe and strangled at 16 Wardle Brook Avenue, the home of Brady and Hindley.

▶ **October 7, 1965**
Brady is arrested for Evans' murder. Hindley is arrested as an accessory to murder on October 11.

▶ **May 6, 1966**
Brady is convicted of murdering Kilbride, Downey, and Evans; Hindley is convicted of murdering Downey and Evans. Their sentence: life in prison.

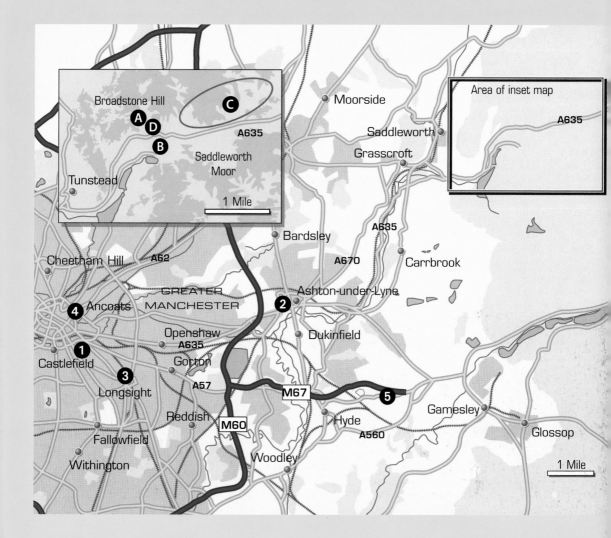

Locations of the Abductions, Murders, and Burial Places

① **Manchester**—Pauline Reade abducted and raped, murdered and then buried on the Saddleworth Moor **Ⓐ**, July 1963

② **Ashton-under-Lyne**—John Kilbride abducted, sexually assaulted then strangled to death and buried on Saddleworth Moor **Ⓑ**, November 1963

③ **Gorton**—Keith Bennett, sexually assaulted, strangled and then buried on Saddleworth Moor,

June 1964; **Ⓒ** (marked with a red oval) shows the area searched for his body

④ **Ancoats, Manchester**—Lesley Ann Downey abducted, tortured, then strangled and buried on Saddleworth Moor **Ⓓ**, December 1964

⑤ **Hattersley**—Edward Evans beaten and strangled, October 1965

Jerry Brudos: The Lust Killer

It was tiring, boring, and stressful, going from door to door trying to persuade reluctant people to buy sets of encyclopedias. But for Linda Slawson, it was a way to get a little extra money to help her through college. Sadly, she would never make it that far.

Vanished

On January 26, 1968, she was selling in a neighborhood in Salem, Oregon, when she disappeared. Her car was later discovered, but there was no sign of anything out of the usual. Nothing was missing, and there was no evidence of a struggle. As the weeks dragged on, nothing new turned up, and Linda gradually became just another missing-person statistic. She would not be the last, however. Her disappearance would be recalled the following year when more young women began to vanish.

Ten months later, on November 26, 1968, another young woman disappeared. Twenty-three-year-old Jan Whitney was driving home to spend Thanksgiving with her family, but she failed to reach her destination. Her car was found at a rest stop near Albany, Oregon. The vehicle was locked, but she was nowhere to be found. Like Linda Slawson, she had disappeared into thin air.

A Pattern Taking Shape? Four months passed before it happened again. On March 27, 1969, 19-year-old Karen Sprinker had been due to have lunch with her mother, but she failed to show up at the restaurant. Her car was found parked in a nearby garage, but she was nowhere to be seen. The only thing that seemed out of the ordinary in the area that day was the appearance of an odd, very large woman. One witness insisted it was a man wearing women's clothing.

Four weeks later, 22-year-old Linda Salee failed to turn up for a date with her boyfriend. She also failed to

Linda Salee, who disappeared from a shopping mall, had been accosted by Brudos, who flashed a fake police badge at her and told her she was being arrested for shoplifting.

arrive at work the next morning. She had last been seen in a shopping mall, where she had been buying a present for her boyfriend.

Investigators, understandably, began to wonder if these missing women could somehow be connected. It seemed odd that the women, including Linda Slawson in January 1968, had all disappeared toward the end of the month. Was it a coincidence? Or was there a reason? If there was a connection, it might mean that a serial killer was on the loose.

Grisly Find in the Long Tom River

Three weeks after Linda Salee had disappeared, a man fishing the Long Tom River, a tributary of the Willamette River, south of Corvallis, Oregon, found the decomposing body of a woman. She had been tied to a car transmission box, presumably to weigh her down. A nylon rope had been used to attach her to the transmission, and whoever had done it had used a particular kind of knot. Detectives noticed that copper wire had been used, and the way it was tied suggested that the killer possibly had an interest in electronics.

A handcuffed Jerry Brudos is taken into custody.

Gruesome Details Emerge. The victim had been strangled, but oddly, there were two puncture marks, one on each side of her body, below her armpits. Each was encircled by burned skin. The authorities identified her from dental records as Linda Salee. Investigators launched a search of the river and several days later found another corpse. This time, the woman, who was identified as Karen Sprinker, had been tied to an engine head. It was immediately obvious from the type of bindings and knots used that the same person who had killed Linda Salee was also responsible for Karen Sprinkler's murder. This time, however, he had removed her breasts, covering them with a black bra that was too big for her. It had been stuffed with paper towels, presumably to absorb the blood.

A Suspect. As part of their investigation, police questioned women attending Oregon State University, where Karen Sprinker had been a student. They became very interested when it emerged that a number of students had been called by a man, claiming to be a lonely Vietnam veteran, wanting to arrange a date. One young woman had actually met him, but she found his manner and conversation slightly disturbing, especially when he had asked her if she was not afraid he might strangle her, referring to the recent murders. She described him as overweight and red-haired. She added that he had freckles, matching the description of a man who had recently tried and failed to abduct two young women in Portland. The police told the student to inform them immediately if he called again.

A few days later, he did, indeed, call her, and they were waiting for him when he turned up to meet her. His name was Jerry Brudos, and he did not seem at all perturbed by their questions. They discovered he was an electrician and began to watch every move he made. On May 30, 1969, five days after the police had developed their first interest in him, he was under arrest.

> "'Do you feel some remorse, Jerry?' Brudos, picking up a piece of paper, screwing it up, and throwing it on the floor, answered: 'That much,' he said, 'I care about those girls as much as that piece of wadded up paper.'"
>
> —BRUDOS WHEN INTERVIEWED BY A POLICE OFFICER

A Fetish for Shoes and Underwear

Brudos was born in South Dakota in 1939. His mother had always wanted a daughter, and, consequently, she never treated him with anything but disdain.

A Troubled Adolescence. By the time Brudos was in his teens, this bad relationship had encouraged him to develop a fantasy life that involved a fetish with women's shoes and underwear. It had begun when he was just five years old and had brought home a pair of high heels from the local dump. When his mother saw him wearing them, she was furious, and women's shoes from that point on seem to have represented something wicked to him. He began to steal shoes and underwear from neighbors' houses.

In 1956, at the age of 17, Brudos was sent to the psychiatric ward of Oregon State Hospital after beating up a 17-year-old girl and forcing her to strip at knifepoint. He had also dug a hole in a hillside where he planned to keep girls prisoners and treat them as sex slaves. Despite this, he was not considered seriously mentally ill or dangerous, and after nine months of treatment, he was released.

Disturbing Behavior. Brudos joined the army in 1959 but was released later that same year following a meeting with an army psychiatrist in which he revealed strange sexual dreams and fantasies. In 1961 he married a 17-year-old girl named Ralphene. He was very controlling, forcing her to remain naked in the house at all times and forbidding her from entering his workshop and the attic where he stored his collection of women's shoes and underwear. They had two children, but in time, Ralphene stopped having sex with him.

Jerry Brudos's house in Salem, Oregon, in which the Oregon State Police found incriminating items— women's underwear, photographs and photographic equipment.

The Confession

After his arrest—he was found to be wearing women's panties at the time—Brudos began to confess. He described battering Linda Slawson on the head with a piece of wood in his garage as she bent down to take an encyclopedia from her bag, and then strangling her. He had then told his wife to take the children out for a meal while he undressed the young woman's lifeless body and hacked off her foot, which he kept in a freezer in the garage. He would enjoy using it to try on shoes.

More Details. Brudos had picked Jan Whitney up when her car broke down. He strangled her in his garage and violated her dead body, taking photographs. He then grotesquely hoisted her into the air on a pulley system and left her there for a few days. A few days after he had killed her, he returned from dropping off his family with relatives for Thanksgiving to find that a car had crashed into a corner of the garage. Luckily for Brudos, amid the wreckage, the police officers failed to notice the body hanging from the ceiling. That night he threw Jan Whitney's body into the Willamette River.

Brudos had abducted Karen Sprinker at gunpoint from a department store parking lot. He took her back to his garage, raped and strangled her, and cut off her breasts before disposing of her body in the Long Tom River.

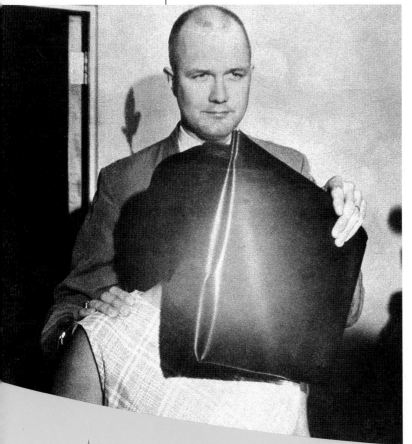

The face of Ralphene Brudos, wife of Jerry Brudos, hidden behind her attorney's briefcase after her indictment on August 7, 1969, on a charge of first degree murder in connection with the death of Karen Sprinker. She was later acquitted.

Women in the Wrong Place at the Wrong Time

Once the investigating officers began to link Jerry Brudos with the murders and the missing women, many pieces of evidence fell into place. Geographical patterns began to emerge that included places of residence, workplaces, and spots where bodies were found.

In January 1968, when Linda Slawson vanished, Brudos had been living in the area in which she had been working. He had moved to Salem, Oregon, in August or September of that year and had worked in Lebanon, Oregon, close to the freeway on which Jan Whitney's car had been found in November 1968. When they picked him up, he was working in Halsey, just 6 miles (9.7 km) from the Long Tom River, where the two bodies had been found. Finally Karen Sprinker had disappeared from the parking lot of the Meier & Frank store in downtown Portland. At the time, Brudos lived just a few blocks away.

Even the geography of these disappearances and murders pointed directly at him as the perpetrator. The science of geographic profiling would undoubtedly have brought investigators to the same conclusion that they reached after following through on the lead provided by the Oregon State student who had met with Brudos and subsequently decided that he was too strange for her.

A Horrific Experiment. He had abducted Linda Salee after pretending to be a police officer, "arresting" her for shoplifting. He raped her in his garage, strangling her as he did so. He now carried out a grotesque experiment, suspending her body by the neck from the ceiling and inserting two hypodermic needles into her sides to which he attached electric wires. When he switched on the current, he had hoped to see the dead woman's body dance, but the current merely burned her skin, leaving the marks that had puzzled investigators.

A Guilty Plea and a Life Sentence. On June 27, 1969, Brudos pleaded guilty to the murders of Jan Whitney, Karen Sprinker, and Linda Salee—Linda Slawson's body was never found—and was sentenced to three terms of life in prison. In prison, he continued to indulge his fetish by having women's shoe catalogs delivered to his cell. He died in 2006 from liver cancer.

Mapping the Crime

Jerry Brudos can be said to have contravened the normal rules of geographic profiling as devised by Dr. Kim Rossmo. Rossmo's methodology stipulates that a serial criminal will normally establish a buffer zone around his home, committing his crimes at a convenient distance from where he lives. Brudos, instead, made his home the scene of his crimes, abducting his victims in various places around Portland or Salem, either through opportunism or by targeting them in parking lots and then bringing them back to his home, where he murdered them. The nearby Willamette River and its tributary, the Long Tom, also featured heavily in Brudos's geography, providing him with convenient places to dispose of the bodies.

Case History: Jerry Brudos

▶ **January 26, 1968**
Linda Slawson (19) disappears in Salem, Oregon, while selling encyclopedias door-to-door. She is killed by Jerry Brudos in his garage, and, although he later confesses to dumping her in the Willamette River, her body is never found.

▶ **November 26, 1968**
Jan Whitney (23) disappears at a freeway rest stop near Albany in Oregon while driving home to spend Thanksgiving with her family. Her body is disposed of in the Willamette River.

▶ **March 27, 1969**
Karen Sprinker (19) fails to meet her mother for lunch. She is abducted by Brudos at gunpoint, raped, and then strangled in his garage. Her body is found in the Long Tom River.

▶ **April 23, 1969**
Linda Salee (22) fails to turn up for a date with her boyfriend. She is murdered by Brudos, and her body is found in the Long Tom River.

▶ **June 27, 1969**
Jerry Brudos pleads guilty to the murders of Jan Whitney, Karen Sprinker, and Linda Salee, and he is sentenced to life in prison.

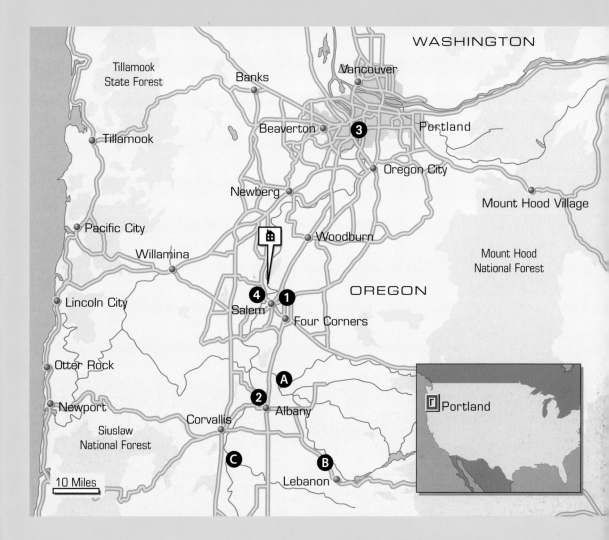

Locations of the Murders

1 Salem, Oregon—Linda Slawson killed by Brudos in his garage in Salem, a suburb of Portland, and later her body is dumped in the Willamette River **A**, January 1968

2 Albany, Oregon—Jan Whitney abducted, murdered, and her body is also dumped in the Willamette River, November 1968; her car was found on the freeway near Lebanon **B**

3 Portland, Oregon—Karen Sprinker disappears from the Meier & Frank store parking lot in downtown Portland; she is raped, strangled, and then mutilated. Her body is then tied to an engine block and dumped in the Long Tom River **C**, March 1969

4 Salem, Oregon—Linda Salee murdered by Brudos, and her body dumped in the Long Tom River, April 1969

Fred and Rosemary West

For some criminals, the most important landscape is the one in the mind, the place where their dreadful fantasies are concocted. Fred West was such a criminal, a man whose world contracted to that of his depraved fantasies and his home, which became the playground where he could act out those fantasies, hidden from the outside world. Inarticulate, uneducated, and unattractive, West had a talent for spotting vulnerable young women that no one would miss. Having been taken in by his apparently good-natured geniality, they would walk, unsuspectingly, into the hell he had created at 25 Cromwell Street in the quiet English town of Gloucester. It was a charnel house, where the remains of nine young women were found in 1994.

Rosemary West. At the age of 16, following the break-up of her parents' marriage, she moved in with her father, who was prone to violence and who repeatedly sexually abused her. He would become a frequent visitor to 25 Cromwell Street where Rose worked as a prostitute.

The Making of a Monster

West grew up in grinding poverty, the latest in a line of poor farm workers. He claimed his father committed incest with his own daughters and that he had himself made his own sister pregnant. A motorcycle accident at age 17 left him with a metal plate in his head and a permanent limp. Afterward, friends and family say, his character changed. He became prone to violent mood swings and unexpected outbursts of anger.

West was constantly in trouble for shoplifting and petty crime and, at age 20, appeared in court yet again, this time accused of getting a 13-year-old girl pregnant. He escaped a jail sentence, but his father threw him out of the family home.

By 1962 West was driving an ice cream truck, an occupation that afforded him ample opportunity to find willing young women. The girl he had married, Catherine "Rena" Costello West, a Scottish prostitute, often refused to indulge some of his more extreme sexual fantasies. After being involved in an accident in his truck in which a boy was killed, West found work in a slaughterhouse. He and Rena and their two children, one of which was West's, moved in with a woman named Ann McFall. She would be Fred West's first victim.

A Deadly Lifestyle

When Rena moved back to Glasgow, West and Ann McFall, by now a couple, moved into a trailer near West's home village of Much Marcle. Tiring of Ann's demands that he marry her, West murdered her, dismembered her body, and buried her, first removing the fetus of their unborn baby, which he buried beside her. He also removed her fingers and toes, a trademark of almost all his murders. Soon Rena was back, and life carried on as normal. She earned money on the streets, while Fred stayed home and molested his stepdaughter, Charmaine.

Fred West, dressed in overalls, working on the renovation of a home for adults suffering from autism in Nailsworth, Gloucestershire. Fred's building skills would become useful at 25 Cromwell Street as he extended the property.

In 1968, Fred West met the love of his life and his future partner in crime. Rosemary Letts was 15. She had always been a bit slow; her family dubbed her "Dozey Rosey." Neighbors remembered her as grossly overweight. She was a sullen, aggressive loner who was always available for sex with the older men of her village.

Soon Rena had gone again, and Rose, by now pregnant, had moved into the trailer with Fred and the two girls. In 1970 their daughter Heather was born. But with Fred in prison for nonpayment of fines, Rose found it almost impossible to look after her new daughter as well as the other two. When Charmaine disappeared, Rose told people that Rena had taken her back to Scotland. The truth was that she had snapped one day and killed the girl. On his release from prison, Fred helped her bury the child's body in a nearby field.

By 1971 Fred and Rose were living in a house on Midland Road in Gloucester. Their life was interrupted, however, when Rena turned up unexpectedly one day asking for her daughter. Fred decided that the only way to keep her quiet was to kill her. He got her drunk one night, strangled her, and buried her dismembered body, except for her toes and fingers, in another Gloucestershire field.

Their lives were becoming increasingly depraved. Fred would bring West Indian immigrants home who paid to have sex with Rose, and he would get his kicks by watching them through a peephole. They began cruising the streets, picking up young girls, bringing them home, and drugging and raping them.

The House of Horrors

Soon they needed a bigger house. Rose's prostitution business was booming, and their family was growing. They moved into 25 Cromwell Street, which had a large basement where they initially planned that Rose would ply her trade. Fred, however, saw an opportunity to bring life to his deepest and most depraved fantasies. He decided to soundproof the space and turn it into a torture chamber.

Their 8-year-old daughter, Anne Marie, was the first occupant. Fred tied her up and repeatedly raped her. He told her that he was merely showing her how to give pleasure to the man she would eventually marry. Then they began to use it for the girls they picked up as they cruised around Gloucester. They held the girls captive in the basement, sometimes for up to a week, subjecting them to sexual abuse and repeated rape before murdering them. The Wests buried the first few bodies under the garage floor and beneath the floorboards of the house. When they decided there was still not enough space, however, Fred enlarged the basement and made the garage an extension of the house.

Three more bodies quickly found their way under the house, while others were held captive. Anne-Marie was one captive, and by now, as well as being raped by her father, she was also being raped by men that he brought home.

> "When murderous criminals are so careful that nobody even realizes they killed anyone, there is nothing to put on a map. Without the pattern of activity there is no 'criminal geography' to profile."
>
> —DAVID CANTER, *MAPPING MURDER: THE SECRETS OF GEOGRAPHIC PROFILING*

Rose, meanwhile, was regularly giving birth. Sometimes the babies were Fred's; at other times their fathers were the other men with whom she had sex. For Fred, of course, the daughters he fathered were no more than opportunities for more sex. When they were old enough, he began to rape his daughters, Heather and Mae.

When Heather said too much to one of her friends, however, she too was murdered and buried beneath the patio, not far from the body of a 17-year-old Swansea girl, Alison Chambers.

In the Absence of a Crime

It is impossible to solve a crime when no one knows that it has even been committed, and that was the case with Fred and Rosemary West. No one linked the disappearances of young women in the Gloucester area. If they had, perhaps they would have been able to compile the criminal geography of the Wests' murderous activity. When people who are marooned on the peripheries of society disappear, often no one notices or cares. Their disappearance is merely confirmation of their already odd behavior or the fact that they simply do not fit in.

For 20 years Fred West raped and murdered such women and girls. Some were reported missing, but no one really cared. Even when police did mount searches, as they did in 1973 when three girls disappeared around Gloucester, the search revealed nothing and was soon abandoned. Added to this was the fact that those victims who survived his crimes were reluctant or afraid to report him. Seventeen-year-old Caroline Owens did, after she was stripped and raped, but the courts merely slapped West on the wrists and fined him, in spite of his long record of sex crimes.

Police excavating the garden at 25 Cromwell Street. Following up on statements taken from social workers that revealed the local joke that Heather was buried under the patio at 25 Cromwell Street, police arrived with a search warrant on February 24, 1994. Two days later, they found Heather's remains. In the days following, the remains of eight more victims were unearthed.

Under the Patio

In May 1992, West was still raping his daughters. Around this time, he filmed himself repeatedly raping one of them. The girl told school friends about it. On August 4, one of her friends told her mom what the girl had told her. She went to the police. Fred was charged with rape and Rosemary with being an accomplice to rape. She was further charged with cruelty and the children were taken into care. On June 7, 1993, however, the case collapsed when the two principal witnesses decided not to testify.

The police remained interested in the Wests, however, and were curious about a story that was making the rounds about their daughter Heather being buried under the patio. Eventually, in February 1994, they obtained a search warrant and began to excavate the garden at 25 Cromwell Street. The following day, they found human bones. Fred was arrested and confessed to Heather's murder, claiming that Rosemary knew nothing about it. She was arrested initially on sex charges, but a murder charge was added later.

Fred West was convicted of the murders of 12 women but hung himself with his bedsheets in prison on New Year's Day, 1995, before a sentence could be passed. Rose was sentenced to life for the murders of the 10 girls found at Cromwell Street, and, after dropping the appeal against her sentence in 2001, she stated that she expects to spend the remainder of her life in prison.

In October 1996, 25 Cromwell Street was demolished. A landscaped footpath now fills the space where Fred West once perpetrated his horrific crimes.

Ten of the Wests' known victims (top row, left to right): Theresa Siegenthaler, Charmaine West, Heather West, Shirley Anne Robinson, Shirley Hubbard; (bottom row, left to right): Lynda Gough, Juanita Mott, Lucy Partington, Carol Ann Cooper, and Alison Chambers.

The Cromwell Street Black Hole

Criminologist David Canter has come as close as anyone to explaining the manner in which people disappeared into the deadly web spun by the Wests without anyone appearing to notice. In his book, *Mapping Murder* (2003), he likens the phenomenon to that of the black hole in space. If no light escapes from a black hole, he wonders, then how could it be seen in the first place? However, it was the very absence of anything that made scientists question what was going on and that finally led them to identify the black hole.

Canter compares the discovery of black holes to the discovery of the murders at the West house at 25 Cromwell Street. All that was recorded of the missing young women the Wests murdered was their absence. The presence of a crime, Canter continues, was not considered. If the disappearances had been pinpointed on a map of the Gloucester area, he points out, it would immediately have become apparent that these disappearances were far from random and that there was a distinct geographical pattern to them. But Fred West had made himself invisible in the Gloucester area, and 25 Cromwell Street had become a kind of black hole into which young girls disappeared forever.

Police stand guard outside the "house of horrors," as the media dubbed it—25 Cromwell Street, Gloucester.

Mapping the Crime

Fred West's victims were on the fringe of society, and many of them were not missed when they disappeared. Profiler David Canter compared Fred West's ability to offend undetected for so many years to the creation of a crime zone "black hole" into which victims disappeared but which left no obvious trace. He suggested the very absence of information can become a starting point for an investigation: These various seemingly unconnected crimes make up a pattern, or "black hole," from which a geographical profile could emerge.

Case History: Fred and Rosemary West

▶ **August 1967**   Ann McFall vanishes. Her remains, minus fingers and toes, were found in June 1994. It matches Fred West's modus operandi, although he was never charged.

▶ **June 1971**   Rosemary West kills Charmaine West (8), Rena Costello's daughter.

▶ **August 1971**   West murders Rena (27) at Midland Road to prevent her from investigating Charmaine's whereabouts.

▶ **April 1973**   Lodger Lynda Gough (19) is killed at Cromwell Street.

▶ **November 1973**   On her way home from the movies, Carol Ann Cooper (15) disappears; she is killed at Cromwell Street by West.

▶ **December 1973**   Lucy Partington (21) disappears after leaving a friend's house to catch a bus home. She is kept alive for several days before being killed and dismembered.

▶ **April 1974**   Swiss student, Theresa Siegenthaler (21), hitchhiking from London to Holyhead, disappears. An investigation uncovers nothing, but her remains are discovered at Cromwell Street in March 1994.

▶ **November 1974**   Shirley Hubbard (15) disappears on her way home from a work experience course in Droitwich in central England.

▶ **April 1975**   Former lodger, Juanita Marion Mott (18), is killed.

▶ **May 1978**   Prostitute Shirley Anne Robinson (19) is murdered after becoming pregnant with Fred West's child.

▶ **August 1979**   Alison Chambers (17) from Swansea is raped and killed.

▶ **June 1987**   Fred and Rose's daughter, Heather (16), is killed and buried

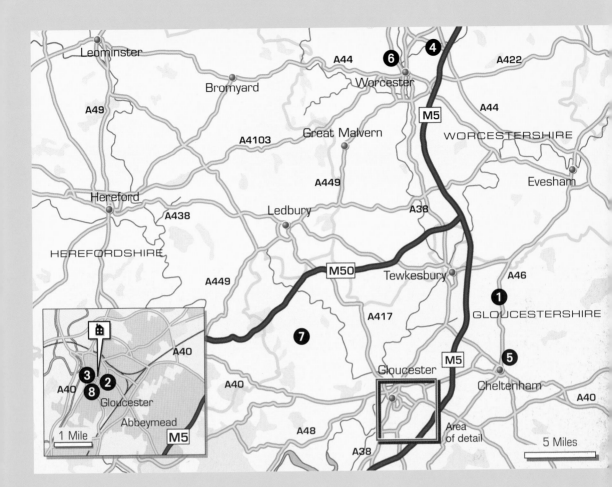

Locations of the Abductions and Murders

❶ Bishop's Cleeve—Ann McFall vanishes while living with West, August 1967

❷ Gloucester—Rosemary West kills Rena Costello's daughter, Charmaine West, in their home in Midland Road, Gloucester, June 1971

❸ Gloucester—Lynda Gough is the first victim at the West's Cromwell Street home, April 1973

❹ Worcester—Carol Ann Cooper abducted from a bus stop in the Warndon area of Worcester, November 1973

❺ Cheltenham—Lucy Partington last seen at a bus stop in Pittville, Cheltenham, December 1973

❻ Worcester—Shirley Hubbard (4) abducted in Worcester, November 1974

❼ Newent—Juanita Mott was standing by the B4215 road near Newent when she disappeared, April 1975

❽ Gloucester—Shirley Anne Robinson, Alison Chambers, and Heather West were all additional victims at Cromwell Street, May 1978 – June 1987

Note: Investigators involved in the West case believe many more people may be buried in the fields and farms of the area.

Kenneth Bianchi and Angelo Buono, Jr.: The Hillside Strangler

Between October 1977 and February 1978, 10 women and girls died horrifically in a spree of murder perpetrated by Kenneth Bianchi and Angelo Buono, Jr., the two men collectively known as the Hillside Strangler. As the sadistic nature of the killings increased, police in and around Los Angeles became even more baffled. But when one of the killers went solo, evidence led directly to him and his partner. They were captured through astute police work and use of a primitive form of the scientific technique that would later become the science of geographic profiling.

The moustachioed Kenneth Bianchi arrives in a sherrif's car at the Criminal Court Building in Los Angeles where he was later arraigned on charges of murdering five women.

Murders in Washington State

On January 12, 1979, two college students, Karen Mandic and Diane Wilder, were reported missing in Bellingham, Washington, while house-sitting for their friend Kenneth Bianchi. A broadcast appeal resulted in the discovery of their car, abandoned in a wooded area. Inside the bodies of the two young women were found. They had been strangled.

Following clues that Bianchi had left behind, Bellingham police apprehended him the next day. The police chief, Terry Mangan, remembered the Hillside Strangler murders in Los Angeles and noted that Bianchi had recently moved to Bellingham from LA. He placed a call to Detective Frank Salerno of the Los Angeles County Sheriff's Department that would break the Hillside Strangler case.

An Early form of Geographic Profiling. Police in Los Angeles began to put together a primitive geographic

profile of Bianchi. It was the days before geographic profiling became the exact science that it is today, but the principles applied instinctively by detectives working on the Hillside Strangler case were similar.

Two murdered women, Cindy Hudspeth and Kristina Weckler, had lived on East Garfield Avenue in Glendale, parts of which are bordered by Los Angeles. Another victim, Kimberly Martin, was a prostitute who had been visiting a client on nearby Tamarind Avenue on the night she disappeared. These streets matched the places at which Kenneth Bianchi had resided while he lived in Los Angeles County.

Physical evidence also linked Bianchi to the killings. Jewelry belonging to Kimberly Martin and another victim, Yolanda Washington, had been found in his house. Hair and fiber evidence further confirmed his guilt.

Making Murder Convenient

As the noted British criminal psychologist and geographic-profiling pioneer David Canter once said, "Like a person going shopping, a criminal will also go to locations that are convenient." Human nature dictates that in selecting a place to commit a crime or dump a body, a criminal is always likely to choose the easiest option. It would, however, be reckless to indulge in serious criminal activity too close to home. That would just make the police's job easier. Therefore, there will always be a buffer zone of some kind around the perpetrator's home or the base of his operations, an area that is off-limits for his criminal acts. Beyond that, there is likely to be a cluster of sites whose locations make it easy for him to get home or that help minimize the likelihood of discovery.

Key Pieces of the Puzzle. Convenience is, therefore, of utmost importance, and that convenience could imply simple familiarity with an area, particularly an area such as that between Glendale (which would become a key piece in the geographic puzzle) and nearby Eagle Rock. In this area, on November 20, 1977, one of the Hillside Strangler's earlier victims, quiet 20-year-old design student Kristina Weckler, was found. Her body had the ligature marks on her neck, wrists, and ankles that would be common to all the victims. Blood flowed from her rectum, and two tiny puncture holes on her arms initially suggested that she was a junkie. The postmortem established, however, that she had been injected with cleaning fluid. As with all of the strangler's victims, Kristina had not died where she was found. She had been dumped, and the rugged nature of the terrain rendered it impossible for her to have been carried by one man. It was likely that at least two people had killed her.

The Body Count Goes Up

Close to Dodger Stadium and not far from where Kristina was found, two other bodies also turned up on November 20. Dolores Cepeda (12) and Sonja Johnson (14) had been seen a few days earlier talking to someone in a two-tone sedan. The conversation had taken place on the passenger side of the car, confirming the premise that more than one person was involved.

Zeroing in on Two. Nine days later, the body of an 18-year-old student, Lauren Wagner, was found in the Glendale-Mount Washington area with the familiar ligature marks, but burns on her palms suggested that she may also have been tortured. A neighbor, who had seen her arguing with two men outside her house at around 9:00 P.M. the previous night, was later telephoned by a man with a New York accent who told her to keep her mouth shut. One of the men was tall and young with acne scars on his face, she told detectives; the other looked Latin, was older and smaller, and had bushy hair.

A Chilling Connection

Investigators now made a connection with three murders that had happened prior to the discovery of Kristina Weckler's body. Prostitute Yolanda Washington had been found raped and strangled on October 18 near Forest Lawn Cemetery, and 16-year-old prostitute Judy Miller had been raped, murdered, and left in La Crescenta, north of Glendale. A small piece of fluff on her eyelid would become a vital clue.

The body of Lissa Kastin, a 21-year-old waitress who had aspirations to get into show business, had been found on November 6, about 6 miles

(9.6 km) from the site where Judy Miller's body had been dumped. It would have taken two people to carry Lissa's body to the hilly area where she was found.

A Temporary Lull in the Killing. The body of Kimberly Diane Martin was found on a steep hillside in Echo Park on December 9. No signs of further killings appeared until February 16, 1978, when the body of a 20-year-old clerk, Cindy Hudspeth, was discovered in the trunk of her orange Datsun, which had been pushed over a cliff in the Angeles Crest area. Ligature abrasions were present and remarkably similar in all cases. The same killers had been at work. Unsurprisingly, panic broke out in Los Angeles, even though the city's residents were not exactly strangers to homicide. Many people, especially women, bought guns, knives, and dogs to protect themselves, and locksmiths did a booming business as Angelenos increased their home security. The media went into overdrive, and, inevitably, the killer—they still believed there was a single person involved—was tagged the "Hillside Strangler."

Meanwhile, investigators had discovered a useful coincidence. Cindy Hudspeth had lived just across the street from one of the stranglers' earlier victims, Kristina Weckler. This seemed to indicate that at least one of the killers lived in Glendale. Detectives began to piece together the geography of the killings, but they were no closer to finding their perpetrators.

A member of the Los Angeles County Coroner's office shouts instructions up a hillside as the Los Angeles Police Hillside Strangler Task Force investigates the body of a woman (her leg can be seen) found in the trunk of a car that has been pushed or driven off the highway. The woman, Cindy Lee Hudspeth (20), was believed to be the 13th victim of the Hillside Strangler.

The Master and His Apprentice

Kenneth Bianchi had had a troubled existence. Born in Rochester, New York, he was adopted when he was three months old. By the age of 5, he was a victim of strange seizures and frightening temper tantrums. He married at age 20, but he was unfaithful, and the marriage foundered.

A Fateful Move to LA. At age 26, Bianchi moved to Los Angeles, living initially with his older cousin, Angelo Buono, Jr., who made a living as a car upholsterer but became a pimp and prostituted young girls on the side. Buono was a habitual abuser—physically and sexually—of women and even his own children. He lived in Glendale.

Bianchi had a son with a woman named Kelli Boyd, whom he had met at work. She refused to marry him due to his often bizarre behavior and attitudes, and she left Los Angeles to return to her hometown of Bellingham, Washington. Bianchi would follow her a few months later, in May 1978, when she agreed to give him another chance. By that time, however, Bianchi and Buono had been deep into their career as the Hillside Strangler.

Angelo Buono, Jr. arrives at Los Angeles Criminal Court Building for arraignment for 10 of the brutal Hillside Strangler murders. His cousin, Kenneth Bianchi, had already pleaded guilty to 5 of the murders, but Buono maintained his innocence.

Confession and Conviction

In custody in Bellingham following his arrest for the murders of Karen Mandic and Diane Wilder in January 1979, Bianchi implicated Angelo Buono in the Hillside killings, explaining how they gained their victims' trust by various means, including impersonating police officers, before abducting them and taking them back to Buono's car upholstery shop. Once there, the pair sexually assaulted and sadistically tortured their victims before killing them.

A Geographic Pattern Emerges. Buono had grown up in Glendale and knew the area like the back of his hand. He was able to use his extensive knowledge of the area in disposing of their victims' bodies. Geographic analysis of the sites where some of the victims had last been seen and the places where their bodies were found suggested that his shop was the scene of the girls' murders. Six of the dump sites were distributed in an obvious cluster around the upholstery shop. The pattern that emerged suggested almost beyond doubt that the victims had died

Geoforensics in the Hillside Strangler Case

Investigators decided that the best way forward in the Hillside Strangler case would be to figure out the most likely location of the murders. The police had a lot of information to work with, most of it in the form of data points telling them where the victims had last been seen and the places where their bodies had been dumped. Armed with this information, investigators could figure out the distance between the key points on a map in each victim's murder. Police computers displayed these distances using Venn diagrams, which use circles to show how two or more different sets (each shown by a circle) share certain elements to form a third set containing elements common to each.

In the Hillside Strangler murders, the center of each circle represented what crime experts call "victim availability"; the circumference of the circle represented "offender capability"; and the radius represented "offender ability." In a typical case, a line was drawn from the location of the abduction to the dump site. This line provided the radius for a circle that covered an area of about 3 square miles (7.8 sq km). Within this area, police believed, they would find the murder location, the killer's base. With enough of these circles placed on a map, each representing a murder, the clustering and intersecting of circles could be used to focus the investigation on key areas that were common to more than one killing.

Two hundred police officers flooded into the area. The operation failed to pinpoint an exact location, but as the police later discovered, Angelo Buono's upholstery workshop was actually very close to the center of the zone. It also seems likely, with hindsight, that the overwhelming police presence in that area forced Bianchi and Buono to temporarily curtail their activities until the police activity died down.

there. This pattern proved to be invaluable evidence at the killers' subsequent trials.

Hard Evidence. Furthermore, the piece of fluff found on Judy Miller's eyelid matched samples of material from Buono's upholstery shop. The fabric had been used as a blindfold. Kenneth Bianchi testified against his cousin and was sentenced to life in prison. He is serving his sentence in Washington State Penitentiary at Walla Walla. Angelo Buono also received a life sentence. He died of a heart attack at age 67 in Calipatria State Prison in California in 2002.

Mapping the Crime

The locations of the murders and the dumpsites used by the Hillside Strangler demonstrate the theories of geographic profiling. There is the reassuring buffer zone where the killer avoids criminal activity. Beyond that, the locations are still within easy access of home, reducing the chance of capture and enabling swift flight if necessary.

Case History: The Hillside Strangler

▶ **October 18, 1977**   Kenneth Bianchi and Angelo Buono murder prostitute Yolanda Washington (19).

▶ **October 31, 1977**   The body of prostitute Judy Miller (16) is found in La Crescenta.

▶ **November 6, 1977**   The body of Lissa Kastin (21) is found on Chevy Chase Drive, beaten, raped, and strangled.

▶ **November 20, 1977**   The naked bodies of Dolores Cepeda (12) and Sonja Johnson (14) are discovered in Elysian Park. The body of Kristina Weckler (20) is discovered a few miles away.

▶ **November 23, 1977**   The body of student Jane King (28) is found close to the Golden State Freeway.

▶ **November 29, 1977**   The body of Lauren Wagner (18) is found. A neighbor provides a description of two men.

▶ **December 9, 1977**   The body of prostitute Kimberly Diane Martin (17) is found in Echo Park.

▶ **February 17, 1978**   The naked body of Cindy Lee Hudspeth (20) is discovered in the trunk of her orange Datsun, which had been pushed off a cliff the day before. Police become convinced the killers live in Glendale.

▶ **January 12, 1979**   In Bellingham, Washington, Diane Wilder (22) and Karen Mandic (27) are found strangled. Kenneth Bianchi, working as a security guard, is arrested.

▶ **October and**   Buono and Bianchi are sentenced to life in prison.

Locations of the Murders

1 Hollywood, Los Angeles—Yolanda Washington murdered and her body dumped near the Forest Lawn Cemetery, October 1977

2 La Crescenta, LA—Judy Miller strangled and left naked in a parkway in a residential area, October 1977

3 Glendale, LA—Lissa Kastin raped, strangled, and her body dumped on Chevy Chase Drive, November 1977

4 Elysian Park, LA—Dolores Cepeda and Sonja Johnson strangled and their bodies dumped in Elysian Park; a few miles away the body of Kristina Weckler found on a hillside near Dodger Stadium, November 1977

5 Elysian Park, LA—Jane King found near the Golden State Freeway, November 1977

6 Glendale, LA—Lauren Wagner tortured and strangled, November 1977

7 Echo Park, LA—Kimberly Diane Martin found murdered on a steep hillside in Alvarado Sreet, December 1977

8 Glendale, LA—Cindy Lee Hudspeth found murdered and naked in the trunk of a Datsun car, February 1978

9 Bellingham, Washington—Diane Wilder and Karen Mandic found strangled, January 1979

Arthur Gary Bishop:
From Molestation to Murder

After his arrest and confession to the murders of four little boys and a teenager, the investigating officers tried to establish what had motivated him to kill them. At first, he claimed to have killed the five boys to prevent them from exposing him, but as time went on, it became increasingly obvious that although that had initially been his reason, he had actually grown to enjoy killing and would undoubtedly have kept killing until stopped or arrested. "I'm glad they caught me," he said, "because I'd do it again."

Arthur Gary Bishop enters Third District Court during his trial in Salt Lake City, Utah. During the trial he cited his obsession with pornography as a major contributing factor to his urge to kill.

Too Much of a Coincidence

It was astonishing that Art Bishop was not caught sooner. Admittedly, the bodies of his victims were unlikely to be discovered, buried deep in the wilderness or in the desert, miles from Salt Lake City. With that vital evidence missing, it was impossible for detectives to complete their jigsaw puzzle. He was arrested in the end because of his proximity to the places where four of the children had vanished. That proximity had meant that the police questioned him each time they made door-to-door inquiries.

An Officer's Interest Aroused. One astute officer noticed this fact and became even more interested in Bishop, or Roger Downs, as he was calling himself, when the officer found that Bishop was actually acquainted with the parents of the fifth child to go missing. It was too much of a coincidence.

Not the Man He Seemed to Be

Bishop's name change had been forced on him in 1978 when, in his hometown of Hinckley, Utah, at the age of

26, he was convicted of embezzling $9,000 from a used-car dealership where he was working as a bookkeeper. Everyone was surprised that the former Eagle Scout from a solid religious background had gone bad.

On the Run. Bishop was given a suspended five-year prison sentence on the condition that he repay all the money. Shortly after, however, he was on the run. He spent five years traveling around under false names, finding whatever work he could, and stealing whenever the opportunity presented itself.

Bishop buried two of his victims—Troy Ward and Graeme Cunningham—in the Twin Peaks Wilderness area.

An Obsession With Child Pornography. Bishop settled in Salt Lake City, adopting the name Roger Downs and using it to enroll with Big Brothers Big Sisters of America, an organization that helps children reach their potential through one-on-one mentoring. The power of hindsight tells us that Art Bishop should not have been allowed near such an organization. He had developed an obsession with child pornography at a very early age and began molesting some of the young boys with whom he became involved in his mentoring role. Soon that obsession would become a deadly one.

The Turn to Murder

Four-year-old Alonzo Daniels lived in the apartment across the hall from Bishop. On October 14, 1979, Bishop enticed the boy into his apartment by promising him candy. He undressed and fondled Alonzo, but when the boy began to cry and said he was going to tell his mother, Bishop panicked.

Victim Number One. He picked up a hammer and smashed the boy's skull before dragging him into the bathroom, where he drowned him in the bathtub. He stuffed the boy's body in a cardboard box and carried it downstairs to his car, on his way passing Alonzo's mother, who was calling her son's name, wondering where he was.

Living so close to Alonzo's apartment, Bishop was one of the first to be questioned, and he of course denied having seen the boy recently. A huge search was mounted, involving hundreds of police officers and civilians, but Bishop had buried the body in the desert, 20 miles (32 km) away, near the town of Cedar Fort, where it was unlikely to be found.

Unsatisfied Bloodlust. After he had killed Alonzo, Bishop began buying puppies—around 20 of them over the course of about a year—and killing them to satisfy his bloodlust. "A puppy whines just like Alonzo did," he later told a detective. Even this form of cruelty wasn't enough to keep Bishop away from children, however, and he continued molesting boys, using his charm and the threat of hurting or killing them to make them promise not to tell their parents.

Victim Number Two. In November 1980, he met an 11-year-old boy, Kim Petersen, at a roller-skating rink. Pretending that he wanted to buy a

Utah State Prison, where Bishop was executed by lethal injection. Prior to his execution, Bishop expressed remorse and said he was "ready and anxious" to die. Mormon bishop Heber Geurts said, "I've dealt with thousands of inmates in 33 years, and he's the most sorrowful and repentant and remorseful man I've ever seen."

pair of skates from the boy, he apparently arranged another meeting with Kim. The boy was never seen alive again. A couple of witnesses reported seeing Kim speaking to a man, and they provided a description and a make of car, but the lead turned out to be a dead end. Critically, the police also failed to link Kim's disappearance to the Alonzo Daniels case.

The Thrill of the Kill

Bishop realized that he enjoyed killing. To free up his time so he could indulge his new habit, he stole $10,000 from a ski shop where he was employed as a bookkeeper and stopped showing up for work. A few weeks later, on October 20, 1981, he found his next victim.

Victim Number Three. Four-year-old Danny Davis was fiddling with a bubble gum machine in a local supermarket, and Bishop offered him some candy. Danny refused it, however, remembering what his mother had told him about accepting gifts from strangers. Bishop immediately left the store, but the boy followed him. By the time Danny's grandmother realized that he was no longer in the store, he was long gone, his body buried in the desert near the remains of Alonzo and Kim. The most extensive search in Salt Lake City's history and a reward offer of $20,000 failed to uncover him.

The Horror Continues

The police were clearly baffled by the killings, and the public was becoming increasingly outraged at their failure to make an arrest. The boys had been taken at different times, on different days. Furthermore, there was no discernable pattern based on race. Kim and Danny had blonde hair and fair skin, and Alonzo was African American.

Victim Number Four. Following the disappearance of Danny Davis, nearly two years passed before the horror returned. On June 23, 1983, Troy Ward vanished from a park on his sixth birthday. Bishop dumped his body in the Twin Peaks Wilderness area, about 65 miles (105 km) from where he had buried the other three boys.

Victim Number Five. Less than one month later, Bishop killed again. He was due to take two boys on a camping trip, but one of them, 13-year-old Graeme Cunningham, disappeared a few days before they were due to leave. Graeme had become Bishop's fifth and final victim, his body buried next to that of Danny Davis. Bishop, still masquerading as Roger Downs, callously visited the house of the missing boy and offered his help.

Another massive search ensued. Lakes, ponds, and rivers were dragged, and the nearby mountains were scoured for any sign of Graeme Cunningham. It was at that point that a detective noticed that the name Roger Downs kept coming up.

"I'd Do It Again"

When he was charged with the murders, the police were astonished to find themselves inundated with calls from parents accusing "Downs" of molesting their children. If these people had called earlier, the authorities reasoned, then perhaps he could have been stopped and not all of the boys would have died.

> "…pornography was a determining factor in my downfall.... All boys became mere sexual objects. My conscience was desensitized and my sexual appetite entirely controlled my actions."
>
> —ARTHUR GARY BISHOP
> IN A LETTER OF CONFESSION

Charged, Convicted, Executed. Bishop was charged with five counts of murder, five of kidnapping, two of forcible sexual assault, and one of sexually abusing a minor. Bishop built his defense around his addiction to pornography. Possibly his statement that he was glad he'd been caught because if he hadn't, "I'd do it again" did little to help his case, and may indeed have helped turn the jury against him. He was found guilty and sentenced to death in 1984. Upon receiving his sentence, Bishop apologized to the victims' families. Four years later, he was executed by lethal injection.

During those four years, Bishop reacquainted himself with the Mormon faith in which he had been raised. He was so eager to find salvation after his death sentence, it was reported, that he read the *Book of Mormon* 10 times from cover to cover.

Criminal Geographic Targeting

As criminologist Dr. Kim Rossmo and others say, the locations of crimes are not totally random or chaotic, though they may seem so initially. Indeed, crime locations are often entirely rational, and as such may be "mapped" once investigators can get a handle on the logic behind them.

Routine Activity Theory suggests that crimes happen where suitable victims and motivated offenders come together. Offenders moving through the geography of their everyday lives—showing up in places where they work, engage in social activity, or reside—create a "mental map," a perception of the area that is derived from their knowledge and experience.

Within that space will be an anchor point, the place they consider to be their base. It could be home, or it could be a bar, a club, or a workplace. Some may even have no specific anchor point because they are transient or are living on the street.

According to criminologists Paul and Patricia Brantingham, a criminal depends on a suitable target coinciding with the criminal's awareness of space. In other words, the victim must be in a place with which the criminal has some level of comfort or familiarity. To find additional targets, an offender may then start to look farther afield, moving out from his or her base. Criminals will also establish a buffer zone close to their bases where their offending activities would be too dangerous.

As difficult as it was at first for the authorities to piece together an approach to Bishop's crimes that pointed to him as the perpetrator, he had little trouble figuring out the easiest, most convenient places to find his young victims—shopping in a supermarket, hanging out at an ice rink, or just being home, as in the case of Alonzo Daniels, his first victim. When the authorities came upon the realization that Bishop was present in various ways in such close proximity to the victims, they were, in effect, using principles of Criminal Geographic Targeting to come up with a "mental map" of spaces based on Bishop's range of daily activity.

This CGT choropleth probability map shows a hypothetical example of a series of crimes committed in British Columbia, Canada. The darker zone represents the most likely area the criminal lives in.

Gary Bishop was eventually arrested simply because of his proximity to the victims. His name kept coming up as having been interviewed, and he was even a friend of the family of one of the victims. Once the "mental map" of Bishop's life was detected, it was, in a sense, surprising that his candidacy as a major suspect was not taken seriously earlier.

Mapping the Crime

Born in the tiny, bone-dry desert town of Hinckley, it was to the desert that Arthur Gary Bishop returned after killing, burying his victims there in remote locations. This was after he had abducted them in Salt Lake City, meeting them in a supermarket, an ice rink, outside his apartment, in a park close to where he lived, or through friendship with the victim's family. It was all local to Bishop, and he selected his victims opportunistically.

Case History: Arthur Gary Bishop

▶ **October 14, 1979**   Alonzo Daniels (4), who lived in the apartment across the hallway from Bishop, is lured into Bishop's apartment with promises of candy and is bludgeoned and drowned in Bishop's bathtub.

▶ **November 8, 1980**   Kim Petersen (11) first meets Bishop at a roller-skating rink and apparently arranges to meet with him again when Bishop claims he wants to buy skates from him. He is abducted and killed, his body buried near that of Alonzo Daniels in the desert.

▶ **October 20, 1981**   Danny Davis (4) is abducted from a supermarket and killed by Bishop, who buries his body near those of his two previous victims.

▶ **June 23, 1983**   Troy Ward (6) is abducted in a park on his sixth birthday. The alarm is raised when he fails to appear at his own birthday party.

▶ **July 14, 1983**   Graeme Cunningham (13) vanishes several days before he is due to go on a camping trip with Bishop. Graeme's disappearance launches a statewide search, but by the time Bishop shows up at the boy's home to offer his "help" to Graeme's family, it is too late. The boy's body has been buried near that of Troy Ward.

▶ **June 10, 1988**   Four years after being tried and convicted of various charges including murder, kidnapping, and sexual assault. Bishop is executed by lethal injection.

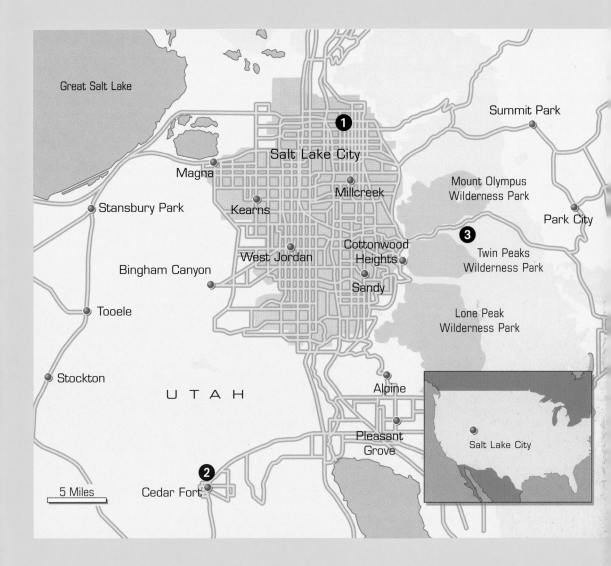

Locations of the Abductions and Murders

❶ Salt Lake City—Arthur Gary Bishop's home and the area where he abducted and murdered Alonzo Daniels (October 1979), Kim Petersen (November 1980), Danny Davis (October 1981), Troy Ward (June 1983), and Graeme Cunningham (July 1983)

❷ Cedar Fort—Bishop shows police the burial site of three of his victims (Daniels, Petersen, and Davis), July 1983

❸ Big Cottonwood Creek—Two skeletons (Ward and Cunningham) found here, July 1983

Jeffrey Dahmer:
The Milwaukee Monster

The police officer opened the refrigerator door and froze in horror. "There's a f**king head in the refrigerator!" he screamed. Actually, he was only partly right. There were, in fact, three heads—two of them in the freezer—wrapped in clear plastic bags, their lifeless eyes staring out at him. Meanwhile, in the hall, the tall, good-looking man with sandy hair shifted uneasily from foot to foot, his earlier, calm demeanor fading. Thirty-one-year-old Jeffrey Dahmer, serial killer of 17 young men and boys, realized it was the end of the road.

The "Weird Dude"

Around midnight on July 22, 1991, Robert Rauth and Rolf Mueller, of the Milwaukee Police Department, were sitting in their cruiser in a Near West Side neighborhood close to Marquette University, when a hysterical young man ran toward them with a pair of handcuffs dangling from one wrist, screaming that someone had tried to kill him. They calmed the man down, learned that his name was Tracy Edwards and that a "weird dude," as Edwards described him, had invited him up to his apartment after meeting him in a mall and had proceeded to snap handcuffs on him and threaten him with a knife. Edwards had managed to keep his attacker from snapping on both cuffs, and he made his escape.

A Nightmare on North 25th Street. The officers suspected the incident was nothing more than a lovers' tiff, but they accompanied Edwards back to apartment 213 in the Oxford Apartments at 924 North 25th Street, where a well-groomed young man opened the door.

The first thing the officers noticed was the smell, as if something had been left to rot. But the man was courteous, telling them his name was Jeffrey Dahmer and that he was sorry if Edwards had believed he had threatened him. He told them he had recently lost his job and was upset and had been drinking. When they asked him to get the key to the handcuffs from the bedroom, however, Edwards shouted that the knife was also in there. One of the officers decided to go and check, but as he walked toward the bedroom, he noticed photographs strewn around that seemed to be of dismembered bodies. He screamed to his colleague to cuff Dahmer, who became hysterical but was quickly subdued. It was at that point that the other officer opened the refrigerator door.

The Early Years
It is well known that the first victim of a serial killer may often be killed on an impulse. For Jeffrey Dahmer, the road to murder began at an early age. Born in 1960, Dahmer was brought up in Akron, Ohio. As he grew up, he became increasingly introverted and found it hard to make friends. He took to collecting dead animals and stripping the flesh from them, and he was drinking heavily from his early teenage years. By the time he graduated from high school, he was an alcoholic. In 1978, when he was 18, his parents divorced. It was also the year he killed for the first time.

The First Fatal Encounter. Stephen Hicks was a 19-year-old hitchhiker whom Dahmer had picked up and brought home. They got drunk together and then had sex, but as Hicks prepared to get back on the road, Dahmer picked up a barbell and brought it down on Hicks' skull, killing him because, he later said, he didn't want him to leave. He buried the body in woods behind the house. Not long after, he enrolled in the Army, after dropping out of Ohio State University. He was discharged for drunkenness, however, and after spending some time in Miami Beach, he ended up back in Milwaukee, where he had been born, living with his grandmother in the suburb of West Allis.

The Milwaukee Monster Comes of Age
In the next four years, Dahmer killed 16 times, 3 times while living at his grandmother's, once at an apartment he lived in after being thrown out of her house, and the remaining 12 in apartment 213 of the Oxford Apartments. Apartment 213 would become infamous in its association with the gruesome crimes committed within its walls.

This police mugshot shows Jeffrey Dahmer shortly after his arrest.

A Grisly Ritual. His methods were invariable. He would pick up a young man at a gay bar and take him back to his apartment, where he would ask him, and sometimes pay him, to pose for photographs. He would then give his victim a drugged drink and strangle him before masturbating over the body or even having sex with it. He dismembered the body, recording the whole process in photographs. He would sometimes boil the skull, removing the flesh and keeping it as a souvenir. He also might paint the skull gray, so it would resemble a plastic model. He also kept other body parts. In time he began to experiment with chemical methods of disposing of the flesh and bones that were piling up in his cupboards and his refrigerator, soaking them in acid and then flushing the resultant sludge down the toilet or pouring it down a drain. He sometimes preserved his victims' genitals in formaldehyde.

Cannibalism and the Need for Total Control. He also ate the flesh of some of his victims, in the deluded belief that they would somehow come alive in him again. He began to add seasoning and used meat tenderizers. Eating human flesh, he said, aroused him sexually. On occasion, he would try a Frankenstein-style "experiment," drugging a victim and then drilling a hole in his skull into which he would use a large syringe to inject muriatic acid. He was attempting, he claimed, to create a "zombie-like" creature over which he could exercise total control. Needless to say, no one survived this horrific treatment.

Work Release at the House of Correction

Dahmer was arrested in 1988, after deciding not to murder a 13-year-old Laotian boy named Somsack Sinthasomphone, whom he had picked up, drugged, and sexually molested. The boy's parents realized what had happened, and Dahmer was arrested. He escaped a prison sentence, however, and instead was given five years' probation and ordered to spend a year in the Milwaukee County House of Correction under a work-release program. This meant that he worked at his

The exterior of the Oxford Apartments in Milwaukee, Wisconsin, where Jeffrey Dahmer lived and where he was arrested. Numerous young men were killed by Dahmer at this address.

job at the Ambrosia Chocolate Factory during the day and returned to jail at night. Ten months later, in 1990, despite a letter from his father pleading with the judge not to release him without treatment, he was freed and moved into the Oxford Apartments.

The Oxford Apartment Years

That year, he killed four men at the Oxford Apartments, and the following year, he killed eight more. On one occasion in 1991, during the period in which he was serving his probationary sentence, Dahmer was almost caught when 14-year-old Konerak Sinthasomphone (coincidentally, a younger brother of the boy Dahmer had sexually molested several years earlier) was found wandering around outside Dahmer's apartment building, naked, drugged, and bleeding. Two young women in the neighborhood called 911. By the time the Milwaukee police arrived, Dahmer was on the scene and was attempting, unsuccessfully, to take the boy back. He was able, however, to convince the officers that Konerak was his 19-year-old boyfriend and that the two had had a quarrel while drinking. The officers accompanied Dahmer and the incoherent boy back to apartment 213, somehow failing to investigate the terrible smell they detected. Had they gone farther into the apartment, they would have discovered that the cause of the smell was the body of Dahmer's previous victim, decomposing in the bedroom. The police ignored the protests of the young women, who knew that the young boy was not 19 years old. Instead, the officers handed the boy over to Dahmer. A few hours later, Konerak would be dead, his body dismembered, and his skull kept as a memento.

MPD Taken to Task. Later, following Dahmer's discovery and arrest, the Milwaukee Police Department would come under heavy criticism for its botched handling of this call. The MPD would also be taken to task for its lack of sensitivity to the situation of the victim, who was Asian and assumed to be gay, and for its failure to take seriously the involvement of the neighbors—all of them young African American women—from the "marginal" Near West Side neighborhood in which Dahmer lived. In the days following the discovery of Dahmer's horrific crimes at the Oxford

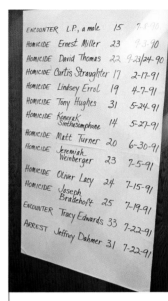

A list of Dahmer's victims' names and the dates of their murders hangs in the courtroom during his trial in Milwaukee.

days following the discovery of Dahmer's horrific crimes at the Oxford Apartments, one report of the unfolding events described "all hell breaking loose." As further details of Dahmer's history became known, and as it became evident that on at least one occasion the police had failed to follow up on a lead that might have prevented one imminent murder and four more that would follow, a radio station in nearby Chicago described a "firestorm" breaking loose in Milwaukee.

A City Eager to Forget. The city of Milwaukee wanted to erase as much of the Dahmer case from its collective memory as possible. Within a week or so of the discovery of Dahmer's crimes in apartment 213, the Oxford Apartments were torn down, leaving a vacant lot.

The Trial

Security for Jeffrey Dahmer's trial was extraordinary. The courthouse was scoured for bombs, and everyone entering the building had to pass through a metal detector. Dahmer was surrounded for his own protection by an 8-foot (2.4-m)-high barrier made of glass and steel. It took the jury just five hours to find Dahmer guilty of the 15 murders with which he was charged. On the day of his sentencing, he read out a statement. "Your Honor, it is now over," he said. "This has never been a case of trying to get free. I didn't ever want freedom. Frankly, I wanted death for myself. This was a case to tell the world that I did what I did, but not for reasons of hate. I hated no one. I knew I was sick or evil or both. Now I believe I was sick. The doctors have told me about my sickness, and now I have some peace. … I believe that only the Lord Jesus Christ can save me from my sins...."

The Sentence and an Unexpected Outcome. Jeffrey Dahmer was sentenced to 15 life sentences, a total of 957 years in prison. He served only a few of those years, however. On November 28, 1994, his skull was smashed by a broom handle wielded by another prisoner, and he was pronounced dead on the way to hospital.

> "...The doctors have told me about my sickness, and now I have some peace. I know how much harm I have caused.... Thank God there will be no more harm that I can do...."
>
> —AN EXTRACT FROM JEFFERY DAHMER'S STATEMENT TO THE COURT

Stealth Killers

According to noted criminologist Dr. Kim Rossmo, Jeffrey Dahmer fell into the category of "stealth predator" or "stealth killer." The murders committed by stealth predators occur in such a way that the authorities do not even realize that a crime has been committed. The easiest targets for such killers are people living on the margins of society, such as prostitutes, drug addicts, or runaways.

So-called custodial killers, too, are noted by Dr. Rossmo as stealth killers. Dr. Harold Shipman was possibly the most notorious custodial killer of all. A man responsible for an unknown number of deaths, but certainly hundreds, Shipman was able to kill in the course of his duties as a physician in the United Kingdom without anyone realizing that his patients were dying of anything other than illness and natural causes. The physician's privileged position, a position of absolute trust, permitted him to engage in his murderous pursuits. Impossible to detect and difficult to investigate, stealth killers are among the most dangerous of murderers. Rossmo, however, has come up with a means of investigating even people who have disappeared off the map. He applies certain techniques of the type used by epidemiologists and other health officials to detect outbreaks of disease. According to these techniques, known as "spatial-temporal clustering," too many reports of a disease in too small an area in an unusually brief period of time—a "cluster," in other words—suggest an epidemic.

Exactly the same method could be applied to missing persons, where an unusually high occurrence has been found. What is important to the application of this method in criminal cases is the follow-up on missing-persons reports from relatives and loved ones. In the Dahmer killings, the local authorities—and in one instance, even the Milwaukee office of the FBI—not only failed to connect the dots between various missing-person reports and inquiries from concerned relatives and neighbors; they failed in many cases even to take seriously the problems that were staring them in the face because the complaints came from people who were themselves socially marginalized. Also, they seemed all too willing to take the word of a calm, pleasant-looking, white male—Dahmer himself—over the agitated pleas of people from the "transitional" community in which the killings took place.

Dr. Harold Shipman was convicted in 2000 of killing 15 patients by lethal injections. He was sentenced to 15 consecutive life terms, and the judge recommended he never be released.

Case History: Jeffrey Dahmer

▶ **June 6, 1978**   Stephen Hicks (19) from Akron, Ohio—attacked while hitchhiking, bludgeoned with a barbell.

▶ **September 15, 1987**   Steven Tuomi (26) murdered in a room at the Ambassador Hotel, Milwaukee, and taken back to Dahmer's grandmother's house to be dismembered.

▶ **January 1988**   James "Jamie" Doxtator (14) from West Allis, Wisconsin, is drugged and strangled; his body disposed of in the trash.

▶ **March 24, 1988**   Richard Guerrero (14) from West Allis, killed and then Dahmer has sex with Guerrero's body.

▶ **March 25, 1989**   Anthony Sears (24) from West Milwaukee.

KILLINGS AT THE OXFORD APARTMENTS

▶ **June 1990**   Eddie Smith (36)—found drugged and murdered.

▶ **July, 1990**   Ricky Beeks (27)—skull kept as a souvenir.

▶ **September 1990**   David Thomas (23)—as Dahmer kills Thomas, he takes photographs.

▶ **February 1991**   Curtis Straughter (19)—another skull that Dahmer keeps.

▶ **April 1991**   Errol Lindsey (19)—again, Dahmer keeps the skull.

▶ **May 24, 1991**   Tony Hughes (31)—Dahmer also keeps the skull of this victim, who is deaf.

▶ **May 27, 1991**   Konerak Sinthasomphone (14)—Dahmer's youngest victim; the sexual assault of his brother, Somsack, had sent Dahmer to work release in 1988.

▶ **June 30, 1991**   Matt Turner (20)—his head is found by police in Dahmer's refrigerator.

▶ **July 5, 1991**   Jeremiah Weinberger (23)—another head found in the refrigerator.

▶ **July 12, 1991**   Oliver Lacy (23)—his head and his heart are found in the refrigerator.

▶ **July 19, 1991**   Joseph Bradehoft (23)—most of his body is dissolved in acid.

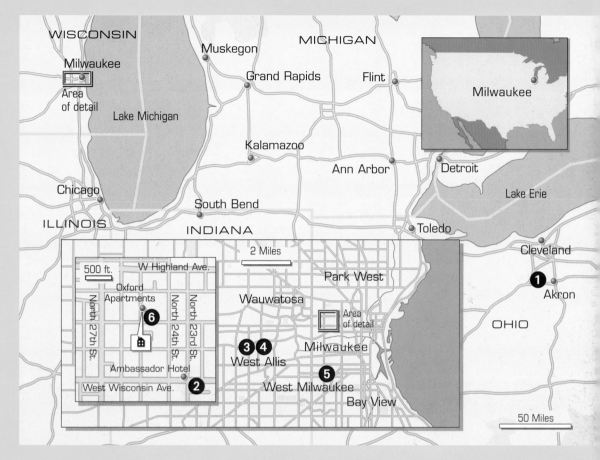

Locations of the Murders

1 **Akron, Ohio**—Stephen Hicks, June 1978

2 **Ambassador Hotel, Milwaukee**—Steven Tuomi, September 1987

3 **West Allis, Wisconsin**—James Doxtator, January 1988

4 **West Allis, Wisconsin**—Richard Guerrero, March 1988

5 **West Milwaukee**—Anthony Sears, March 1989

6 **Apartment 213, Oxford Apartments, 924 North 25th Street, Milwaukee**

—Eddie Smith, June 1990

—Ricky Beeks, July 1990

—David Thomas, September 1990

—Curtis Straughter, February 1991

—Errol Lindsey, April 1991

—Tony Hughes, May 1991

—Konerak Sinthasomphone, May 1991

—Matt Turner, June 1991

—Jeremiah Weinberger, July 1991

—Oliver Lacy, July 1991

—Joseph Bradehoft, July 1991

Paul Bernardo and Karla Homolka:
The Ken and Barbie Killers

Outwardly they appeared to be the perfect couple, but ever since the world found out the horrors they perpetrated, they have been called "the perfect storm of personalities." Paul Bernardo was a monster—a sadistic, woman-hating rapist—but Karla Homolka loved him to the point where she would do anything for him. In doing so, Homolka became an accomplice in an increasing spiral of depravity and evil.

Her Own Sister

Karla Homolka worked in a veterinary clinic, and Paul Bernardo was a junior accountant with Price Waterhouse, a large accounting firm. They met in 1987, and by 1990 they were engaged. There was one thing that really irritated Paul about Karla, however. She had not been a virgin when he met her. Therefore, he reasoned, it was up to her to find some way in which he could take the virginity of her younger sister, Tammy. Karla's work in the clinic provided her with the opportunity to obtain drugs that would knock Tammy out long enough for Paul to rape her.

A Twisted Plan... On December 23, 1990, the family was enjoying the run-up to Christmas together at the house of Karla and Tammy's parents. Paul plied Tammy with drinks into which he had put quantities of the sedative Halcion, and before long she was asleep on the sofa. When everyone else went to bed, Paul and Karla stayed up, and Paul raped Tammy while filming with a handheld video camera. Karla, meanwhile, was holding a rag over Tammy's face, soaked in halothane, a sedative given to animals prior to surgery. When Paul had finished, he ordered Karla to sexually assault her own sister.

... Gone Wrong. All of a sudden, however, Tammy started to throw up. Karla panicked, desperately trying to clear her sister's airways as Tammy began to choke on her own vomit. Her efforts were futile, however;

Tammy was dead. The couple came up with a plan, quickly hiding the camera and cleaning Tammy up before calling an ambulance. No one suspected anything other than a tragic accident.

A Sick Wedding Gift

As the date for their wedding approached, Karla decided on a special wedding gift for her man. She invited a 15-year-old girl over to their home and slipped sedatives into her drinks. When the girl was unconscious on the sofa, she called Paul. This time, Karla was filmed assaulting the girl first before Paul raped her. They put the girl to bed, and when she awoke the next morning, she knew nothing about what had happened while she was knocked out. She merely thought she had drunk too much and had awakened with some strange aches and pains.

The Scarborough Rapist

Three years earlier, in 1987, Paul Bernardo had begun to rape girls and young women in his neighborhood of Scarborough, a suburb of Toronto, Ontario. His method was generally the same. He pounced on a victim as she got off a bus, grabbing her from behind and pulling her to the ground, where he would rape her and force her to perform sex acts on him, talking to her all the while. He would then set her free and take off.

Missed Opportunities. One victim, raped just before Christmas 1987, had provided detectives with a good description of her attacker. Strangely, however, the composite picture, which bore an almost exact likeness to Paul Bernardo, was never released to the press or the public. It was not the only mistake the police made. One of Paul's former girlfriends had informed police about his sexual violence, believing it closely resembled the behavior of the rapist, but the report joined all the others and was never followed up. Paul Bernardo also drove a fairly distinctive white Capri, just like the car the rapist had been reported

Karla Homolka earned notoriety as the most hated woman in Canada.

driving. That, coupled with the fact that he lived in the vicinity of the attacks, should have made him a suspect. But nobody bothered to investigate him.

A Break. In May 1990, however, the picture compiled from the victim's description was finally released, and Paul Bernardo's former colleagues at Price Waterhouse—he had quit and was now living solely off the proceeds of a cigarette-smuggling business—immediately recognized him and reported the fact to the police. Again, it was added to the burgeoning pile of tip-offs and leads and was never investigated.

Placed on the Back Burner. When an increasing number of people began to contact the police about Paul Bernardo, a detective finally paid him a visit and persuaded him to give blood, hair, and saliva samples. Samples taken from 230 suspects were narrowed down to just 5, 1 of which was Paul's. By the time those remaining samples were due to be tested, however, the Scarborough rapes had stopped. The Scarborough Rapist seemed to have ended his career, and the case lost its sense of urgency. The authorities moved on to other investigations, and the samples were forgotten.

Encased in Concrete

On Friday June 14, 1991, Paul Bernardo was out looking for a license plate to steal in Burlington, Ontario. He needed the plate for his frequent smuggling trips across the U.S.-Canadian border. At about 2:00 A.M., he encountered 14-year-old Leslie Mahaffy, who had been locked out of her home by her parents for yet again breaking her curfew. Pulling a knife, he grabbed the girl, forced her into his car, and drove her to the house in St.

Paul Bernardo leaves a Kingston, Ontario, courthouse after seeking a court-appointed lawyer to fight his appeal.

Catharines, Ontario, in which he and Karla, now married, were living. He stripped Leslie and blindfolded her, filming her with his video camera as he assaulted her. When Karla awoke, she enthusiastically joined in as Paul directed her actions. He then started to brutally rape Leslie. A short while later, the girl was dead. Leslie's body, identified from the braces on her teeth, was found two weeks later in Lake Gibson, dismembered and encased in five blocks of concrete.

Police forensic investigators outside the house in St. Catharines that had been rented by Paul Bernardo and Karla Homolka.

The Last Killing

On April 16, 1992, Paul Bernardo and Karla Homolka abducted 15-year-old Kristen French as she walked home from school in St. Catharines. For the next three days, she was horrifically tortured, sexually abused, and raped by the couple—all captured on tape—before her body was dumped naked in a ditch 45 minutes from St. Catharines. When Kristen's body was found on April 30, it had been washed clean to remove any evidence, and, to make identification difficult, her hair had been shorn.

Old Evidence Dug Up. Paul Bernardo's name surfaced again in this inquiry, and a couple of officers paid him a visit. They were still far from convinced that he was the killer, but as he carelessly let slip that he had been questioned in connection with the Scarborough Rapist case, they contacted the officer who had worked on it. In February 1993, the samples from several years earlier were dug out and finally analyzed. They proved conclusively that he had raped three of the Scarborough Rapist's victims.

Investigators put him under surveillance and hauled Karla in for questioning. By now he was being violent toward her, and she had had enough. She also realized that the police had made the connection between the Scarborough rapes and the St. Catharines murders. She told them everything she knew in exchange for a plea bargain.

Two Trials, Two Convictions

When their house was searched, incriminating evidence was found but police were unaware that on May 6, Homolka's defense lawyer, Ken Murray, had gained access to the house and from above a ceiling light fixture in the upstairs bathroom had retrieved the videotapes showing Bernardo and Homolka torturing and raping their victims. Murray would hold on to these for the next 17 months, only handing them over to his successor, John Rosen, after he quit. Rosen handed the tapes over to investigators later that month. There was little doubt of Homolka's guilt, but Karla was tried first, and there was outrage when, on June 28, 1993, a plea bargain, which was struck well before the full extent of her crimes became known, got her off with a relatively light sentence of 12 years for manslaughter.

"Don't make me mad. Don't make me hurt you...."

—REMARKS ATTRIBUTED TO PAUL BERNARDO WHEN HE WAS ASSAULTING KRISTIN FRENCH

Condemned. Paul, on the other hand, was sentenced to 25 years in prison on September 1, 1995. Convicted for a number of offenses, including two murders and two sexual assaults, he was condemned by Karla's detailed testimony as well as the overwhelming physical evidence. In the years following his conviction, suspicions linger about the role that he and Karla may have played in a number of other deaths and sexual assaults.

In 2006 Paul Bernardo gave an interview in which he claimed he had reformed. Officials appear to be unmoved by his claim, and he is serving his term in an isolation unit where he spends 23 hours of every day locked in his cell.

A Deal with the Devil? Karla Homolka was released from prison in July 2005, amid a media frenzy over what many observers considered to be the worst deal ever made with a criminal in Canada's history. In fact, the plea bargain was made before the incriminating videotapes had been

A Behavioral and Geographic Profile

After six women had been attacked, a profile on the Scarborough Rapist was compiled from his verbal, sexual, and physical behavior during the commission of the attacks. According to the profile, the offender used bus stops for staking-out points. Some crimes were opportunistic rather than premeditated, which means that the victims just happened to be in the wrong place at the wrong time when the rapist decided to strike.

In addition to the women and girls who had become victims, analysts believed Bernardo had seen potential victims in passing but either had no urge to attack or had seen potential victims and the moment was inopportune. Successful attacks occurred when three things coincided—urge, opportunity, and victims. Furthermore victims were being targeted in areas in which attacks had already happened, and the profile stated that the offender was in all likelihood attacking in an area with which he was familiar. He derived security and comfort from the fact that he could easily plan escape routes, if necessary.

Additionally, the profile said, the rapist was probably an inhabitant of the Scarborough area and in fact lived within walking distance of the first, second, and fifth attacks, and because of this, it was very important that his victims did not see his face. Investigators believed this to be the case because of the simple fact that he attacked his victims from behind. He always forced them to the ground face down or ordered them to close their eyes.

Despite these consistent factors, however, as in other cases involving a defined geographic area, such as the Railway Rapist case in the United Kingdom and the Hillside Strangler case in Los Angeles, police activity was believed to have had an effect on the range of the Scarborough Rapist. On May 25, 1988, a police officer conducting surveillance on a Scarborough bus stop unsuccessfully pursued a suspect whom he had seen lurking in some trees in the vicinity of the bus stop. Four days later, a young woman was stalked and raped in the Mississauga area. It was undoubtedly the Scarborough Rapist, but this time, he approached her from the front, asking for directions. He was not in his home area and would have been less concerned about being recognized.

handed over to the authorities. Prosecutors insisted that they would not have agreed to the plea bargain if they had known about the existence of the tapes. Ken Murray was later charged with obstruction of justice but was acquitted.

Mapping the Crime

There can be few examples of serial criminals pursuing two careers, like Paul Bernardo, in two places not terribly far apart from each other: St. Catharines, where he and Karla Homolka

Case History: Bernardo and Homolka

▶ **May 4, 1987**
Paul Bernardo's first known rape in Scarborough, Ontario, is of a 21-year-old woman; the attack lasted more than 30 minutes.

▶ **May 14, 1987**
Bernardo attacks a 19-year-old woman in the backyard of her parents' house for over an hour.

▶ **July 27, 1987**
Bernardo abandons an attack after victim fights back.

▶ **December 16, 1987**
Bernardo rapes a 15-year-old girl.

▶ **December 23, 1987**
After Bernardo rapes a 17-year-old girl, the name "Scarborough Rapist" is coined.

▶ **April 18, 1988**
Bernardo rapes a 17-year-old girl.

▶ **May 25, 1988**
Bernardo is almost caught by a uniformed Metro Toronto investigator staking out a bus shelter. Noticing him hiding under a tree, the investigator pursues him on foot, but Bernardo escapes.

▶ **May 30, 1988**
Bernardo rapes an 18-year-old in Clarkson.

▶ **October 4, 1988 – May 26, 1990**
Bernardo makes at least eight more attacks in the Scarborough area. On May 26, 1990, he rapes a woman (19) whose description allows police to make a computer composite photograph.

▶ **December 23, 1990**
Bernardo and Homolka drug and rape Homolka's younger sister, Tammy. Tammy dies.

▶ **June 15, 1991**
Driving through Burlington, Ontario, Bernardo comes across Leslie Mahaffy (14), who has been locked out of her house. He drives her to St. Catharines, where he and Homolka sexually assault Leslie. Leslie dies, and her body is disposed of in Lake Gibson.

▶ **April 16, 1992**
Bernardo and Homolka abduct Kristen French (15) in St. Catharines and hold her for several days, raping and torturing her before killing her. Kristen's body is dumped in a ditch in Burlington.

murdered Leslie Mahaffy and Kristen French, and Scarborough, located in the city of Toronto, just across Lake Ontario. In Scarborough, Bernardo was careful not to carry out his attacks too close to home. In St. Catharines, he and Homolka murdered in their home, the bodies being disposed of some distance away.

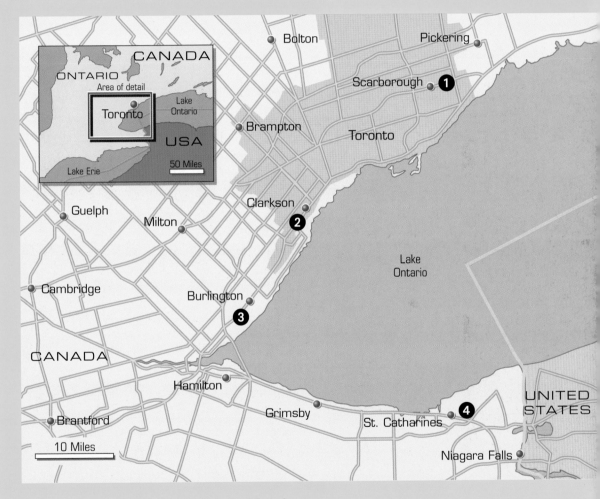

Locations of the Attacks and Murders

❶ **Scarborough**—The site of 11 rapes known to have been committed by Bernardo between May 1987 and May 1990

❷ **Clarkson**—Bernardo rapes an 18-year-old woman in Clarkson, May 1988

❸ **Burlington**—Abducts Leslie Mahaffy and takes her to St. Catharines, where she is assaulted and killed, June 1991

❹ **St. Catharines**—Kristen French abducted, raped, tortured, and killed, April 1992

Michel Fourniret:
The Ogre of the Ardennes

When they caught Michel Fourniret in 2003, he confessed to having committed 10 murders, although some believe that he possibly killed closer to 40 people. As details of his horrific crimes began to emerge, police across Europe began to reopen unsolved murder files in order to ascertain whether the "Ogre of the Ardennes," as the media dubbed him, might have been responsible.

French forestry worker Michel Fourniret, pictured at the courthouse in Dinant in Belgium after confessing to the murders of six girls in Belgium and France.

The Chatelaine of Death

The base for Michel Fourniret's forays into the surrounding French countryside or across the border into Belgium was the eighteenth-century Château du Sautou, situated near the village of Donchery in the Ardennes region in the north of France. From there he would set out on what he and his wife, Monique Olivier, called their "hunts for virgins."

A Deadly Visit. Michel Fourniret had bought the chateau after learning from another prison inmate—a member of the gang of bank robbers known as the Gang des Postiches—that his wife was looking after the spoils of their robberies, some $30,000 in gold bars. When he was released from prison, Fourniret found the woman and forced her to tell him where the money was. He killed her and used the money toward the purchase of the château and its 32 acres (13 hectares) of land. The grounds of Château du Sautou would become the resting place for a number of Fourniret's unfortunate young victims.

A Poison-Pen Pal

Michel Fourniret had qualified as a draftsman and opened his own tool-making business near Paris. In

1966 at the age of 24, he was convicted of abducting and sexually abusing a young girl in his hometown of Sedan. Further convictions followed, and he was locked up in 1984 after a series of abductions and sexual assaults in the Paris area. In prison he advertised for a pen pal and received a reply from a woman named Monique Olivier.

A Grisly Partnership. Olivier had been married twice and had two children but was estranged from them. An intense, depraved correspondence began in which, among other things, they discussed raping young virgins. In one letter, Fourniret grotesquely described virgins as "membranes on legs."

In 1987 Fourniret was sentenced to seven years for rape and the indecent assault of minors. Having already spent three years awaiting trial, however, he was released just four months into his sentence. Olivier was waiting for him at the prison gates, and they moved to the village of Saint-Cyr-les-Colons in northern Burgundy, where Fourniret found a job working in a school lunchroom.

"Hunting for Virgins"

On December 11, 1987, just six weeks after Fourniret and Olivier arrived in Saint-Cyr-les-Colons, 17-year-old Isabelle Laville disappeared.

The Killing Begins. Fourniret and Olivier devised a plan involving two cars. Driving one of the cars, Olivier pulled up next to Isabelle to ask for directions and managed to persuade Isabelle to get into the vehicle and show her the way. A little way along the road, they came upon another car beside which Fourniret was signaling for help, claiming that he had run out of gas. Olivier pulled over, and Fourniret climbed into the back seat. As Olivier set off again, he reached over into the front seat, where Isabelle was sitting, and stretched a cord around her neck. They then drugged her and drove back to their house. Fourniret, unable to become

Monique Olivier, wife of self-confessed killer, Michel Fourniret, appears in court at the opening of her trial in Charleville-Meziers in northern France. She was accused of participating in one of the murders and of supporting her husband in four others.

sufficiently aroused to rape Isabelle, had to be stimulated by Olivier. They then killed Isabelle and threw her body into a deep, abandoned well in the countryside. In July 1988 Fourniret killed 20-year-old Fabienne Leroy. She disappeared in Mourmelon and was later found in woods not far away.

Homegrown Horror. Soon, however, Fourniret was burying his victims on his own land, digging a shallow, 3-foot (1-m)-deep grave in readiness before climbing into his car and driving off in search of a young girl that he thought might be a virgin.

Olivier Cracks

In 2003, Fourniret had been arrested for the attempted abduction of a 13-year-old Belgian girl. Meanwhile, back home, with mounting horror, Monique Olivier was following the progress of the trial of the Belgian pedophile, Mark Dutroux.

A Frightening Parallel. When Marc Dutroux's wife, Michelle Martin, was sentenced to 25 years in prison for trying to cover up her husband's crimes, Olivier was terrified, especially as she had played a far bigger role in her husband's abductions than Michelle Martin had in Marc Dutroux's case. She rode in the car in order to reassure the girls they had picked up. Sometimes, she had even taken their young son, Selim, with them on their expeditions to add extra reassurance.

Giving up Michel Fourniret. Anxious to save her own skin, Olivier went to the police and denounced her husband, providing details of nine murders in France and Belgium while claiming that she played no part in them. Before long, however, it became clear that she was intrinsic to the success of his activities.

Often Fourniret would order her to look on as he raped and killed, and sometimes she helped him arrive at a state of sufficient arousal in order to carry out a rape. In 2008, Both Fourniret and Olivier were sentenced to life imprisonment.

The Murder of Joanna Parrish— a Link to Michel Fourniret?

In 2005, Monique Olivier sat in an interrogation room in Dinant in southern Belgium. For seven months, she had said nothing, but suddenly she began talking, describing the abduction and murder of one young woman who investigators believed might have been 19-year-old Marie-Angèle Domece.

> "I dream of a guillotine whose blade would be controlled by a rope long enough so that all the people who have something against me can join together and eliminate me. I owe them that."
>
> —MICHEL FOURNIRET TO INVESTIGATORS FOLLOWING HIS CAPTURE

A Possible Connection Emerges. Then, she began to describe another murder, and it became clear to the two detectives in the room with her that she was talking about the young British woman, Joanna Parrish, whose mysterious 1990 death had puzzled French police since her body had been found by a fisherman in the River Yonne. She had been drugged, tied up, raped, and thrown into the river.

A Deadly Rendezvous? Joanna, from Gloucestershire, England, was a student of Modern Languages at Leeds University who was spending part of her course of studies teaching at a school in Auxerre. Eager to earn some extra cash, she had placed an advertisement in a local newspaper offering English lessons, and a local man had replied. They had agreed to meet in a square in the town at 7:00 P.M. one evening. A friend accompanied her to the square, and the two separated. Joanna was never seen alive again.

A Case Left Unsettled. The police bungled the case, failing to mount a thorough search of the vicinity and then permitting the public onto the land while it was still a crime scene. Furthermore, bite marks on Joanna's body seem to have been ignored, and none of the local male population was subjected to DNA tests. Olivier told the officers that she had driven the van in which Joanne was abducted, her husband in the back savagely beating Joanna into unconsciousness before raping her. They took her to the river and threw her lifeless body into the waters. As recently as 2010—a full 20 years after Joanna's death—the parents of the young student and teacher expressed the fear the case of their daughter's murder may be closed without any formal charges ever being filed against Michel Fourniret.

Weapons and other items used by Michel Fourniret in the abduction and murder of his victims.

Deadly Postscript

In 2006 there was speculation that Michel Fourniret might have been responsible for the notorious 1974 murder of eight-year-old Marie-Dolorès Rambla in Marseilles, France. Christian Ranucci, one of the last people to be executed in France before the death penalty was ended, was guillotined for the young girl's murder in 1976. Doubts about his conviction contributed to the eventual decision to stop beheading convicted killers.

Marie-Dolorès was abducted by a man who told her he needed help finding his dog. His car was involved in a collision with another vehicle an hour later, but he quickly drove off. Ranucci was arrested because he had been involved in a car crash that same day and had been seen carrying a large package.

Despite circumstantial evidence that eventually proved strong enough to convict Ranucci in the murder of Marie-Dolorès, there was a wealth of other evidence that was weak and inconclusive. Ranucci drove a Peugeot 304. Although the car that Marie-Dolorès was seen getting into that day was identified as a Simca 1100, the Simca had a rear that was similar to that of the Peugeot. Another piece of evidence that turned out to be questionable was a red pullover that the driver of the car was seen wearing. The pullover that was later found lying at the roadside was several sizes too small for Ranucci.

Furthermore, a pair of pants in Ranucci's car had traces of dried blood on them, of the same blood type as that of the little girl who had by this time been found stabbed to death. Ranucci was unlucky enough to have the same blood type as Marie-Dolorès. Although the bloodstains were later proved to be old and the blood was believed to belong to Ranucci, he was convicted and paid the ultimate penalty—death.

After Fourniret's arrest for his crimes, it emerged that he had actually been vacationing in Marseilles at the time of Marie-Dolorès's murder. Additionally, the story of the lost dog was one used by Fourniret in his later abductions. The most chilling piece of evidence complicating the conviction of Ranucci, however, is a photograph taken at the courthouse during his trial. Standing in the crowd is a bearded man with glasses who bares an uncanny resemblance to the "Ogre of the Ardennes," Michel Fourniret.

Christian Ranucci being escorted by two detectives following his arrest for the murder of Marie-Dolorès Rambla (8) in Marseilles in 1974.

Mapping the Crime

The true number of murders committed by Michel Fourniret may never be known. He initially claimed to have murdered a man in order to rob him. His wife claimed that he also murdered the couple's live-in helper as well as another couple of young women, including Joanna Parrish, the British student who was killed in 1990. The following is a list of the murders of girls and young women to which Fourniret has so far confessed.

Case History: Michel Fourniret

▶ **December 11, 1987** Isabelle Laville (17) disappears in Auxerre on her way home from school. Her remains are found in 2006 at the bottom of an abandoned well north of Auxerre.

▶ **March 1988** Fourniret kills Farida Hellegouarch (30), the girlfriend of a member of the Gang des Postiches bank robbers, after helping her recover 34 gold ingots and thousands of gold coins from a tomb in a cemetery in Val d'Oise.

▶ **July 8, 1988** Fabienne Leroy (20) disappears from a supermarket parking lot in Châlons-en-Champagne, east of Paris. Her body is discovered in wooded countryside outside a military base the next day.

▶ **March 18, 1989** Law student Jeanne-Marie Desramault (22) is kidnapped outside the railway station in Charleville-Mezieres. She is killed and buried in the grounds of Château du Sautou.

▶ **December 20, 1989** Elisabeth Brichet (12) is kidnapped on her way home from a friend's house in Namur in Belgium. She is murdered, but Fourniret denies raping her.

▶ **November 21, 1990** Natacha Danais (13) is kidnapped while out shopping with her mother near Nantes, in western France. Three days later her body is found on a beach.

▶ **May 16, 2000** Céline Saison (18) disappears after taking an exam in Charleville-Mezieres. Two months later her body is found in the woods in Belgium.

▶ **May 5, 2001** Mananya Thumphong (13) disappears from Sedan. Her remains are found in 2002 in the Nollevaux forest.

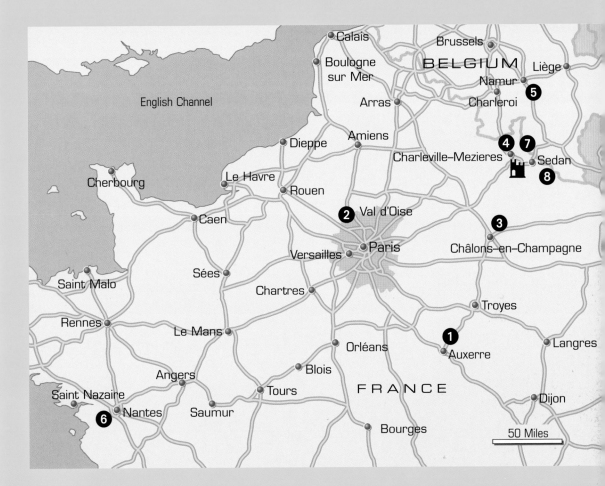

Locations of the Abductions and Murders

❶ Auxerre—Isabelle Laville was murdered and her body dumped in a well, December 1987

❷ Val d'Oise—Farida Hellegouarch was killed after revealing the location of money belonging to a group of bank robbers, March 1988

❸ Châlons-en-Champagne—Fabienne Leroy was killed by a bullet in the chest, July 1988

❹ Charleville-Mezieres—Jeanne-Marie Desramault was killed and then buried, March 1989

❺ Namur, Belgium—Elisabeth Brichet was kidnapped and murdered, December 1989

❻ Nantes, France—Natacha Danais was sexually assaulted and stabbed to death, November 1990

❼ Charleville-Mezieres—Céline Saison's body is found in woods, two months after she went missing, May 2000

❽ Sedan—Mananya Thumphong disappears from the French town of Sedan and, a year later, her body is found in the Nollevaux forest in Belgium, May 2001

Marc Dutroux: The Belgian Child Rapist and Serial Killer

Beneath the house in the grim Charleroi suburb of Marcinelle, Belgium, was a large basement. It was the reason Marc Dutroux had bought the house. Inside it, cleverly hidden behind a bookcase, was a massive concrete door. Behind the door was a soundproof dungeon in which lay a cage 7 feet (2 m) long by less than 3 feet (1 m) wide and about 5 feet (1.5 m) high. Here, young girls were tortured, abused, and ultimately killed. It was a case characterized by police bungling, a disastrous legal system, and rumors of the involvement of important people in a pedophile ring. Its ramifications went all the way to the top, almost bringing down the Belgian government.

A portrait of Marc Dutroux following his arrest for abduction, sexual assault, and murder.

A Life of Crime

Although unemployed and drawing welfare from the state, Marc Dutroux had little problem in earning money. Dealing drugs, trading stolen cars, and trafficking young women across Europe to be used in prostitution left him fairly well off—so well off, in fact, that he owned no fewer than seven houses in Belgium, most of which were vacant.

Rough Beginnings. Marc Dutroux had been born in Brussels in 1956 but grew up in the Belgian Congo, where his parents, both teachers, had found jobs. It was a loveless family, in which the young Marc Dutroux suffered regular beatings. He returned to Belgium in 1971, working for a while as a male prostitute and beginning to establish an extensive criminal record, mostly for drug dealing, car theft, and mugging. Eventually he became involved in a relationship with a woman named Michelle Martin, whom he married in 1989 while they were both in prison.

Signs of Trouble to Come. By the time Dutroux was divorced from his first wife in 1983, he and Martin had already been having an affair. In 1985, the couple was arrested for the abduction and rape of five young girls. Martin was sentenced to five years in prison, and Dutroux was sentenced to 13.5 years, but not long after he was incarcerated, the Belgian Justice Minister, Melchior Wathelet, announced that a large number of Belgium's sex offenders were to be released. This incredible leniency set free some of the country's worst offenders, among them Marc Dutroux, who had served just six years of his sentence.

A Description of a Killer

On June 24, 1995, two 8-year-old friends, Julie Lejeune and Mélissa Russo, were last seen waving to traffic from a bridge over a highway near Liege. They disappeared and were never seen alive again. As the police seemed to be making slow progress with their investigation, the girls' parents brought in a criminal profiler to try to build a picture of a person who might have abducted their daughters.

The profiler deduced that the abductor was probably unemployed and married with children. Further, this was probably not the first time he had abducted girls and had perhaps done it a number of times. It was a perfect fit for Marc Dutroux, but when the investigators were handed the profile, they did nothing about it.

A Vacation Nightmare

A couple of weeks later, on August 22, 17-year-old An Marchal and 19-year-old Eefje Lambrecks, who were on vacation with friends in Blankenberge on the Belgian coast, failed to return to their campsite after attending a show in town. When their friends went to police to report their concerns about their missing friends, the officers merely laughed and told them that the girls were probably off with boyfriends; they would turn up.

Unfortunately they did not. Even when it finally sank in that the girls were missing, however, no connection was made with the disappearance of the other girls.

Hidden Voices

Three weeks later, police in Charleroi received a letter from a woman saying that she believed her son was holding two girls captive in his house. The woman was the mother of Marc Dutroux, and she was concerned about the activities of her son. Astonishingly, however, the police did nothing.

Earlier Clues Left Unheeded. It was not the first time the authorities had been informed about Marc Dutroux. Small-time crook and sometimes-informant Claude Thirault had already gone to police in 1993 after Dutroux had talked to him about helping him abduct some girls, even offering to pay him. Dutroux had told Thirault that he was building a room in which to keep girls, referring, no doubt, to the room at his house in Marcinelle. The police had done nothing then, and even when others, suspicious of Dutroux's activities, began to inform on him, nothing was done.

When Dutroux was arrested for car theft in December 1995, police searched the Marcinelle house. One officer, René Michaud, even went down into the cellar with a locksmith. At one point, they heard the sounds of young girls' voices, but Michaud brushed them aside as coming from the street outside. Those voices belonged to Julie Lejeune and Mélissa Russo.

Law Enforcement at War with Itself. There seemed to be no end to the number of mistakes and miscues committed by police at various levels. Local police, the national law enforcement agency known as the Gendarmie, and a branch known as the judicial police were constantly at war with each other, and each withheld vital information from the other. In another instance of astonishing incompetence, a judicial official involved in the case even neglected to inform another official taking over for her that children had gone missing.

Hidden Voices Gone Silent. The voices from beyond the wall would soon be silent. Dutroux served four months in prison on car theft charges, instructing an associate, Bernard Weinstein, to feed the two girls.

> "We don't know everything about what happened, but we do know that if the authorities had done their jobs properly, our children would be alive today."
>
> —PAUL MARCHAL, THE FATHER OF ONE OF THE MURDERED GIRLS

Weinstein failed to do so. Michelle Martin did not bother to give them food and drink either, even though she went to the house regularly to feed her dogs. Julie and Mélissa starved to death.

When he was released from prison, Dutroux was furious. He tortured Weinstein before burying him alive next to the bodies of Julie and Mélissa.

Abducted and Brainwashed

On May 28, 1996, 12-year-old Sabine Dardenne was taken and imprisoned by Dutroux with the help of his accomplice, a junkie named Michel Lelièvre. Dutroux told Sabine that her parents had refused to pay a ransom and persuaded her that he was part of a gang, and that he was protecting her from the rest of them. She began to be conditioned into believing he was helping her.

A Lead too Strong to Ignore. On August 9, 14-year-old Laetitia Delhez joined Sabine in the dungeon. When she was taken, however, a witness saw a white van and remembered part of its license plate number. Police were able to match it to a vehicle owned by Dutroux, who was arrested on August 13, 1996, along with Michelle Martin and Lelièvre. Eventually, Lelièvre cracked under intense questioning, and the police found Sabine and Laetitia at Marcinelle. They had been so brainwashed, they would only leave their cage when Dutroux told them it was safe to do so. The graves of the others were found shortly after.

Outrage

The Belgian public was outraged as details of the incompetence of the authorities began to emerge and as rumors of a pedophile ring involving

Police excavate an area near Dutroux's home in the search for evidence during the investigation, 1996.

high-ranking officials began to circulate. Dutroux encouraged such rumors by claiming that he was nothing more than a pawn for influential people. Three hundred thousand people staged a "White March" in Brussels to protest the corrupt Belgian justice system. Another shocking development occurred when Dutroux escaped from custody while being transferred from the courthouse to prison, but he was recaptured a few hours later.

A Long List of Crimes

Dutroux's trial eventually began on March 1, 2004, more than seven years after his arrest. He was charged with three counts of murder, all of which he denied. The charges against him also included a long list of other crimes— auto theft, abduction, attempted murder, attempted abduction, molestation, and the rapes of three Slovakian women.

The dungeon in the house in Marcinelle hidden behind a massive concrete door disguised as a set of shelves. The dungeon was seven feet long by less than three feet wide and five feet high.

Dutroux, Martin, and Lelièvre appeared in court in a bulletproof glass cage to protect them from attack by members of the public. Another man sat beside them—Jean-Michel Nihoul, who Dutroux claimed was the leader of the pedophile network. Rumors suggested that Nihoul had organized an orgy at a Belgian château that had been attended by several government officials, police officers, and a former European Commissioner. More arrests in connection with the network, including some police officers, would follow. Nihoul, however, would be acquitted on murder and kidnapping charges—although he was sentenced to prison for five years on drug-related charges.

Guilty as Charged. On June 17, 2004, after a trial lasting three months, Michelle Martin was sentenced to 30 years, Michel Lelièvre to 25 years, and Marc Dutroux to the maximum sentence of life in prison.

Using the Map to One's Criminal Advantage

A number of factors contributed to Marc Dutroux's being able to continue to abduct girls and young women in spite of a national outcry, a huge manhunt, and even police surveillance of his own properties. Some of these factors had to do with the quality of police work and, some would argue, the integrity of the police themselves. Others had to do with the way in which Dutroux took advantage of the geography of Belgium, a relatively small country that allowed him to travel from one end of the country to the other, using the city of Charleroi as a base.

He traveled between jurisdictions that simply could not cooperate well enough to conduct a competent investigation. The rivalry among competing factions of various Belgian police forces meant that officers often focused more on each other than on catching the perpetrator. Every town in Belgium has a police force that is separate from the national force, which is called the Gendarmerie. Another section of the Gendarmerie, the BSR, is targeted at organized crime. Yet another agency, the judicial police, is present in every city. The judicial police and the BSR were at odds over the missing girls, each desperate to gain the glory of solving the case by itself.

Police incompetence also helped Dutroux avoid detection. At one point, he succeeded in smuggling An Marchal and Eefje Lambrecks into his Charleroi house, even though he was under surveillance by the BSR. Dutroux was well aware of the shortcomings of the Belgian police and must have been confident he would remain undetected. These and other inexcusable deficiencies on the part of nearly every level of law enforcement in Belgium seemed too blatant, almost too "perfect," to be attributed solely to incompetence. The conclusion of many was that there was an element of corruption in the Belgian police forces. Indeed, during the months following Dutroux's arrest many calls went out for reforms at various levels of Belgium's law enforcement and judicial systems.

The police failed to connect the dots in their investigation of Dutroux's crimes for many reasons, but the principles of geographic profiling very much applied to Marc Dutroux's crimes. Only in this case, it seemed as if the criminal rather than the cops who had the upper hand.

Thousands of Belgians took part in the "White March" in Brussels, protesting systematic corruption and incompetence in the Belgian justice system.

Mapping the Crime

In *Mapping Murder: The Secrets of Geographical Profiling*, British criminologist David Canter argues that Marc Dutroux purposefully plotted his crimes across the entire country of Belgium, knowing that this would minimize his chances of being caught in a country with a highly regionalized judiciary system. As a trader in stolen cars, he was also able to travel the country in a variety of vehicles that would not have any obvious connection with each other. He was also careful to avoid unneccesary risk by returning to places he may have been spotted earlier.

Case History: Marc Dutroux

▶ **June 24, 1995**   Julie Lejeune (8) and Mélissa Russo (8) are kidnapped close to a highway near Liège, Belgium. Dutroux holds them briefly at one of his houses before moving them to a house in Marcinelle that he has equipped with a soundproof dungeon.

▶ **August 22, 1995**   An Marchal (17) and Eefje Lambrecks (19) disappear while on vacation in Blankenberge. The victims are drugged and buried alive.

▶ **December 1995**   Dutroux goes to prison for four months for car theft. Julie and Mélissa are allowed to starve to death by Bernard Weinstein and Michelle Martin.

▶ **May 28, 1996**   Sabine Dardenne (12) is abducted by Dutroux and Michel Lelièvre on her way to school. She is held in the Marcinelle cellar.

▶ **August 9, 1996**   Laetitia Delhez (14) is abducted by Dutroux and Lelièvre on her way home from a swimming pool. She is held with Sabine in Marcinelle.

▶ **August 13, 1996**   Marc Dutroux, his wife, Michelle Martin, and another accomplice, Michel Lelièvre, are arrested.

▶ **August 15, 1996**   Sabine and Laetitia are found alive by police.

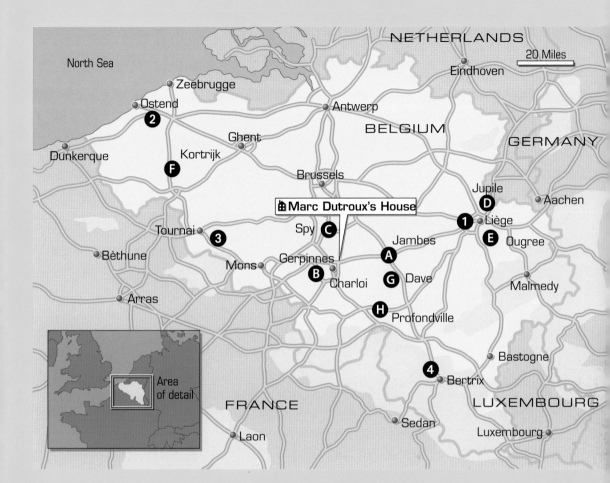

Locations of the Abductions

1 **Liège, Belgium**—Julie Lejeune and Mélissa Russo are kidnapped, June 1995

2 **Blankenberge, Ostend**—An Marchal and Eefje Lambrecks abducted, chained, drugged, and then buried alive, August 1995

3 **Kain, near Tournai**—Sabine Dardenne was abducted by Dutroux and Lelièvre and held in the Marcinelle cellar, May 1996

4 **Bertrix**—Laetitia Delhez abducted by Dutroux; Lelièvre and also held in the Marcinelle cellar, August 1996

....

Locations of the Attempted Abductions

A **Jambes**—Natacha, April 1992

B **Gerpinnes**—Aurelie, June 1995

C **Spy**—Thyfene, June 1995

D **Jupile**—Lindsay and Stephanie, May/June 1995

E **Ougree**—Vanessa and Dikana, June 1995

F **Kortrijk**—Sylvia, June 1995

G **Dave**—Samantha, May 1996

H **Profondville**—Tiffany, July 1996

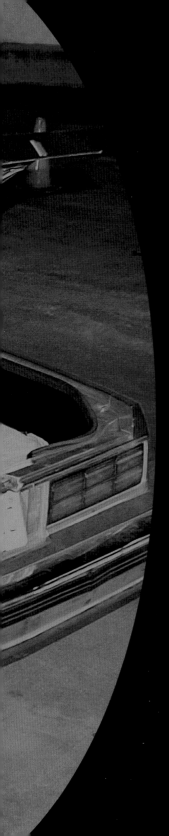

Transports of Death

David Berkowitz, "Son of Sam," mainly attacked courting couples sitting in their cars in the early hours; the English Railway Rapists, John Duffy and David Mulcahy, attacked their victims at railway stations in southern England; Aileen Wuornos was the hitchhiker from hell, killing seven men who stopped to give her a ride; and the Washington Snipers, John Allen Muhammad and Lee Boyd Malvo, remodeled their 1990 Chevrolet Caprice so that they could fire on their victims from inside the vehicle.

- David Berkowitz
- Robert Lee Yates, Jr.
- John Duffy and David Mulcahy
- Aileen Wuornos
- John Allen Muhammad and Lee Boyd Malvo

The 1990 Chevrolet Caprice used by convicted killers John Allen Muhammad and Lee Boyd Malvo, the Washington Snipers.

David Berkowitz: The Son of Sam

David Berkowitz grew up in the Bronx, the New York City borough where he also committed his first murder. When he moved to Yonkers, a city in neighboring Westchester County, away from the familiarity of his home streets, he became a nomadic killer who commuted, traveling into New York City in search of the courting couples and longhaired young women that he targeted. His horrific, random crimes are among the most terrifying in U.S. criminal history.

A Paranoid, Frustrated Loner

Berkowitz was always big for his age and lacked social skills. Adopted shortly after birth by a Jewish couple, he soon became a handful for his parents. His adoptive mother died in 1967, when he was 14. Berkowitz was devastated by his mother's death, and he became reclusive and began to suffer from paranoid delusions that her death was part of a plan to destroy him. His father remarried to a woman with whom Berkowitz didn't get along, and when the couple moved to Florida, Berkowitz was, at the age of 18, left alone with his delusions in New York.

A spell in the Army failed to help, and he became increasingly frustrated with his inability to form relationships with women. He vented those frustrations by setting fires—1,488 of them—in New York, but his paranoia got worse. He shut himself away in his apartment for a month, covering the walls with crazed slogans.

His attention moved from buildings to people on Christmas Eve, 1977, when he drove out into New York's streets armed with a hunting knife, determined to hurt people. He stabbed two women that night, but both survived. Six months later, he hit the streets again, but this time he carried a gun.

A smiling David Berkowitz is taken from a police car prior to a criminal court arraignment in connection with the "Son of Sam" murders.

Random Mayhem

Berkowitz killed for the first time on July 29, 1976. Eighteen-year-old Donna Lauria and 19-year-old Jody Valenti were talking in Jody's car outside Donna's parents' apartment building in the Pelham Bay section of the Bronx. It was 1:00 A.M., and Donna was startled to see a figure of a man at her window. The man suddenly pulled a handgun—a .44 caliber Bulldog—out of a paper bag he was carrying and rapidly pumped five bullets into the car. Donna was dead before the fifth bullet had left the barrel, and Jody was hit in the thigh but survived.

The investigating officers were puzzled by what appeared to be the random nature of the shooting. If it was not a case of mistaken identity, it had to be the work of a psycho, someone killing for pleasure, they surmised.

Just the Beginning. A few months later, during the early hours of October 23, 20-year-old Carl Denaro and 18-year-old Rosemary Keenan were talking in Rosemary's Volkswagen Beetle near her home in the Flushing neighborhood of the New York City borough of Queens. Suddenly a figure appeared at the passenger window and shots rang out. Carl was hit in the head, but Rosemary immediately slammed her foot on the accelerator and sped away, escaping their assailant. Carl was seriously injured, but he survived.

No Pattern Detected Yet. Berkowitz had shot people in two different boroughs—and police precincts—of New York City. Critical to Berkowitz's ability to avoid detection was the fact that detectives in varying precincts worked in isolation from one another. This was almost 20 years before the establishment of the National Center for the Analysis of Violent Crime at Quantico, Virginia, which was created to find similarities between crimes committed in different parts of the country. Therefore, at this point in the investigation, investigating

FINAL **DAILY NEWS**

New York, Monday, June 27, 1977 — Price: 20 cents

.44 KILLER HITS AGAIN, WOUNDS 2

Jimmy Breslin's Exclusive Interview With Victim

Shot in Car in Queens

Jody Placido, 17, of the Bronx and boy friend, Sal Lupo, were wounded as they sat in a car parked in Bayside, Queens. They were wounded by four .44 caliber bullets fired at close range. Police said Son of Sam had struck again.

Stories on pages 3 and 29; other pictures in centerfold   Sal Lupo, arm bandaged, is wheeled from Flushing Hospital emergency room.

42 Die in Tennessee Jail Fire

Story on Page 3

The front page from the *New York Daily News*, dated June 27, 1977, features reporter Jimmy Breslin's interview with victim Judy Placido (left) of the Bronx. The page also shows a bandaged Sal Lupo being wheeled from the Flushing Hospital emergency room.

officers in Queens and the Bronx were unaware that they were dealing with the same shooter. On November 26, 16-year-old Donna DeMasi and 18-year-old Joanne Lomino were accosted by a man as they talked outside Joanne's home in Queens. He started to ask them for directions in a bizarre, high-pitched voice but suddenly pulled a gun and fired, bringing people from their houses and forcing him to flee. Both girls were hit but survived.

A Deadly Victory. Berkowitz had more success the next time. On January 30, 1977, he shot at a young couple, 26-year-old Christine Freund and her fiancé, John Diel, as they sat in John's car in the Ridgewood neighborhood of Queens. John, who drove off when the shots were fired, suffered minor wounds, but Christine died a few hours later in the hospital.

> "I am deeply hurt by your calling me a woman hater. I am not…. But I am a monster. I am the Son of Sam."
>
> —BERKOWITZ WROTE THE ABOVE IN A NOTE ADDRESSED TO CAPTAIN JOSEPH BORELLI

A Serial Killer Emerges. Police had now matched the bullets from each incident and realized that a serial killer was on the loose. But they were puzzled. There was nothing to connect the victims, and they could only presume that their perpetrator was a lone psycho with a grudge against young women. The random nature of the murders made it impossible to predict where he would strike next. All they had was an inadequate description: "a white male, 25 to 36 years old, 6 feet (1.83 m) tall, of medium build and with dark hair." Deputy Inspector Timothy O'Dowd was put in charge of a task force named Omega.

Letters to the Detectives. On March 8, 1977, Virginia Voskerichian, a 19-year-old Columbia University student, was shot as she walked home from a class in Manhattan. She died immediately. On the night of April 17, another pair of young lovers, 18-year-old Valentina Suriani and 20-year-old Alexander Esau, died in a hail of bullets when a car pulled up next to theirs near the Hutchinson River Parkway in the Bronx. Nearby an envelope was found containing a letter addressed to Captain Joseph Borelli, one of the investigating detectives. Among its misspelled ramblings were the words, "I am deeply hurt by your calling me a wemon [sic] hater. I am not. But I am a monster. I am the Son of Sam." The media latched onto the name immediately.

The 1970 Ford Galaxie owned by David Berkowitz sits in the garage of the Manhattan police headquarters. Berkowitz was arrested as he sat at the wheel of the Galaxie in front of his Yonkers apartment. A .44 caliber Bulldog revolver found under the seat of the car was identified as the gun used in eight attacks in the previous year.

Son of Sam Goes Public. The writer claimed that his father, "Sam," had ordered him to go out and kill. Another letter, sent to Jimmy Breslin, a columnist for the *New York Daily News* who had been covering the killings, made references to "Sam" and furthered the legend of the Son of Sam. New York was gripped by panic. As the killer's victims all had long, dark hair, thousands of women in the city cut their hair or even dyed it. Blond wigs sold out in beauty stores, and when summer came, despite the boiling hot temperatures, people stayed home at night, doors and windows firmly locked.

The .44 Caliber Killer's Final Victims. The panic was heightened when, on June 26, Salvatore Lupo (20) and Judy Placido (17) were wounded in their car in Bayside, Queens. On July 31, Berkowitz—by now known as both the Son of Sam and the .44 Caliber Killer—struck in Brooklyn. Stacy Moskowitz and Robert Violante, both 20 years old, were kissing in their car near a park. They had parked beneath a streetlight, believing that would protect them from whatever was out there. Suddenly a man walked out of the darkness and fired several times into the vehicle, hitting both in the head. Stacy died a few hours later in the hospital. Robert survived, although he lost an eye. It would be the Son of Sam's last shooting.

Just Sane Enough

Walking her dog near the scene of the Moskowitz-Violante shootings, Cacilia Davis saw the police put a parking ticket on a Ford Galaxie parked across the road from her. Shortly after, a man came running up, grabbed the ticket, and threw it away angrily before jumping into the car and speeding off. She told the police, and it took several more days before they located the ticket, traced the registration, and came up with a name—David Berkowitz.

A Quick Capture and Confession. On August 10, 1977, when Berkowitz was met by Detective John Falotico outside his apartment, his first words reportedly were, "You got me. What took you so long?" In the bag he was carrying, they found his .44 Bulldog, and in the car was a duffel bag filled with ammunition and maps of the crime scenes. There was also a letter that spoke of more murders. In custody a short while later, Berkowitz confessed to the killings.

The name Sam seems to have come from a neighbor, Sam Carr, whose black Labrador, Harvey, had angered Berkowitz by barking at night and keeping him awake. He wrote rambling, anonymous letters to Carr and eventually shot the dog but failed to kill it. He claimed under questioning that Harvey was possessed by a demon that issued orders for Berkowitz to kill people.

The Trial, Sentencing, and Conversion. The trial of David Berkowitz began on May 8, 1978. Although there were obvious questions about his sanity, he was judged fit to stand trial. On June 12, 1978, he received six life sentences, a prison term of 365 years.

Berkowitz, now a born-again Christian, remains in prison. He no longer seeks parole. In 2002, he wrote a letter to then-governor of New York, George Pataki, in which he states, "In all honesty, I believe that I deserve to be in prison for the rest of my life. I have, with God's help, long ago come to terms with my situation, and I have accepted my punishment."

Investigators examine the car in which Berkowitz shot his last victims, Stacy Moscowitz and Robert Violante, at Shore Parkway and 16th Street in Brooklyn on July 31, 1977.

The Letters

The Son of Sam investigation provides a perfect example of how law enforcement officers can be so overwhelmed by leads and information that even when the culprit is pointed out to them, they miss what seems obvious.

Jack Cassara, a resident of the city of New Rochelle in Westchester County, New York, was the recipient of a bizarre "get well" note expressing the hope that he was getting better after his fall. It also included a photograph of a dog. It was signed by a "Mr. Carr" and his wife, who, the note said, lived in nearby Yonkers. Cassara had not, in fact, had a fall, and he did not have a clue who "Mr. Carr" was. He called "Mr. Carr"—who turned out to be Sam Carr—and learned that he had also been receiving odd letters. Carr also told Cassara that his dog had recently been shot.

Cassara's son, Stephen, recalled a strange man who had rented a room at their house and had left without collecting his deposit. Stephen also remembered that their renter did not like dogs and that his name was David Berkowitz. The Carrs' daughter, Wheat, worked for the Yonkers Police Department and asked officers to investigate. They discovered that another man, a deputy sheriff named Craig Glassman, had received a ranting letter from his neighbor, David Berkowitz, claiming that Glassman and the Cassaras and the Carrs were part of a devil-worshiping cult. Nothing came of the investigation, but a little later two Yonkers detectives decided to investigate the letters and the shootings of a couple of dogs. As they looked at a description of Berkowitz in their files, they realized that he resembled the man described by witnesses to the murders.

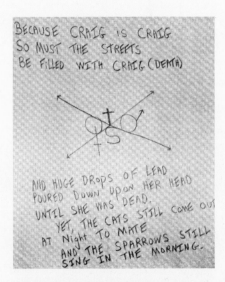

A **poem by Berkowitz** addressed to his neighbor, Craig Glassman, that was found on him when he was arrested. The full text reads: "Because Craig is Craig/So must the streets/Be filled with Craig (Death)/And huge drops of lead/Poured down upon her head/Until she was dead/Yet, the cats still come out/At night to mate/And the sparrows still/Sing in the morning."

Glassman showed the police letters he had received that were in the same handwriting as those received by the Carrs and the Cassaras. It all came to nothing, however. When Carr went to the Omega task force headquarters to persuade them that Berkowitz was the Son of Sam, he was simply told that he was just one of hundreds of people who were sure they knew who the killer was.

Mapping the Crime

Although he lived in Yonkers, most of David Berkowitz's criminal activity was in nearby Queens. In Queens he carried out four attacks, shooting seven people, one of whom died. The other attacks were spread across other New York boroughs: the Bronx, where three people died in two attacks; Manhattan, where Virginia Voskerichian died; and Brooklyn, where Stacy Moskowitz and Robert Violante died.

Case History: David Berkowitz

▶ **July 29, 1976** — Berkowitz fires into a car containing Donna Lauria (18) and Jody Valenti (19) outside Donna's parents' apartment in the Bronx. Donna dies; Jody is wounded.

▶ **October 23, 1976** — Berkowitz shoots Carl Denaro (20) and Rosemary Keenan (18) in their car in Queens. Rosemary is injured by flying glass; Carl is shot in the head but survives.

▶ **November 26, 1976** — Berkowitz shoots Donna DeMasi (16) and Joanne Lomino (18). Both are wounded and survive, although Joanne is paralyzed.

▶ **January 30, 1977** — Christine Freund (26) is shot dead when Berkowitz attacks the car in which she is sitting with boyfriend John Diel in Queens.

▶ **March 8, 1977** — Virginia Voskerichian (19) is killed as she walks home from a class at Columbia University in Manhattan.

▶ **April 17, 1977** — Alexander Esau (20) and Valentina Suriani (18) are both shot dead in their car in the Bronx. Berkowitz leaves behind a letter describing himself as "Son of Sam."

▶ **June 26, 1977** — Sal Lupo (20) and Judy Placido (17) receive minor wounds when Berkowitz attacks them in the Bayside area of Queens.

▶ **July 31, 1977** — Stacy Moskowitz and Robert Violante are both shot in the head as they kiss in their car in Brooklyn. Stacy dies later in the hospital and Violante survives. Berkowitz receives a parking ticket and is seen by Cacilia Davis. She informs the police, who later arrest Berkowitz for the Son of Sam murders.

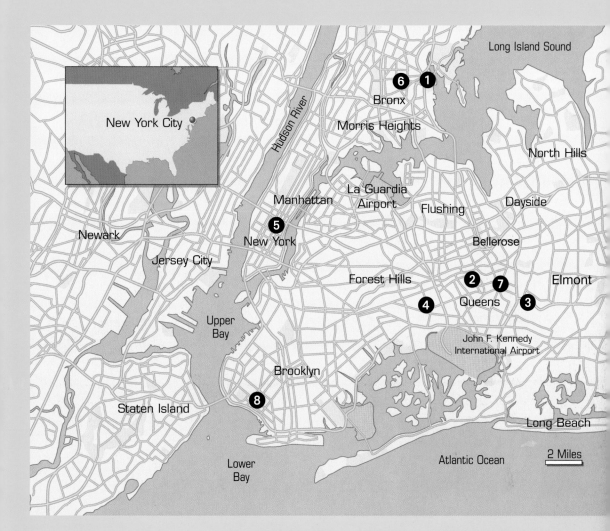

Locations of the Murders

1 **Bronx**—Donna Lauria is shot dead and her friend Jody Valenti is wounded, July 1976

2 **Queens**—Carl Denaro and Rosemary Keenan shot by Berkowitz in their car—both survive, October 1976

3 **Queens**—Donna DeMasi and Joanne Lomino shot but survive; Joanne is paralyzed, November 1976

4 **Queens**—Christine Freud is shot dead, January 1977

5 **Manhattan**—Virginia Voskerichian is killed on her way home from Columbia University, March 1977

6 **Bronx**—Alexander Esau and Valentina Suriani are shot dead in their car, April 1977

7 **Queens**—Sal Lupo and Judy Placido are both shot but survive, June 1977

8 **Brooklyn**—Stacy Moskowitz and Robert Violante are both shot—Stacy dies, Violante survives; July 1977

Robert Lee Yates, Jr.:
The Spokane Serial Killer

He seemed like an ordinary, middle-aged guy. Married with five children, he had a religious upbringing and had been a good student. Later, he became a military helicopter pilot and served with notable bravery around the world, winning numerous medals and citations. There was another side to Robert Lee Yates, Jr., however. In Washington state, between 1975 and 1998, he brutally murdered at least 21 people, most of whom were prostitutes.

Robert Lee Yates, Jr. escorted by Spokane County Sheriff Deputies out of a Superior courtroom in Spokane, Washington, on May 31, 2000. Yates had pleaded not guilty to eight first-degree murder charges.

A Killer of Spokane's Own

In one spate of killing in Spokane, seven prostitutes were found dead in the last five months of 1997, four of them in the last few weeks of the year. At first police thought the Green River Killer, who had been terrorizing and killing prostitutes in Seattle, had moved to Spokane. Sadly, however, this killer turned out to be one of Spokane's own.

Decades of Killing. Most of the Spokane killings took place between 1996 and 1998, but the total span of time covered by the murders would turn out to be considerably greater—dating, by the killer's own reckoning, back to 1975. The first body was found on February 22, 1990, near the Spokane River. A 26-year-old prostitute, Yolanda Sapp, had been shot a number of times with a small-caliber handgun. She was naked, and none of her clothing or belongings was found in the area. The absence of shell casings suggested that she had probably been killed elsewhere and brought to this spot. She had last been seen two days earlier.

More Victims, More Similarities. Just over a month later, another body was found. Nickie Lowe, a 34-year-old woman, had also been shot to death. Like the previous victim, she had worked the streets and had a history of drug abuse. A 22-caliber bullet was retrieved intact from her body, and similarities between the two cases made it almost certain that the same man had killed both women.

Seven weeks passed without incident, but on May 15, a nude body was found in the Trent and Pines area, again close to the Spokane River. As with the other two victims, small-caliber bullets were extracted from the corpse of 38-year-old Kathleen Brisbois. She appeared also to have been beaten, however. Tire tracks were found near the scene. Investigators now had no doubt, given the similarity of the murders, the fact that the victims had all been prostitutes, and the fact that the weapon used had been the same small-caliber handgun, that a serial killer was at work in Spokane.

Pierce County Superior Court Judge John McCarthy addresses jurors on location at a city maintenance building where the van driven by Robert Lee Yates, Jr. is stored. Yates is visible, second from top left, whispering to his defense attorney Roger Hunko.

Taking a Break

Nothing happened for two years, and the police began to believe that their unsub (short for unknown subject of an investigation) had moved away. But on May 13, 1992, 19-year-old Sherry Anne Palmer was found, shot dead, near Mount Spokane Park Drive. Twelve days earlier, she had left a motel in which she had been working as a prostitute, to keep an appointment with her boyfriend, but she had failed to arrive. It was evident once again, from the lack of shell casings and pooling of blood, that she had died elsewhere. The police collected hair, fibers, and swabs of other evidence from her body.

The killer took another break, three years this time. As studies have shown, serial killers rarely change their hunting and killing methods, and this one was carried out in exactly the same manner as the previous ones. The only difference this time was that the killer had traveled to a different locale, Kitsap County, northwest of Spokane. The body of Patricia Barnes was found on August 25, 1995. Her body was covered in foliage that, investigators noted with interest, had not originated at the scene of her discovery. Again she had not been killed where she lay. In fact, a second pile of foliage 1 mile (1.6 km) away covered blood and plastic bags containing hair curlers belonging to the victim.

Nearly a Year Later, Another Body. The body of 39-year-old Shannon R. Zielinski was found in June 1996. Yet a year later, in August 1997, two bodies turned up in one day. As before, the bodies of both of these victims—Heather Hernandez and Jennifer Joseph—had been dragged to their final resting places from the sites of their murders. In the case of Jennifer Joseph, detectives at last got a break. A witness recalled and reported seeing her in a car with a white male. His age, the witness told detectives, seemed to be between 30 and 40. The car was a white Corvette.

Mounting Clues and a Body Count to Match

On Wednesday, September 24, 1997, a police officer in Spokane stopped a white Corvette for a minor traffic violation. The driver, given a ticket and allowed to proceed, was named Robert L. Yates, Jr. In addition to not picking up on the similarity between Yates's car and the one noted just weeks earlier, the police officer mistakenly recorded the vehicle make as a Camaro instead of a Corvette, and the connection was not made with the vehicle in which Jennifer Joseph had been driven to her death.

Trademarks of a Serial Killer. Before the end of 1997, another five bodies turned up. They all bore the trademarks of the Spokane killer: The victims had been shot, and pieces of clothing were missing from each. Police surmised that the killer took "souvenirs" of his deeds. One victim had last been seen in the company of a man driving a burgundy-colored minivan. The last two, discovered the day after Christmas, were covered with vegetation. The body of Sunny Oster was found on February 28, 1998, and on April 1, 34-year-old Linda

"I've taken away the love, the compassion and the tenderness of your loved ones... In my struggle to overcome my guilt and shame, I have turned to God... I hope that God will replace your... sorrow with peace."

—ROBERT LEE YATES'S COURTROOM EXPRESSION OF REMORSE TO HIS VICTIMS' FAMILIES, WHICH WAS MET WITH BOOS

Maybin's body was found beneath a pile of vegetation that once again was not from the area.

The Killing Ends. The last three victims turned up in May, July, and October of 1998, bringing the body count for the Spokane serial killer to 17. Police, however, believed that there may have been many bodies still not discovered and that the tally could be much higher.

Connecting the Dots

Ballistic evidence linked the bullets found in a number of the bodies to the same .22 pistol. Sherry Anne Palmer, however, had been shot with a .32 semiautomatic, and Shannon Zielinski had been killed with a .25 caliber weapon, as had several other victims. Hair and fiber evidence taken from the scenes of the crimes was discovered to have originated from a variety of sources, and sperm was found in several cases that was confirmed to be from the same man. The police now had DNA evidence that could prove conclusive. All they had to do was find a suspect.

Prosecutor Jerry Costello points to the entry paths of the bullets that were fired into the head of Melody A. Murfin, at the murder trial of Robert Lee Yates, Jr. in Tacoma, on September 17, 2002.

A Missed Opportunity. Robert Yates, Jr. had another brush with the law on the night of November 10, 1998, when he was stopped and questioned after pulling over to speak to a young prostitute named Jennifer Robinson. Yates and Jennifer quickly dreamed up a story, and Yates told the officer that Jennifer's father had asked him to find her and drive her home. Jennifer also wanted to stay out of trouble, and she was only too happy to confirm the story. On the basis of what seems in hindsight to be a flimsy story at best—but one that both Yates and his intended victim agreed was true—the officer figured that there was nothing more he could do. Clearly fortune had smiled on Jennifer that night.

Meanwhile a report was uncovered of a prostitute, 30-year-old Christine Smith, who had been picked up by a man driving a van with a bed in the back. In an unguarded moment, the man had told her he had five children and was a helicopter pilot. They climbed into the back and began to have sex, but then Christine suddenly felt something hit her on the head. She did not lose consciousness and managed to struggle with her attacker and escape. Later when her injury was checked out, she learned that she had actually been shot. Although Christine didn't have a name for her "date," she was able to identify him as a father of five and a helicopter pilot. With both of these details pointing squarely at Robert Yates, Jr., he became the number-one suspect.

Working Up a History

Once investigators began examining Yates's background, they learned that while serving as an Army National Guard helicopter pilot, he had been grounded pending medical evaluations from the spring of 1997 until the spring of 1998, the period when the majority of the murders had been committed. Furthermore, his wife told detectives, he had come home one morning with a substantial amount of blood in the back of his van that he claimed came from a dog he had run over and taken to a veterinarian. When Yates arrived home, his wife reported, he went to work cleaning up the back of the van and replaced the old mattress with a new one. That incident happened the morning after the night that Christine Smith had been picked up, shot, and managed to escape.

Fiber Samples from a 'Vette. The Corvette had been sold, but the new owner confirmed that Yates had told her he had changed the car's carpeting. It emerged, in fact, that he had changed it twice in two years. Fiber samples taken from the car were found to match those found during the investigation into Jennifer Joseph's murder.

Arrest and Conviction

Yates was arrested on April 18, 2000, and initially charged with 8 counts of first-degree murder, later increased to 13 counts of first-degree murder and 1 count of attempted first-degree murder. To avoid the death penalty, however, he decided to plead guilty to the charges, and he promised to provide investigators with the location of the body of another woman he was suspected of killing. The body of 43-year-old Melody Murfin was found in a shallow grave outside Yates' bedroom window. He confessed to

Unsub

The term *unsub* has been coined in law enforcement to describe an *unknown subject* of an investigation. The term's usage varies from agency to agency and place to place. Some officers still prefer to use the older term *perp*, which is short for *perpetrator*. Profilers invariably use unsub. In recent years, the term has been used in a number of films and television shows, notably the 1996 movie *Ransom*, the 2002 movie, *Catch Me if You Can*, the NBC-TV series *Unsub*, which ran for one season in 1989, and the long-running CBS-TV series *Criminal Minds*, which premiered in 2005. In all four of these, the term is used by members of the FBI; in the two TV shows, the agents are members of elite investigative squads—an FBI forensics unit in *Unsub*, and in *Criminal Minds*, a team of profilers from the FBI's Behavioral Analysis Unit (BAU).

The term *unsub* has in this way become associated with action thrillers and police procedural dramas. The reality behind a subject being unknown may, however, be rooted in causes that are more down-to-earth than the popular media would suggest. For one thing, it takes time for material gathered from a crime scene to be processed and analyzed, and the investigating officers may wish to move to apprehend their suspect before that process is completed. Or the evidence may point to a suspect who has never been in trouble before, meaning that he or she may not be present on any criminal database. The suspect, therefore, remains unknown.

Of course the evidence may be compromised in some way that also means the suspect will be termed *unknown*. Although the subject is unknown—and perhaps because of it—the authorities publish information about him or her, hoping to reach anyone who might be able to provide them with vital leads.

the murders of a young couple he apparently met while they were out on a picnic in Walla Walla in 1975 when he was working as a prison guard there. He also confessed to the murder—in Skagit County in 1988—of a young woman who is believed to be the first prostitute killed by Yates.

On October 26, 2000, Yates was sentenced to 408 years in prison, but in 2001 he was charged with the murders of two more women, both prostitutes in Pierce County, in 1997 and 1998. There was no deal to be made this time, and he was sentenced to death by lethal injection on October 4, 2002. He is currently being held on death row at Washington State Penitentiary.

Case History: Robert Lee Yates, Jr.

▶ **July 13, 1975**
Patrick Oliver (22) and Susan Savage (21) killed while picnicking on Mill Creek, just east of Walla Walla.

▶ **December 28, 1988**
Stacy E. Hawn (23) is found in Skagit County, Washington.

▶ **February 22, 1990**
Yolanda Sapp (26) is found on the embankment near the Spokane River on the 3200 block of East Sprague.

▶ **March 25, 1990**
Nickie Lowe (34) is found in the road at the 3200 block of East South Riverton.

▶ **May 15, 1990**
Kathleen Brisbois (38) is found in the Trent and Pines area near the banks of the Spokane River.

▶ **May 13, 1992**
Sherry Anne Palmer (19) is found on Bill Gulch Road.

▶ **August 25, 1995**
Patricia Barnes (60) is found in the vicinity of the 15900 block of Peacock Hill Road in Kitsap County.

▶ **June 14, 1996**
Shannon Zielinski (39) is found near the intersection of Mount Spokane Park Drive and Holcomb Road.

▶ **August 26, 1997**
Heather Hernandez (20) and Jennifer Joseph (16) are found on the same day, Hernandez in a field behind 1817 E. Springfield in Spokane, Joseph near the north 9800 block of Forker Road.

▶ **November 5, 1997**
Darla Scott (29) is found in a shallow grave near South 12600 Hangman Valley Road.

▶ **December 7, 1997**
Melinda L. Mercer (24) is found in the 5000 block of South Adams Street.

▶ **December 17, 1997**
Shawn Johnson (36) is found in the 11400 block of Hangman Valley Road.

▶ **December 26, 1997**
Laurel Wason (31) and Shawn A. McClenahan (39) are found on the same day in the 4800 block of East 14th Avenue.

▶ **February 28, 1998**
Sunny Oster (41) is found in a ditch on Graham Road in a rural area of Spokane County.

▶ **April 1, 1998**
Linda Maybin (34) is found dumped in East 14th Avenue.

▶ **July 7, 1998**
Michelyn Derning (47) is found near 218 N. Crestline.

▶ **October 13, 1998**
Connie LaFontaine Ellis (35) is found near the 1700 block of 108th Street South, Tacoma.

▶ **May 12, 1998**
Melody Murfin (43) is found buried in Yates's yard after he makes a plea bargain with investigators.

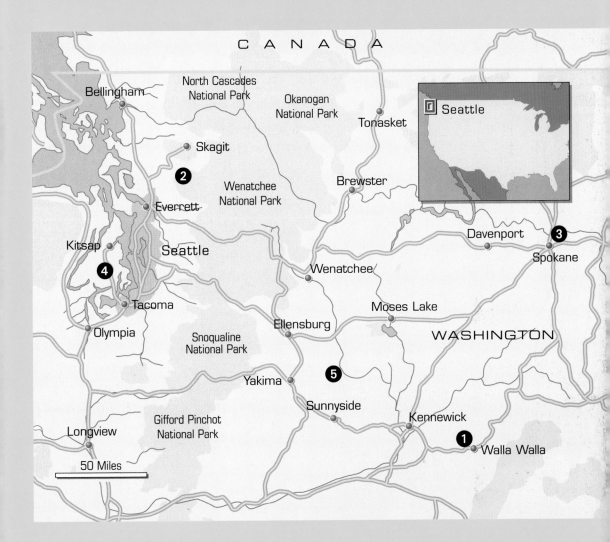

Locations of the Murders

1 **Walla Walla, Washington**—Patrick Oliver and Susan Savage killed while Yates was working as a prison guard, July 1975

2 **Skagit County, Washington**—Stacy Elizabeth Hawn was last seen alive in Seattle, July 1988

3 **Spokane, Washington**—The bodies of 15 women discovered, February 1990–July 1998

4 **Kitsap County, Washington**—Patricia Barnes murdered, August 1995

5 **Pierce County, Washington**—Melinda L. Mercer murdered in 1997 and Connie LaFontaine Ellis in 1998

John Duffy and David Mulcahy:
The Railway Rapists

As leading criminologist David Canter has pointed out, sometimes the journey that killers take to murder is a tortuous one. This certainly seems to have been true of the Railway Rapists, the name given to the perpetrators of a series of attacks in the 1980s—rapes and murders—that were characterized by the fact that many of their locations were in the vicinity of railroad lines in the south of England. The assaults had begun as what seemed to be opportunistic and unplanned rapes but had graduated into planned, premeditated, and horrific murders.

An Attempt to Learn from Past Mistakes

The Yorkshire Ripper case (1971–1985) had not only shocked the nation; it had also shaken the British police to the core. During that investigation, authorities had been swamped with information, most of it in the form of letters and phone calls suggesting likely suspects. But investigators had also conducted thousands of door-to-door interviews and spoken to thousands of men who may have handled a £5 bill that had been found at one of the crime scenes and was considered a key component of the investigation.

A Scathing Report. In addition to the £5 note, the police were stymied in their efforts to connect a set of tire tracks to one of the 100,000 or so vehicles that could have left the tracks. The Byford Report following the Ripper case had been scathing of the investigation, in particular its poor management of police

John Duffy (left) and David Mulcahy pictured as teenagers in what looks like a photo-booth shot and issued as a handout by police at the time of the investigation.

records. Staff working on the Railway Rapist case in 1985 had taken note and put in place an excellent computerized information-recording system. Still, however, it failed to bring them closer to solving the case and finding the man, or men, responsible.

The Rapes Begin. The first rape took place in 1982 when a woman was attacked by two men near the Hampstead Heath station. During the following 12 months, 18 more women were raped. More followed in 1984, and then, in 1985, three women were attacked on the same night in the Hendon area. When the tally of rapes spiraled to around 40, police urgently set up an investigation, code named Operation Hart, to find the perpetrators of these terrible crimes. Before long, however, raping alone seemed to have ceased to adequately satisfy the attackers' needs. They now needed to kill.

Hackney Wick station in London where the body of Alison Day (19) was found after being dragged off a train, repeatedly raped, and strangled with a piece of string on December 29, 1985.

When Rape Is Not Enough

The first murder was carried out on December 29, 1985, when 19-year-old Alison Day was attacked as she got off a train at Hackney Wick station in East London. She was repeatedly raped and then strangled with a piece of string.

On April 17, 1986, 15-year-old Maartje Tamboezer was attacked in West Horsley as she cycled through woodland close to a railroad station. She was pulled from her bike and dragged through the woods for a distance of 0.5 mile (0.8 km) before being raped and murdered. It was suggested at the time that an unknown suspect had been seen in the area for a few days, likely looking for a victim, it was surmised. It was a piece of evidence that supported David Canter's theory that the rapist had switched his status from opportunist to planner. A month later, on May 18, Anne Locke, a 29-year-old secretary with a television company, was raped and murdered after getting off a train at Brookman's Park in Hertfordshire.

> "...a bit of a joke, a bit of a game. You get into the pattern of offending— it is very difficult to stop."
>
> —DESCRIPTION BY DUFFY WHEN ASKED ABOUT HIS CRIMES

A Killer Profile

The Byford Report that came out of the Yorkshire Ripper case had recommended the use of scientists where appropriate, and the investigators on the Railway Rapist case decided to call in David Canter. Canter began by overlaying the locations on a map of London and investigating how the crimes had unfolded over time. He discovered that in 1982, the rapes had been limited to one area. In 1984 that area had widened, and in 1985 and 1986, it had widened even more. This increase in the area of the rapists' activity was coupled with a development in the way the crimes were being committed. The earlier rapes had involved two individuals and tended to take place on weekends. The later ones took place on weekdays and tended to be committed by only one man. Furthermore they appeared to be much more premeditated and better planned.

Narrowing the Search. The 1982 rapes had been far more opportunistic, and it was therefore likely, Canter argued, that they were committed not a great distance from where the perpetrators lived. He told police that they were likely to be based in the Kilburn area of North West London.

The police had a list of thousands of suspects, but only one lived in the area that Canter was referring to—John Duffy. Duffy had been interviewed, along with his childhood friend David Mulcahy, in July 1985, but they had not been charged. Shortly after that time, they had turned to murder.

A Portrait of a Serial Rapist and Killer. Canter provided a profile of the killer. He described him as living in the area circumscribed by the first three cases that occurred in 1982 and 1983; he probably lived with a wife or girlfriend and was aged in his mid- to late-20s; it was likely that he did not have any children; he was right-handed and had a semiskilled or skilled job with weekend work; he had an excellent knowledge of the railroad system; and he had a criminal record involving violence.

When John Duffy was eventually arrested in November 1986, he was found to be living in Kilburn in North London, was separated from his wife, was in his late 20s, was right-handed, and worked as a traveling carpenter for British Rail, which gave him an excellent knowledge of the rail system. Regarding a criminal record, he was known to the police for having raped his wife at knifepoint.

A picture issued by police showing the various weapons recovered from David Mulcahy's house after his arrest.

The Match is Made. The police charged Duffy with three murders and 7 rapes and sexual assaults. He was later charged with 17 more rapes. Several years later, police believed that those numbers might have been much higher.

Balaclavas and Knives

For years following his arrest in 1986, Duffy refused to talk about who his accomplice might have been. In 1998, however, to clear his conscience, as he put it, he finally began to open up. He named David Mulcahy and described how they had realized that there were very often lone women getting off trains late at night or in the dark at railroad stations. They would drive around, therefore, visiting railroad stations and looking out for a likely victim.

David Mulcahy shortly before his arrest in 2000.

The "Thriller Killers." Many people had assumed that the rapist had actually been a train traveler who had followed a victim off a train, but this was not the case. Duffy and Mulcahy called it "hunting," and they would sing along to the soundtrack of Michael Jackson's *Thriller* as they waited. When this fact became known, the Railway Rapists also became known as the "Thriller Killers."

Keeping Ahead of the Police. Duffy told how they changed their geographical location once they read that police were looking for men the papers were calling the North London Rapists. Their attacks spread farther from their home areas into other areas of London and surrounding counties. They wore tight-fitting, hooded garments called balaclavas and armed themselves with knives. Duffy described it as, ". . . a bit of a joke, a bit of a game. You get into the pattern of offending—it is very difficult to stop."

And Mulcahy Makes Two

By the time Mulcahy appeared at the central criminal court in London, Old Bailey, in 2000, Duffy had been in prison for 14 years. Duffy testified for the prosecution and spent 14 days in the witness box. In February 2001, David Mulcahy was given three life sentences for the rape and murder of three women and for seven additional rapes.

Duffy and Mulcahy will in all likelihood never be released, but police fear that they may well have been responsible for many more deaths than the ones for which they were sentenced.

David Canter

David Canter is a British psychologist who began his career studying the relationships between people and buildings. He was involved in the design of countless buildings—offices, schools, residences, and prisons as well as other types of structures. An element of his work involved studies of human reactions to emergency situations, such as fires.

Canter is probably best known for his groundbreaking work on offender profiling in Britain. He helped police on the 1985 Railway Rapist case, and, while professor of Psychology at the University of Surrey, he developed the new science of Investigative Psychology. This deals with the identifying and retrieval of investigative information and using that information, along with the support of various systems derived from scientific research, to help police make critical decisions in their investigations.

Professor Canter developed a "geographic prioritization computer package," called Dragnet, that uses the locations of a series of crimes to prioritize the surrounding areas

in relation to the likely location of the offender's base. The investigator inputs the crime locations, and an offense map is produced with a crime scene represented by a dot. A prioritized map is then produced, indicating where the offender is likely to live or base his operations.

Criminologist David Canter is one of the pioneers of offender profiling in the United Kingdom.

Mapping the Crime

The crimes of Duffy and Mulcahy developed from casual, opportunistic assault to premeditated, vicious murder. They also developed from crimes committed in familiar areas as part of the killers' daily routines to crimes carried out farther away. The earliest rapes took place in the north London areas of Kilburn and West Hampstead, but the murders occurred farther out. It was later discovered, after Mulcahy was arrested, that most of the rapes happened between their two residences.

Case History: John Duffy & David Mulcahy

June 1982
A woman is raped close to Hampstead Station.

Summer 1983
Between the summer of 1983 and early 1984, 18 women are raped near train stations.

Autumn 1983
The attacks abruptly stop. Police will later learn that at this time Duffy was separating from his wife.

Early 1984
The attacks start again, this time in West London and North London. The police are unsure whether they are looking for one or two suspects.

July 1985
Three women are raped on the same night in the Hendon–Hampstead area of north London.

September 1985
After being attacked in Barnet, a woman gives a description that fits Duffy, but fails to pick him in a police lineup.

December 29, 1985
John Duffy murders Alison Day (19).

April 17, 1986
Duffy murders Maartje Tamboezer (15).

May 12, 1986
Duffy is arrested near North Weald station carrying a knife, but is later released due to lack of evidence.

May 18, 1986
Anne Locke (29), a secretary, is raped and murdered after getting off a train in Hertfordshire.

November 1986
Duffy is arrested after stalking a woman in a park.

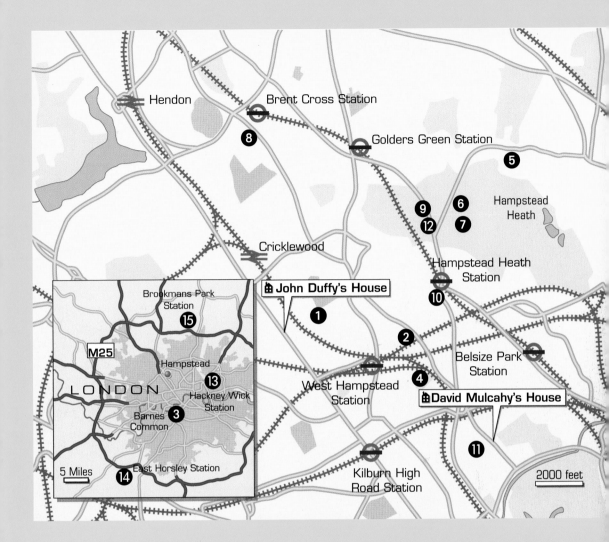

Locations of the Rapes* and Murders

① October 21, 1982

② March 26, 1983

③ January 20, 1984

④ June 3, 1984

⑤ July 8, 1984

⑥ July 15, 1984

⑦ July 15, 1984

⑧ January 26, 1985

⑨ January 30, 1985

⑩ February 2, 1985

⑪ February 3, 1985

⑫ March 3, 1985

⑬ **Hackney Wick Station**—Alison Day murdered, December 1985

⑭ **East Horsley Station**—Maartje Tamboezer murdered, April 1986

⑮ **Brookman's Park Station**—Anne Locke murdered, May 1986

* The rape victims cannot be named for legal reasons.

Aileen Wuornos: The Damsel of Death

Investigators knew the killer had to be a woman. In those unstable times, no one was likely to stop and pick up a man hitchhiking at the side of the road. A woman, however, posed little threat. Or at least that is what the seven men who were killed by Aileen "Lee" Wuornos thought as she took her revenge on the gender that had made so much of her life miserable.

A Doomed Life

She was born in 1956 to Diane and Leo Dale Pittman. Her father was a psychotic child molester who hanged himself in prison in 1969. At the age of 4, she was handed over to her grandparents in Troy, Michigan, to be cared for, taking their name, Wuornos. Throughout her childhood, she believed that her grandparents were actually her parents. It was only at the age of 12 that she would learn otherwise.

A smiling Aileen **Wuornos** in court during her trial for the murder of seven men.

A Rotten Childhood. It was a strict upbringing in a family devoid of love. Her grandfather was a chronic alcoholic and violently disciplined Aileen and her brother Keith. The kids were themselves difficult to control, and Aileen became sexually active at an early age. She was pregnant at the age of 14 and gave up the baby for adoption. When her grandmother died that same year, 1971, Aileen decided to hit the road, hitchhiking and using prostitution to earn enough money to live on.

Debauchery, Drunkenness, and Marriage. In a life that presented few opportunities, she had an extraordinary piece of luck when she was picked up one day hitchhiking by a man named Lewis Fell, a well-off 69-year-old who was president of a Florida yacht club. The two embarked on an intense relationship, and before long they were married. But, Wuornos was unable to escape the spiral of debauchery and drunkenness that had constituted her life. When she was eventually jailed for assault, Fell realized he had made a mistake. The marriage was annulled, and Aileen Wuornos hit the road again.

The next 10 years took her on an increasing spiral of doomed relationships, drugs, prostitution, and general lawbreaking. She was involved in forgery and even armed robbery, and she later said that she had hit rock bottom and that at one point she had tried to kill herself.

The Last Resort Bar in Port Orange, Florida, where Aileen Wuornos was arrested.

The Love of Her Life. Just when it all seemed pointless, in 1989 Wuornos met the love of her life. Tyria Moore was a pretty, 24-year-old chambermaid, and soon she and Wuornos were living together, Wuornos supporting them with her earnings from prostitution. It was getting tougher, though. She was in her 30s by now and was losing out to younger, better-looking girls in her work as a prostitute. She had to find another way to earn enough to be able to keep her lover. Robbing the men who picked her up was the only way, and to do that, she decided, she would have to kill them.

Hitchhiker from Hell

The first was Richard Mallory, a middle-aged proprietor of an electronics repair business who was also a convicted rapist. Mallory was known to be in the habit of disappearing for days, partying somewhere. No one worried, therefore, when he was nowhere to be found in December 1989; he always came back when his cash ran out. Not this time, however.

The Florida Killings Begin. Mallory's 1977 Cadillac was discovered abandoned outside Daytona, Florida, on a back road near Interstate 95. On December 13, his body was found, wrapped in a carpet in a wooded area not far away. Three bullets fired at close range from a .22 caliber pistol had killed him.

1990: A Very Bad Year. About six months later, on June 1, 1990, the naked body of 43-year-old heavy equipment operator David Spears was found in the woods near Highway 19 in Citrus County, 40 miles (64 km) north of Tampa. Missing since May 19, when he was driving his truck to Orlando, he had been killed by six bullets from a .22. There was a used condom close to his body.

June 6 turned up another corpse, close to Interstate 75 in Pasco County. Forty-year-old part-time rodeo worker Charles Carskaddon had been killed by nine bullets from a .22.

> "I wanted to confess to you that Richard Mallory did violently rape me as I've told you. But these others did not. [They] only began to start to."
>
> —AN EXTRACT FROM THE STATEMENT READ BY WUORNOS TO THE COURT IN 1992

A Wreck and More Deaths

On July 4, 1990, a car crashed off State Road 315, near Orange Springs, Florida. From it staggered two women who appeared to be drunk. It was Aileen Wuornos and Tyria Moore, who were arguing with each other and swearing loudly. When a passerby stopped and asked if they needed help, however, Wuornos calmed down, begging him not to call the police, claiming that she lived just down the road and her father would sort things out.

Missing Men. The abandoned wreck was later checked by detectives, who found it to be registered to Peter Siems, a 65-year-old retired merchant seaman from Jupiter, Florida. Siems had set out to visit family out of state on June 7, 1990, and he has not been seen since.

Four weeks later, on July 31, sausage deliveryman Troy Burress failed to return to his depot. The next morning, his truck was found 20 miles (32 km) east of the town of Ocala. They found his body five days later in the Ocala National Forest, shot with two slugs from a .22.

The Count Rises to Seven. They kept on coming. On September 12, the body of retired Air Force major, former police chief, and Florida state child abuse investigator Charles "Dick" Humphreys was found in Marion County. He had been shot six times in the head and body.

Aileen Wuornos's seventh and last victim was 62-year-old Walter Gino Antonio, whose body was found on November 19, 1990, close to a remote logging road in Dixie County. He was almost naked and had been shot four times in the back and head. His car was found five days later.

A Suspect Emerges

The police soon found a suspect in the disappearance of Peter Siems. A palm print found in his car was identified as belonging to Aileen Wuornos. At the same time, they were beginning to connect her to some of the other murders through goods that she had pawned, such as Richard Mallory's camera. A manhunt was launched.

Capture and Confession. Wuornos was eventually found by plainclothes officers posing as drug dealers at a biker bar in Port Orange and was arrested on January 9, 1991. On January 16, she confessed, emphasizing that her lover, Tyria Moore, had no involvement in the killings. Wuornos claimed to have killed only in self-defense, that her victims had all tried to rape her or had threatened her in some way. But there was little consistency in her statements, and she seemed to be embellishing them as she went along.

Peter Siems, a victim of Aileen Wuornos. Wuornos and Moore were seen abandoning his car in Orange Springs, Florida, but his body has never been found.

A Helper and Protector

Another bizarre twist in the already tortuous life of Aileen Wuornos occurred when a born-again Christian, 44-year-old Marion County horse breeder Arlene Pralle, claimed to have been ordered by Jesus to write to Wuornos, who was in jail awaiting trial. The two began corresponding in January 1991, and Pralle became Wuornos's advisor and protector, raising a huge amount of pretrial publicity about the case on television and in the press.

Pralle constantly referred to what she believed to be the mitigating factors of Wuornos's miserable background. Then, on November 22, 1991, she announced that she and her husband had legally adopted Aileen Wuornos, claiming that they had been ordered to do so by God.

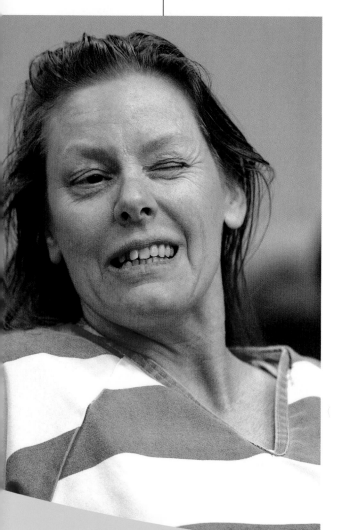

Aileen Wuornos makes a face during her trial.

"Scumbags of America!"

In the midst of an extraordinary ongoing media circus, Aileen Wuornos went to trial for the murder of Richard Mallory. When she was found guilty on January 27, 1992, she was furious, screaming at the jury, "I'm innocent! I was raped! I hope you get raped! Scumbags of America!"

Four days later, she received the death penalty. Her conviction was aided by testimony by Tyria Moore. Police had tracked Moore down to a motel in Pennsylvania and brought her back to Florida with an agreement that her help in the case would spare her being charged as an accomplice.

More Convictions and Death Sentences.
In March 1992, Wuornos pleaded "no contest" to the murders of Dick Humphreys, Troy Burress, and David Spears. This time she read out a comparatively dignified statement: "I wanted to confess to you that Richard

Nomad on the Loose

In the view of noted Canadian criminologist Dr. Kim Rossmo, Aileen "Lee" Wuornos was a "nomadic killer." She lived in various motels and in different cities. Even as a nomadic killer, however, her base can be shown, from analysis of the locations of her murders, to have been Wildwood, Florida. It was from a truck stop there, on Interstate 75, that she would hitchhike and meet her victims.

Nomadic killers are notoriously difficult to find, but the only way to truly avoid detection is to give up the trappings of everyday existence such as bank accounts, credit cards, and cell phones and live, in a way, outside of society. Even in doing that, however, we still leave traces of ourselves wherever we go.

Investigators traced the movements of Aileen Wuornos and Tyria Moore from late September to mid-December 1990 through trailer parks, motels, and several different identities. The identity that finally paid off was that of Cammie Marsh Greene, used by Wuornos while the couple stayed in Daytona.

Officers visited pawnshops in Daytona and came up with a list of items, including a camera and a radar detector that had belonged to Richard Mallory. In Ormond Beach, they came up with a set of tools that had been taken from David Spears's truck.

Meanwhile some old-fashioned forensics finally nailed the culprit when a thumbprint taken from Peter Siems's car was identified as belonging to one Lori Grody. Lori Grody was a known alias of Aileen Wuornos.

Mallory did violently rape me as I've told you. But these others did not. [They] only began to start to." As another three death sentences were delivered, however, she turned to the Assistant State Attorney Ric Ridgeway and snarled, "I hope your wife and children get raped…." Additional death sentences were delivered at trials later in the year for the murders of Charles Carskaddon and Walter Antonio. Peter Siems's body was never found.

Aileen Wuornos was executed by lethal injection at 9:47 A.M. on Wednesday October 9, 2002. The relationship with her adoptive mother, Arlene Pralle, had soured by this time, and Pralle did not even know the date of the execution.

Mapping the Crime

Highway, 19, Interstate 75, Interstate 95—these were the roads that Aileen Wuornos traveled in search of her victims, taking revenge on men for what other men had done to her and stealing what she could to pawn after she had dispatched them and dumped their bodies in isolated locations. She would stick out her thumb at rest stops and take a trip to wherever the driver thought he was going. It was Wuornos, however, who decided the ultimate destination.

Case History: Aileen Wuornos

▶ **November 30, 1989**   Aileen Wuornos's first victim, electronics store owner, Richard Mallory (51), is shot with a .22. His body is found on December 13.

▶ **June 1, 1990**   The body of Winter Garden construction worker David Spears (43) is found alongside Highway 19 in Citrus County, Florida. He had been missing since May 19.

▶ **June 6, 1990**   The body of part-time rodeo worker Charles Carskaddon (40) is found in Pasco County Florida.

▶ **July 4, 1990**   Police find a car apparently abandoned by Aileen Wuornos and Tyria Moore and owned by a former merchant seaman named Peter Siems (65). His body is never found, but Wuornos will later confess to the crime.

▶ **August 4, 1990**   Sausage delivery truck driver Troy Burress (50), who has been missing since July 30, is found dead near State Road 19 in Marion County.

▶ **September 12, 1990**   Retired Air Force major, former police chief, and Florida state child abuse investigator Dick Humphreys (56) is found dead in Marion County.

▶ **November 19, 1990**   The body of Walter Gino Antonio (62) is found near a remote logging road in Dixie County.

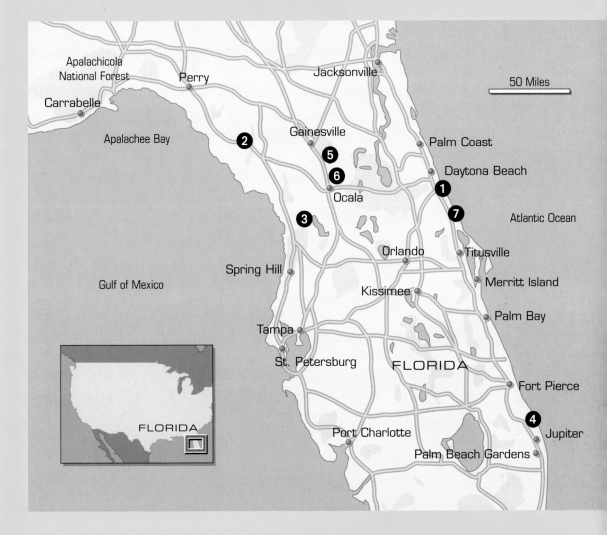

Locations of the Abductions and Murders

❶ Volusia County—Richard Mallory shot three times with a .22, November 1989

❷ Citrus County—David Spears's body found near Highway 19, June 1990

❸ Pasco County—Body of Charles Carskaddon, found June 1990

❹ South Florida—Peter Siems is murdered; his body is never found, June 1990

❺ Marion County—Troy Burress found dead on State Road 19, August 1990

❻ Marion County—Dick Humphreys found shot, September 1990

❼ Dixie County—Walter Gino Antonio found dead on remote logging road, November 1990

John Allen Muhammad and Lee Boyd Malvo: The Beltway Snipers

The 13 killings were random. Age, sex, race—nothing seemed to matter. During those awful three weeks in October 2002, if you found yourself in the wrong place at the wrong time in Washington, D.C., and suburban communities in Maryland and Virginia, filling your car with gasoline, loading your trunk with groceries, or just going about your daily business, you stood a chance of being gunned down. Gas stations erected tarpaulins to block the view of people standing at the pumps, many schools closed, and at those that remained open, police officers were called in to nervously patrol playgrounds and perimeter fences.

A Plan to Kill Six People a Day

The Beltway Sniper, named after the circular highway that ringed Washington, D.C., was actually two men—41-year-old former soldier John Allen Muhammad and 17-year-old Jamaican immigrant Lee Boyd Malvo.

John Allen Muhammad. Muhammad had been born John Williams but had changed his name when he converted to Islam in the 1980s. This conversion is sometimes used to explain the motive for the killings, some suggesting that Muhammad was waging jihad, or holy war, on the United States. Others point to the messy divorce he had gone through that had given his ex-wife custody of their three children. He had either snapped and decided to avenge himself on society or planned to use these killings to disguise his ultimate goal, the murder of his ex-wife.

Muhammad certainly did not lack the skills to be a sniper. He had been in the U.S. Army for nine years, serving in the first Gulf War and becoming a specialist in M16 rifle marksmanship.

Lee Boyd Malvo. Muhammad had recruited the compliant Lee Malvo to his cause, telling him that they would extract $10 million from the government as a payment for stopping the shootings. This would be used to found a home for 140 homeless African-American children. To force the government's hand, Muhammad told Malvo, they would kill six people a day.

Cross-Country Killers

It all began in Hammond, Louisiana, on August 1, 2002, when they shot a man named John Gaeta but failed to kill him. Then, on September 6, Paul LaRuffa was seriously wounded by six bullets in the chest, fired at close range as he locked up his pizzeria in Clinton, Maryland. The shooters got away with his laptop, which would still be in their car when they were eventually arrested.

Their first murder occurred on September 21, 2002, in Montgomery, Alabama, when they shot Claudine Parker, a clerk in a liquor store they were robbing. Parker's coworker, Kellie Adams, was also shot, but she survived her injuries. They then headed for Washington, D.C.

The Beltway Killings Begin. Without warning, at 5:20 P.M. on October 2, the window of a craft store in Aspen Hill, Maryland, exploded as it was hit by a bullet from a high-velocity .223 caliber rifle. No one was hurt there, but just over an hour later, 55-year-old program analyst James Martin fell to the ground, shot and killed by a bullet in the parking lot of a grocery store in Glenmont, a couple of miles from Aspen Hill.

Lee Boyd Malvo is escorted from a hearing at Fairfax County juvenile court by Fairfax County sheriffs on November 15, 2003.

The **1990 Chevrolet Caprice** used by Muhammad and Malvo is seen at the Montgomery County Judicial Center after being entered as evidence in the murder trial.

Their spree had begun, and the following day would bring dreadful carnage to affluent suburban Montgomery County, Maryland, with four people being shot dead at different locations in the space of two hours.

A Day of Carnage

At 7:41 A.M., the life of James "Sonny" Buchanan, a 39-year-old landscape gardener, was ended by a single shot to the chest as he mowed the lawn at the Fitzgerald Auto Mall, near Rockville, Maryland. At 8:12 A.M., 54-year-old part-time taxi driver Premkumar Walekar died as he filled his taxi's tank at a Mobil gas station at the junction of Aspen Hill Road and Connecticut Avenue in Aspen Hill.

Just 25 minutes later, at 8:37 A.M., with local emergency services roaring through the streets, another fatal shooting was reported. A 34-year-old housekeeper, Sarah Ramos, was shot dead as she read a book on a bench at a bus stop at the Leisure World Shopping Center in Aspen Hill.

No End to the Day's Killings. As dispatchers waited nervously for another call to come in, time passed and they dared to think it was all over. At 9:58 A.M., however, another fatality was called in. Twenty-five-year-old Lori-Ann Lewis-Rivera had been shot dead at a gas station in Kensington as she vacuumed her camper.

All was quiet until 9:15 P.M., when 72-year-old Pascal Charlot was hit on Georgia Avenue in Washington. He died an hour later. The murder rate in the area had risen by 30 percent in one day.

No One Is Safe

On October 4, a woman was shot but only wounded, but three days later, the sniper sent a shock wave through the nation. Responding to a statement by the authorities that schoolchildren were safe, he shot and seriously wounded 13-year-old Iran Brown as he arrived at the Benjamin Tasker Middle School in Bowie, Maryland. A Tarot card was found in a wooded area 50 yards (45 m) from where he was hot. It was the card signifying death, and on the front was written: "Call me God." The back of the card read, "For you mr. Police"; "Code: Call me God"; and "Do not release to the press."

The Shootings Continue. On October 9, a bullet in the head at a gas station in Manassas, Virginia, killed 53-year-old Dean Harold Meyers, and on October 11, at another gas station just outside Fredericksburg, Virginia, 53-year-old father of six Kenneth Bridges was shot dead. Three days later, FBI analyst Linda Franklin was shot to death as she left a store in Falls Church, Virginia. On October 21, 37-year-old Jeffrey Hopper was shot and wounded outside a steakhouse in Ashland, Virginia. A rambling four-page letter from the sniper was found in nearby woods.

A drawing made by Lee Boyd Malvo while he was incarcerated awaiting trial. The drawing, which includes references to jihad, or "holy war," was entered into evidence on December 3, 2003, during his trial at the Chesapeake Circuit Court in Chesapeake, Virginia.

The Killers Begin to Slip Up. As Muhammad and Malvo continued their killing spree in the D.C. area, they started becoming over-confident. They taunted the police with phone calls, during one of which they made reference to a liquor store robbery in Montgomery, Alabama. On October 17, a fingerprint from that robbery was matched to one found at the school where Iran Brown had been shot. It was identified as belonging to Lee Malvo, and after further investigation of other criminal records, detectives learned that he had close ties with John Allen Muhammad stretching over jurisdictions outside the D.C. area. The names and the registration of the blue 1990 Chevrolet Caprice in which they were traveling were released to the public.

Muhammad and Malvo killed their tenth and final victim on October 22, 2002. Bus driver Conrad Johnson was shot dead as he stood on the steps of his bus in Aspen Hill.

The End of the Road

On October 23, police received a call from a truck driver, Ron Lantz, who had parked his rig across the exit of a rest stop on Interstate 70 in Maryland, northwest of Washington. Sleeping soundly in their car at the rest stop were Malvo and Muhammad, whose vehicle the eagle-eyed Lantz had recognized.

The Bushmaster rifle used by John Allen Muhammad and Lee Boyd Malvo to shoot their victims.

The Authorities Move In. Within an hour, law enforcement officials swarmed over the scene, staking out the car and moving in on the sleeping killers. After apprehending the duo, officers discovered that Muhammad and Malvo had cut a hole in the trunk of their car. They had also cut sheet metal separating the backseat from the trunk, allowing them to fire at their victims from within the vehicle. As described by the FBI, the vehicle "was, in effect, a rolling sniper's nest."

Tried, Convicted, and Sentenced. With these clues and items found in the car, along with other information the authorities had gathered in their investigation, the authorities were able to piece together enough evidence to convict both Beltway Snipers of their crimes. In multiple court cases in Maryland and Virginia, both John Allen Muhammad and Lee Boyd Malvo were sentenced to life in prison. Muhammad was also sentenced to death in Virginia, where he died by lethal injection on November 10, 2009. Lee Boyd Malvo, too young to be executed, is serving six consecutive life sentences with no possibility of parole.

In addition to the killings in Alabama, Louisiana, and Greater Washington, D.C., Muhammad and Malvo have been linked to killings in Arizona, California, Washington state, and Texas. Most of these connections are based on statements made by Malvo following his capture.

Beating Geographic Profiling

The Beltway Sniper case appeared at first glance to be the perfect case for geographic profiling. The killer or killers seemed to move across the Washington, D.C., area like ghosts, committing an act and then fading back into the traffic flow on the Beltway around Washington, D.C., leaving not a scrap of DNA or other physical evidence behind.

The hi-tech gizmos of modern policing—such as using gas chromatographs to perform chemical analysis and scanning electron microscopes to create super-magnified images—were useless in the face of such agility at leaving the scene of the crime without a trace of evidence to analyze. On the other hand, the lifeblood of geo-forensics—data points on a map—were being left. Every time they opened fire, the killers were providing information about their whereabouts that could be used for geographic profiling.

Respected Canadian geographic profiler Dr. Kim Rossmo was brought into the investigation at an early stage. It seemed that the situation was made for him. After all, it was not DNA he required, but data points—and the snipers were providing him with plenty of those. He ran the points through his computer program, Rigel, which established the center of activity for the killers to be in the northern suburbs of the nation's capital. As investigators later discovered, however, Muhammad and Malvo's center of activity was actually the car in which they traveled the Beltway. They never remained in one place for very long. Therefore, like every other profiler who weighed in on this case, Rossmo got it wrong because the information available was just too variable and the killers too mobile.

Like Andrew Cunanan (the killer of clothing designer Gianni Versace) and Aileen Wuornos (who murdered seven men in Florida after they picked her up as a hitchhiker), the movements of Muhammad and Malvo did not follow the patterns typically found with geographic profiling. Whoever was committing the crimes was killing not in areas they knew, but in areas of a generic character, similar to places they knew—shopping mall parking lots and gas stations.

An attorney indicates a point on a map at the trial of John Allen Muhammad for the murder of Dean Harold Meyers in Virginia Beach, Virginia, on November 12, 2003.

se History: The Beltway Snipers

August 1, 2002   John Gaeta (54) is shot in Hammond, Louisiana, but he survives.

September 6, 2002   Paul LaRuffa (55) survives being shot six times in the chest as he closes his restaurant in Clinton, Maryland.

September 21, 2002 Claudine Parker (52) is shot dead during a liquor store robbery in Montgomery, Alabama. Her coworker, Kellie Adams (24), is also shot, but she survives.

October 2, 2002   James Martin (55) is killed in a grocery store parking lot in Glenmont, Maryland.

October 3, 2002:   7:41 A.M.: James "Sonny" Buchanan (39) is shot dead mowing a lawn near Rockville, Maryland.

8:12 A.M.: Premkumar Walekar (54) is shot dead at a gas station in Aspen Hill, Maryland.

8:37 A.M.: Sarah Ramos (34) is killed at a bus stop in Aspen Hill.

9:58 A.M.: Lori-Ann Lewis-Rivera (25) is killed at a gas station in Kensington, Maryland.

9:15 P.M.: Pascal Charlot (72) is shot dead on a street in Washington, D.C.

October 4, 2002   Caroline Seawell (43) is wounded in a parking lot in Spotsylvania, Virginia.

October 7, 2002   Iran Brown (13) survives being shot as he arrives at school in Bowie, Maryland.

October 9, 2002   Dean Harold Meyers (53) is killed at a gas station in Manassas, Virginia.

October 11, 2002   Kenneth Bridges (53) is shot dead at a gas station just outside Fredericksburg, Virginia.

October 14, 2002   Linda Franklin (47) is shot dead outside a store in Falls Church, Virginia.

October 21, 2002   Jeffrey Hopper (37) is wounded in the parking lot of the Ponderosa Steakhouse in Ashland, Virginia.

October 22, 2002   Bus driver Conrad Johnson (35) is shot dead while

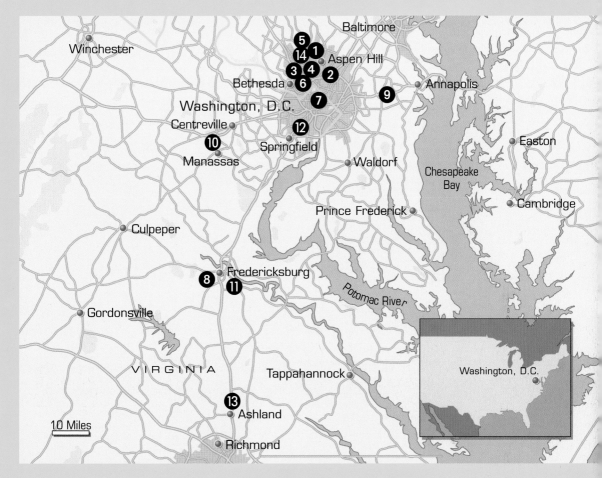

Locations of the Shootings

1 **Aspen Hill, Maryland**—Windows shot out of store on Georgia Avenue; no injuries, October 2

2 **Glenmont, Maryland**—James D. Martin killed, October 2

3 **Rockville, Maryland**—James Buchanan killed, October 3

4 **Aspen Hill, Maryland**—Premkumar Walekar murdered, October 3

5 **Aspen Hill**—Sarah Ramos shot dead, October 3

6 **Kensington, Maryland**—Lori-Ann Lewis-Rivera murdered, October 3

7 **Washington, D.C.**—Pascal Charlot killed, October 3

8 **Spotsylvania, Virginia**—Caroline Seawell wounded, October 4

9 **Bowie, Maryland**—Iran Brown wounded at the Benjamin Tasker Middle School, October 7

10 **Manassas, Virginia**—Dean Harold Meyers killed, October 9

11 **Fredericksburg, Virginia**—Kenneth Bridges killed, October 11

12 **Falls Church, Virginia**—Linda Franklin shot dead, October 14

13 **Ashland, Virginia**—Jeffrey Hopper wounded, October 21

14 **Aspen Hill, Maryland**—Conrad Johnson shot dead, October 22

Nomads

The nomadic serial killer, taking advantage of the country's infrastructure to move quickly from place to place, is a growing phenomenon. Law enforcement agencies in the United States have been forced to introduce new data management systems between states and agencies in order to deal with the deadly threat it poses. None was more of a nomad than Christopher Wilder, who killed in half a dozen different states across North America.

- George Metesky
- John Norman Collins
- Peter Sutcliffe
- Christopher Wilder
- Robert Black
- Edgar Pearce

Detectives examine the remains of Vera Millward, one of the victims of Peter Sutcliffe, the Yorkshire Ripper.

159

George Metesky: The Mad Bomber of New York City

"CON EDISON CROOKS, THIS IS FOR YOU." The words were written in neat capitals on a note that had been wrapped around the small pipe bomb that was found in a wooden toolbox on a windowsill at the Consolidated Edison building on West 64th Street on November 16, 1940. The device had not exploded, and it was obvious from the existence of the note that its maker had never intended it to go off. For the next 16 years, however, the man the media dubbed the "Mad Bomber" planted at least 33 bombs in theaters, bus and railroad terminals, libraries, and offices. Important and busy public buildings would become targets. It would be an early use of offender profiling that would eventually bring to justice the man responsible—disgruntled former Con Edison employee George Metesky.

A smiling George Metesky, also known as "The Mad Bomber," entering the Waterbury, Connecticut, police station, where he was charged with attempted murder, damaging a building by explosion, maliciously endangering life, and violation of New York State's Sullivan Law by carrying concealed weapons—his bombs.

A Bomber and a Patriot

The United States had not yet entered World War II, but events going on elsewhere easily overshadowed the newsworthiness of this one discovery. It never even made the evening papers, and after a few weeks the incident was forgotten.

Another Year, Another Bomb. Less than a year later, however, in September 1941, another device was found lying on 19th Street, wrapped in a sock, just a few blocks from the Con Ed offices. This one was also not intended to explode, as its alarm clock detonator had not been wound. Its construction was similar to that of the first bomb, however, and investigators surmised that the bomber had dropped it in the street for some unknown reason on his way to the Con Ed offices. Again the incident did not make the news. It all became academic a few months later when the Japanese bombed Pearl

Harbor and the United States entered World War II. The bomber, it seemed, was a patriot. Following the bombing of Pearl Harbor, he wrote a letter to the New York Police Department, mailed from Westchester County, just north of New York City. The note read:

"I WILL MAKE NO MORE BOMB UNITS FOR THE DURATION OF THE WAR—MY PATRIOTIC FEELINGS HAVE MADE ME DECIDE THIS—LATER I WILL BRING THE CON EDISON TO JUSTICE—THEY MUST PAY FOR THEIR DASTARDLY DEEDS."

He kept his word, and there were no more bombs for the next nine years. He did, however, send a series of threatening notes to Con Edison, newspapers, hotels, and stores. They were signed "F.P."

The Campaign Resumes

On March 29, 1951, just as anyone who remembered the earlier bomb incidents was beginning to assume that F.P. had either given up or died, a bomb exploded near the Oyster Bar on the lower level of Grand Central Station. The bomb was made in a much more skillful way than the first two and was more powerful, but no one was hurt.

A New Wave Begins. Shortly after, in April 1951, another exploded in a phone booth at the New York Public Library. A new wave of bombings had begun. It would last until the end of 1956—and while the previous bombs placed in New York had probably not been designed to go off, many in the next wave would explode, setting off a reign of worry and panic among New York residents, visitors, and investigators alike.

Injuries Begin. In the next three years, a dozen more exploded. No one was injured by any of these devices until 1954, when three men were slightly hurt in a small explosion in a men's room at Grand Central. Then, in November of that year, four people were hurt when a bomb that had been stuffed into the cushion of a seat at Radio City Music Hall exploded.

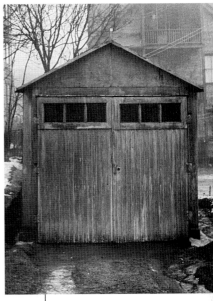

The garage in which George Metesky stored his materials and manufactured his bombs.

Explosion of Anger

Four of six bombs planted in 1955 exploded, and it was noticeable that they were becoming increasingly sophisticated and powerful. The bomber was also becoming increasingly angry, as his stream of letters and telephone calls to newspapers made clear. He insisted that the bombings—numbered by him as 54 in one letter—would continue until Con Edison was finally brought to justice.

Following the serious injury, in 1956, of a 74-year-old men's-room attendant when a bomb in a toilet exploded, the bomber's anger erupted with even more fury on December 2, 1956, when a device exploded at the Paramount movie theater in Brooklyn. As with other bombs left in theaters, he had slashed a hole in a seat and slipped the device inside. Six people were hurt, three of them seriously, on this occasion.

The First Clue

Soon after the Paramount Theater bombing, the *New York Journal American* published an editorial, offering the bomber free publicity for his cause in return for surrendering himself to the authorities. The response of the bomber contained some hints about going after certain senior officials. He also provided a list of 14 devices he had planted during 1956, a number of which had not been discovered.

Nearly Spilling the Beans. He wrote again, soon after, and provided some clues as to his identity and his motives in attacking the city. "I was injured on a job at Consolidated Edison," he wrote. "As a result, I am adjudged totally and permanently disabled. I did not receive aid of any kind from the company—that I did not pay for myself—while fighting for my life…."

An Uncooperative Filing System. The hope was to use employee records at Con Edison to compile a portrait of the bomber based on the information he was giving them. Sadly, however, the personnel records at Con Ed were complex. The company had been created by the mergers of several smaller utility companies in the late 1920s and early 1930s, and consequently, the files were poorly organized. It was an impossible task.

A Profiler Comes Through. The investigation received an additional boost, however, when Inspector Howard E. Finney of the New York Police Crime Laboratory decided to call in a psychiatrist, Dr. James A. Brussel, who provided a profile of the man they were looking for. The major New York newspapers all ran the profile, unleashing a flood of cranks who all claimed to be the "Mad Bomber." None, however, was able to accurately describe the bombs, details of which had been deliberately kept from the media.

"Dastardly Deeds": A Recurring Theme

Meanwhile the bomber was still corresponding with the *New York Journal American*, and one of his letters was to provide the clue that would blow the case wide open. One section read, "I was injured on the job at Con Edison—September 15, 1931."

Excited detectives searched what records there were at Consolidated Edison and for the first time in 16 years had some luck. On September 15, 1931, a Polish immigrant named George Metesky had been injured in a boiler blast. Afterward, he had suffered from pneumonia and tuberculosis, but all he had received by way of compensation was $180. It was discovered that Metesky had sent several angry letters to Con Ed, one phrasing its promise for revenge for the firm's misdeeds in terms that would eventually become a clue to the identity of the writer: "dastardly deeds."

The Man in the Crazy House

George Metesky lived in Waterbury, Connecticut, with his two unmarried sisters. He was described by neighbors as distant, and local children are said to have called his house "The Crazy House."

Neighbors Take Notice. Neighbors wondered what he did on his frequent trips into New York City and why he spent so much time—day and

Members of the New York Police Department's bomb squad haul a mesh iron sealer containing a bomb planted by George Metesky from the side entrance of the Paramount Theater to the truck that will take it to Fort Tilden in Queens to be detonated.

night—in his workshop. It was noticed that around the time Dr. Brussel's profile of the bomber was being publicized in the newspapers, Metesky's behavior changed. He suddenly became friendlier and spoke to the local children.

"Fair Play." The neighbors soon understood some of the reasons behind Metesky's behavior when, in January 1957, police arrived with a warrant for his arrest. In his garage they found a lathe and a length of piping similar to that used in the manufacture of the bombs. In his bedroom was the typewriter on which he had composed many letters, signed F.P. In custody, he happily confessed to being the "Mad Bomber." "F.P.," he added, stood for "Fair Play."

Legally Insane

On hearing from psychiatric experts who had examined George Metesky, a New York judge declared Metesky legally insane and unfit to stand trial. On April 18, 1957, the judge committed Metesky to the Matteawan Hospital for the Criminally Insane at Beacon, New York.

Efforts to Gain Release. During his time at Matteawan, Metesky tried to obtain his release on the grounds that he had been mentally incompetent at the time of his arrest and as such was unable to understand his rights. His appeal was denied, but in 1973 the U.S. Supreme Court ruled that a mentally ill defendant could not be committed to a facility within the corrections system unless found dangerous by a jury. Metesky was then transferred to Creedmoor Psychiatric Center in Queens, New York, which is not a part of the corrections system. There it was determined that he was harmless.

Police remove a lathe found in George Metesky's garage that was used in the manufacture of the bombs that terrorized New York City for more than 16 years.

James Brussel and the Profiling of the "Mad Bomber"

Traditional police methods were proving futile in tracking down the "Mad Bomber." One of the difficulties was the erratic nature of Metesky's campaign. After his initial attempts to bomb Consolidated Edison, he changed his modus operandi and chose random targets, often busy public places that would be difficult to effectively police and where he could merge into crowds. The police decided to adopt a more unorthodox approach, introducing the fledgling science of criminal profiling to try to understand the type of man they were looking for.

Dr. James A. Brussel, a criminologist and psychiatrist living in the Greenwich Village neighborhood of New York City, had over 20 years of experience in working with the criminally insane and immediately deduced that the offender in this case was suffering from acute paranoia. He said that the bomber would be male—historically, most bombers were male—and would be aged around 40 to 50, as paranoia develops slowly. His letters were the work of a neat, tidy individual who was probably not born in the United States. The letters contained no Americanisms and some odd words and phrases, such as "dastardly deeds." Brussel deduced that the writer was probably Slavic, a notion further supported by the knowledge that bombs were commonly used in Eastern Europe. He was, therefore, an immigrant, or the son of an immigrant.

The odd shape of the "W" in the letters, resembling female breasts, suggested to Brussel that the writer was possibly fixated on his mother. Brussel characterized the bomber as a loner, a man who had little interest in women, and who may even be a virgin. He probably lived in Connecticut, where many Slavs had settled.

Remarkably Brussel also threw in an additional piece of information—a prediction that, when caught, the bomber would likely be wearing a double-breasted suit. Moreover it would be buttoned. When detectives arrested Metesky at his home in Waterbury, Connecticut, they ordered him into his bedroom to change out of his pajamas. When Metesky emerged, he was wearing a double-breasted suit—and it was buttoned!

Still Angry. He was released in December 1973; even after so much time, he remained angry about the way he had been treated by Consolidated Edison. After his release, he told a reporter that he had written 900 letters to the Mayor, to the Police Commissioner, and to the newspapers, without receiving a single reply. Metesky returned to his home in Waterbury, Connecticut, where he lived for another 20 years before dying at the age of 90 in 1994.

Case History: George Metesky

▶ September 15, 1931 George Metesky, a Polish immigrant employed by New York utility company Consolidated Edison, is injured in a boiler explosion at one of their plants. He subsequently suffers from pneumonia and tuberculosis that he believes are a direct result of the explosion.

▶ November 16, 1940 An explosive device is found in a wooden toolbox at the Consolidated Edison building in New York City. It appears that it has not been intended to explode as a note is wrapped around it announcing that the bomb was intended for "CON EDISON CROOKS."

▶ September 1941 A second device is found in the street, close to the Con Ed building. There is no note, and like the previous device, it does not go off.

▶ December 1941 Shortly after Japan attacks the U.S. Navy base at Pearl Harbor, Hawaii, drawing the United States into World War II, the bomber, George Metesky, announces in a letter that he will stop planting bombs while the country is at war.

▶ 1941–1951 There are no bombs, but Metesky bombards police stations, newspapers, private citizens, and, of course, Consolidated Edison with letters.

▶ March 29, 1951 The campaign resumes when a bomb detonates in Grand Central Station. A few weeks later, another bomb goes off in a phone booth at the New York Public Library. No one is hurt in either blast.

▶ 1951–1954 The new wave of bombings targets public buildings; in this period, Metesky plants at least a dozen devices. Three men are injured by one explosion in a men's room at Grand Central. On November 7, 1954, four people are injured by an explosion at Radio City Music Hall.

▶ 1955 Metesky plants six devices during this year that are known of; he claims in a letter that he has at that point planted 54 bombs.

▶ 1956 A 74-year-old men's-room attendant suffers the first serious injury at the hands of the bomber when a bomb in a toilet explodes. On December 2, six patrons of the Paramount Theater in Brooklyn are injured in an explosion. Metesky writes to the *New York Journal American* listing 14 bombs planted that year.

▶ January 1957 Metesky is arrested and, in April, judged to be legally insane and, as such, incompetent to stand trial. He is committed to a hospital for the criminally insane.

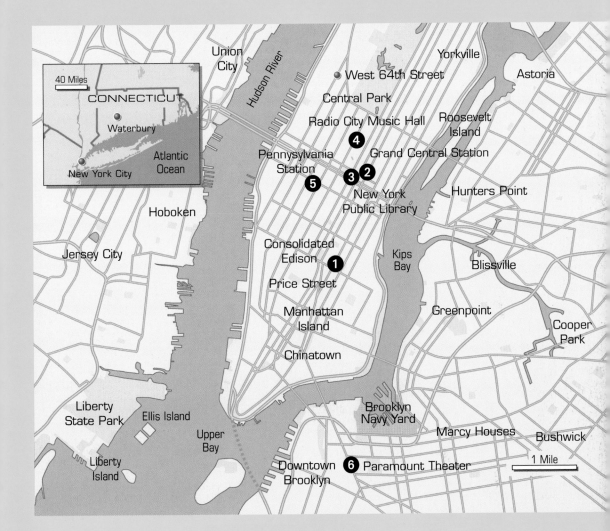

Locations of Bombings

1 **Consolidated Edison Building**—Device found in November 1940; another device planted here, September 1941

2 **Grand Central Station**—Bomb detonated in March 1951; another bomb injures three men in a men's room, March 1954

3 **New York Public Library**—Bomb detonated in phone booth, April 1951

4 **Radio City Music Hall**—Bomb injures four people, November 1954

5 **Pennsylvania Station**—Man seriously injured in a blast in a men's room, 1956

6 **Paramount Theater**—Six people injured after an explosion, December 1956

John Norman Collins: The Co-ed Killer

At the start of a murder spree, a killer is, naturally, less confident and tends to center his activities around places he knows, often staying close to where he lives. Victims, too, are often the type of people with whom he is already familiar. He needs no surprises in the perpetration of a murder. In the case of the Ypsilanti, Michigan, murders, this proved to be exactly the case. John Collins, the man eventually associated with the murders of 7 girls—although he may have killed at least 15—did indeed live close to the Eastern Michigan University campus near which a number of his victims lived. He had attended the school himself. In certain key ways, his victims were just like him.

John Norman Collins arrives at the Washtenaw County Courthouse in Michigan on July 20, 1970, during his trial.

Geographic Similarities

The killings were well organized and certainly premeditated. Collins would cruise an area, checking it out before approaching a potential victim. He drove the bodies away from where he committed the murders, blurring any clues that he might have left. Only once did he leave the state of Michigan to do his killing—in the case of Roxie Phillips, whom Collins killed while he was in California. Even then, he made sure to create some distance between the scene of his crime—Salinas, where he'd picked her up—and where he dumped her body—a canyon close to the nearby town of Carmel.

The First Fatal Encounter

Nineteen-year-old Mary Fleszar was a student at Eastern Michigan. On July 9, 1967, she left her apartment in Ypsilanti to take a walk. A witness saw a bluish gray Chevy driven by a young man pull up beside her as she walked. The man appeared to talk to her, but she shook her head and walked on. He pulled up beside her again a few paces further on. Again, the witness recalled, she seemed to be saying no to whatever he was asking. The car accelerated, its tires screaming, and sped off. Mary continued to her building, but she was never seen alive again.

A Disturbing Discovery. On August 7, two 15-year-old boys saw a car pull up at a farm near Geddes and LaForge Roads. They crept toward the farm, hoping to be able to spy on a courting couple, but the car pulled away. Instead of a courting couple, they discovered the naked, decomposing body of a young woman. Mary Fleszar had been viciously beaten and stabbed repeatedly in the chest. She was missing one forearm and hand, and the fingers of her other hand were also absent.

A curious factor in Collins's dumping of his victims' bodies was that he left most of them outside, making little effort to conceal them. He seems even to have returned several times to the body of Mary Fleszar, moving her in order to make it easier for her to be found.

The Man without a Camera. Just before Mary's funeral, an odd, chilling incident occurred when a young man walked into the funeral home, claiming to have been a family friend and asking to take a photograph of her. The employees of course informed him that he could not, and he left, but it was only later that someone recalled that he was not even carrying a camera. The police surmised that it had been Mary's killer.

More Bodies

It would be nearly a year before another young woman disappeared. Late in the night of June 30, 1968, 20-year-old art major Joan Schell was hitchhiking in front of the EMU student union. Her lifeless body was

> "If a person holds a gun on somebody—it's up to him to decide whether to take the other's life or not. The point is: It's not society's judgment that's important, but the individual's own choice of will and intellect."
>
> —COLLINS, IN AN ENGLISH PAPER WRITTEN AT COLLEGE

found outside Ann Arbor on July 6. She had been sexually assaulted, her throat had been slashed, and she had been stabbed five times.

The Michigan Murders. Twenty-three-year-old freshman law student Jane Mixer told friends on March 20, 1969, that she was meeting a young man named David Johnson who had offered her a lift home on his motorcycle. The next day, her body was found in a cemetery in Denton Township, with two .22 bullets in her head. This time the body was fully clothed, and it would later emerge that she had been killed by 62-year-old Gary Leiterman. At the time, however, her death was believed to be another in the sequence of killings, and it added to the panic over what was later called "the Michigan Murders" when Collins began his next wave of terror.

The Wave Continues. Sixteen-year-old high school dropout Maralynn Skelton also disappeared while hitchhiking, on March 24, 1969. She was found close to the dumping site of Joan Schell's body, sexually assaulted with her skull smashed. A garter belt was knotted around her neck.

Thirteen-year-old Dawn Basom of Ypsilanti disappeared on April 15, 1969, and was found strangled and stabbed the next day. Dawn would be the youngest of Collins's victims.

Three more young women died before the end of that year, two in Michigan and one in California. On June 7, 23-year-old Alice Kalom, a University of Michigan graduate, was seen at a party in Ann Arbor dancing with a young man with long hair. Her body was found near a farm. She had been shot in the head and stabbed.

In a killing that occurred while Collins was in California, 17-year-old Roxie Phillips disappeared on June 30 and was found dead two weeks later. Less than a month later, on July 23, after Collins had returned to Michigan, 18-year-old EMU student Karen Sue Beineman accepted a ride on a motorcycle from a man and was found beaten and stabbed to death.

Under Suspicion

John Norman Collins had been a suspect in the murder of Joan Schell. He lived across the street from her and had been seen in her company on

July 1, 1968. When questioned by police, he claimed to have been with his mother at the time that Joan was murdered. He seemed clean-cut and personable; they believed him.

A Young Cop Begins to Work Up a Profile. Collins re-entered the investigation, however, when a young policeman named Larry Matthewson became suspicious of him. He knew that Collins had been driving around campus on the day that Jane Mixer disappeared. He obtained a photograph of him and showed it to a young woman who had seen "David Johnson" on his motorcycle. She identified Collins. Unfortunately, by the time Matthewson got to Collins, he had removed all incriminating evidence from his apartment. He had also cleaned out his car.

A New Twist, and a Break. The investigation of Collins got a boost from an unlikely source—Collins' uncle, who was a Michigan state trooper. Collins had recently been looking after his uncle's home and dog while his uncle had left with his family for a vacation. When his family returned, they noticed some things amiss, including a newly painted area of the basement floor and a missing paint can, ammonia bottle, and detergent

Washtenaw County Sheriff Douglas Harvey points to the spot on an isolated rural road where the body of Dawn Basom (13) was found. She was the fifth girl found slain in the same general area in the previous 21 months.

box. When the uncle found out that his nephew had been a suspect in the murder of Joan Schell, he reported his own suspicions to his superiors.

Forensic Evidence Emerges. When police scientists checked out the basement of the uncle's house, they found hair clippings as well as what appeared to be droplets of blood on the floor. Tests revealed the hairs matched some found on Karen Beineman's underwear. The bloodstains were found to be human. Additionally, Collins's car was examined, and blood matching Alice Kanom's blood type was found. Further, it later emerged that Joan Schell had been picked up by three men—one of them being Collins. The other two had gone their separate ways, leaving Collins with Joan. He claimed he had left her at an empty parking lot.

A California connection. Collins had been in Salinas, California, when Roxie Phillips disappeared. A friend told police that she had met a man named "John" from Michigan who drove motorcycles, like Collins. Roxie was found in a grove of poison oak, and Collins turned out to have been treated in a hospital in Salinas that week for poison-oak stings.

Trial and Imprisonment

The trial of John Norman Collins began on June 30, 1970, with the prosecution focusing on the murder of Karen Beineman.

One Conviction, Many Deaths. On August 19, 1970, Collins was found guilty of that murder and sentenced to life imprisonment with no possibility of parole. Although Collins is believed to be the killer of the

Defense Attorneys Joseph Louisell and Neil Fink are seen leaving the Washtenaw County Building during the trial of John Collins, July 1970.

The John Collins Investigation

The number of variables that have to be taken into consideration when trying to create a picture or profile of an unsub, or unknown subject, are extraordinary. The relatively new science of geoforensics has added to that list of variables, but it provides an invaluable new addition to the weaponry of those hunting homicidal predators. Victim selection area, the location of the actual crime, how the killer got the body to the eventual dump site, how he left the bodies, and the type of location in which he left them all provide invaluable insights into the criminal.

In the case of John Norman Collins, also called the Ypsilanti Killer and the Co-ed Killer, analysis of such information helped capture him and eventually convict him. Many of his victims were students. Therefore, it was likely that the killer hunted for them around the area of the university. Six of the seven bodies were eventually found in countryside areas between the university towns of Ann Arbor and Ypsilanti, and five of the locations where bodies were found formed an interesting circle. In fact they formed such a close circle that many came to the conclusion that Jane Mixer, whose body was not found within that area, had probably been murdered by someone else, as was proved when Gary Leiterman was convicted of her murder in 2005.

The establishment of such a pattern and evidence that Collins had used an abandoned farmhouse to murder at least two of his victims confirm that an unsub's knowledge of a local area and his familiarity with a "comfort zone" are important geographic variables in an investigation of multiple crimes.

six other young murder victims, he has not been formally charged in those crimes (or with any others that have also been associated with him), and those six murders remain officially "unsolved."

An Odd Change of Name. In the early 1980s, Collins bizarrely changed his name to Chapman, which was his mother's maiden name. It was also the surname of Mark David Chapman, the man who assassinated John Lennon, however, and many suspected that Collins wished to be associated with him in the public's mind.

Now in his mid-60s, Collins is serving his sentence in Michigan's Upper Peninsula, at the Marquette Branch Prison in Marquette.

Mapping the Crime

The "Michigan Murders," as they were called by various media outlets and local people, were carried out in the Ann Arbor/Ypsilanti area of Southeastern Michigan, terrifying the inhabitants of Washtenaw County between 1967 and 1969. Collins was also unable to resist killing while away, however. While on vacation in Monterey, California, in June 1969, he murdered Roxie Philips.

Case History: John Norman Collins

▶ **July 9, 1967**
Mary Fleszar (19) disappears from the campus at Eastern Michigan University in Ypsilanti. Her body is found on August 7 by two 15-year-old boys.

▶ **June 30–July 1, 1968**
Joan Schell (20) disappears. She is last seen with John Norman Collins. Her body is found a week later outside Ann Arbor.

▶ **March 20, 1969**
Jane Mixer (23) disappears after being offered a lift by "David Johnson" on his motorcycle. Her body is found the next day in a cemetery in Denton Township. Her death is initially linked to Collins's series of killings, but in 2005 another man is convicted of her murder.

▶ **March 24, 1969**
Maralynn Skelton (16) disappears while hitchhiking outside Arborland Shopping Center. Her body is found the following day with its skull smashed.

▶ **April 15, 1969**
Dawn Basom (13) is abducted near the EMU campus. She is found strangled and stabbed the next day.

▶ **June 7, 1969**
Alice Kalom (23) disappears after a party in Ann Arbor. She is found shot dead outside the city.

▶ **June 30, 1969**
Roxie Phillips (17) disappears while mailing a letter in Salinas, California. A friend thinks Roxie may have met a young man named "John" who rode a motorcycle. Her body is discovered a week later in Pescadero Canyon, north of Carmel, California.

▶ **July 23, 1969**
Karen Sue Beineman (18) accepts a ride on a motorcycle from a young man and is last seen leaving a wig shop with him. She is found in a ravine in Ann Arbor, naked and with her face battered. DNA evidence found on her will lead to Collins's conviction on August 19, 1970.

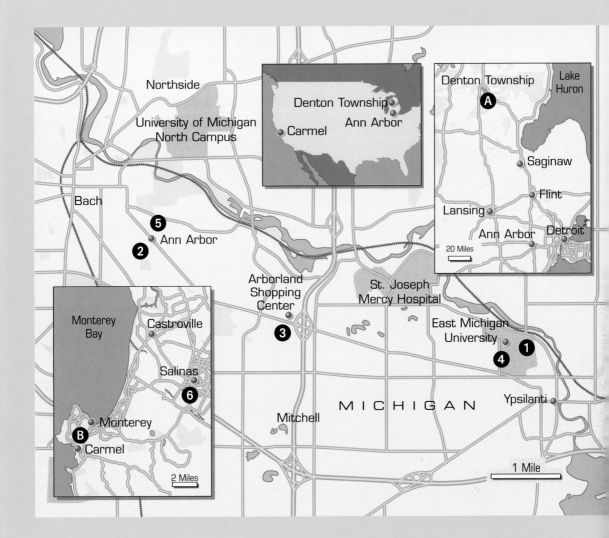

Locations of the Abductions and Murders

❶ East Michigan University, Ypsilanti—Mary Fleszar disappears, July 1967

❷ Ann Arbor—Joan Schell disappears; her body is discovered outside Ann Arbor, June 1968

❸ Aborland Shopping Center, Michigan—Maralynn Skelton disappears, March 1969

❹ East Michigan University, Ypsilanti—Dawn Basom disappears, April 1969

❺ Ann Arbor—Alice Kalom disappears, her body is discovered outsid the city, June 1969

❻ Salinas, CA—Roxie Phillips disappears, June 1969

Ⓐ Denton Township—The body of Jane Mixer is discovered, March 1969

Ⓑ Pescadero Canyon—Body of Roxie Phillips is discovered a week after her disappearance, June 1969

Peter Sutcliffe: The Yorkshire Ripper

Pioneering criminologist, Dr. Kim Rossmo, has described geographic profiling as an "information management system." The information gathered about a series of crimes can be harnessed to build the geography of the crime and ultimately lead investigators to the perpetrator. If ever there was a case that required such a system, it was that of "the Yorkshire Ripper," Peter Sutcliffe, murderer of 13 women between 1975 and 1981 in northern England. The statistics of the investigation into these murders are staggering. There was an index of 268,000 names, 27,000 houses were visited in the course of door-to-door inquiries, 5.4 million car registration numbers were recorded, and 31,000 statements were taken.

Peter Sutcliffe, the Yorkshire Ripper, photographed with his wife, Sonia.

Every day, more than 1,000 letters containing tip-offs were received from the public. The investigation involved 250 detectives working for a three-year period—around 5 million hours of police time—at a cost estimated at £4 million, which would amount to more than £10 million in today's terms.

Cruising the Red Light Districts

To most people, Peter Sutcliffe would seem an unlikely serial killer, a soft-spoken man who worked as a truck driver and kept to himself. In 1974 at age 20, he married Sonia Szurma. He appeared to everyone to be an unassuming man who thought the world of his wife.

All was not as it seemed, however. Sutcliffe frequented prostitutes. He was often in the company of his friend, Trevor Birdsall, who at one point in the later investigation would report suspicions about his friend

to the police, suspicions sadly lost in the mountain of tip-offs. In the mid-1970s, however, he spent a great deal of time cruising Yorkshire's red-light districts with Peter Sutcliffe.

The Tools of a Killer

Sutcliffe struck twice before his first murder but was interrupted both times before he could finish the job. In each case he used the tools of his newfound trade—a heavy ball-peen hammer and a knife. He beat each woman to the ground with the hammer and then slashed them across their lower bodies. It would be three years before police would link these two incidents to each other and to the deaths that followed.

Killing Begins. Two months after his second unsuccessful assault, on October 30, 1975, he killed for the first time. A mother of four, Wilma McCann was found by a milkman just 100 yards (91 m) from her front

The scene in Sheffield of Peter Sutcliffe's arrest on January 4, 1981, for questioning in relation to the "Yorkshire Ripper" murders.

door. She had been bludgeoned on the back of the head before being stabbed repeatedly in a frenzied attack. There was semen on her clothing, but she had not been raped. More than 150 police officers undertook the thankless task of conducting 7,000 door-to-door interviews, but the killer's identity remained unknown.

Sutcliffe killed again on January 20, 1976. Part-time prostitute Emily Jackson had been working in Roundhay Road in Leeds. She was found with her skull smashed and 51 stab wounds on her body, probably made by a sharpened Phillips screwdriver. The imprint of a size 7 Dunlop Warwick Wellington boot nearby provided police with their first clue.

On May 9, he struck once more but again failed to kill his victim. A 20-year-old prostitute, Marcella Claxton, was struck on the head in the field where he had taken her for sex. He masturbated as she lay semiconscious on the ground and then stuffed a £5 note in her hand before driving off. She crawled to a phone booth and called for help. It was another break for the investigation as she was able to give police the first description of the killer.

The Yorkshire Ripper case sparked a justifiable media frenzy, especially after Sutcliffe's arrest for questioning.

The Yorkshire Ripper Is Born

Panic began to stalk the red light districts of northern England, a situation not helped by the media's coining of a name for the killer—"the Yorkshire Ripper." The media compared him to the unknown killer of prostitutes, called "Jack the Ripper," who had created a similar hysteria on the streets of London's East End 90 years previously.

When Sutcliffe viciously murdered Irene Richardson on February 5, 1977, there was some excitement as tire tracks were found at the scene. It very quickly turned to disappointment, however, when the police learned that the tracks could belong to any one of 100,000 vehicles.

Patricia Atkinson died at his hands on April 23, and 16-year-old Jayne MacDonald was bludgeoned and stabbed in a playground on June 26. This time, however, there was a difference. Jayne was not a prostitute. The public sat up and took notice, and police were inundated with even more information.

An unnamed victim of the Yorkshire Ripper lies in an isolated spot.

Sutcliffe failed to kill Maureen Long in Bradford on July 9, but a witness told police that he drove a white Ford Corsair. Unfortunately, so did thousands of taxi drivers in the Leeds-Bradford area.

He picked up prostitute Jean Jordan on October 1, 1977. She had agreed to have sex with him for £5, and he gave her the money before striking her no fewer than 13 times with his hammer. Eight days later, remembering that the £5 note was still in her bag, he returned to her well-concealed body to recover it. Unable to find her purse, however, he became furious and, in a frenzy, mutilated her corpse, almost decapitating it.

When police eventually found her and the purse, it seemed they had their biggest clue when the serial number of the note was traced to payrolls distributed in the Bradford and Shipley area. Eight thousand men, including Sutcliffe, were interviewed but nothing came to light.

"This man had dealings with prostitutes.... He is a long distance lorry driver, collecting engineering items, etc.... His name and address is Peter Sutcliffe, 3 Garden Lane, Heaton, Bradford...."

—AN EXTRACT FROM THE LETTER SENT TO THE POLICE BY TREVOR BIRDSALL

Spreading His Net. It was becoming difficult for Sutcliffe to target prostitutes because they were sticking together and looking out for each

other. He chose to spread his net wider. He killed in Bradford, Huddersfield, and Manchester before murdering a savings-and-loan clerk in April 1979 and a student in September 1979. He killed a 47-year-old civil servant in August 1980 and after failing to kill two women in November, 20-year-old Jacqueline Hill, a student at Leeds University, became his final murder victim on November 17. He had been killing for more than five years.

Emotions run high in the crowd that gathers outside the court in Dewsbury where Peter Sutcliffe appeared, charged with the murder of Leeds University student Jacqueline Hill.

Panic and Frustration in the Ranks

Around this time, Lawrence Byford, Her Majesty's Inspector of Constabulary, the official with the statutory right to inspect police forces and review activity, launched a review of the case. He formed an advisory group consisting of senior officers and a Home Office forensic scientist. Detectives argued over where they believed the killer lived. George Oldfield, the chief investigating officer, believed he was from the Sunderland area. Others, however, thought that he was from West Yorkshire, where the most of the attacks had occurred. The advisory group decided, after an intensive review of all the evidence, that the latter conclusion was the correct one.

Killing at God's Command

It came too late, however, and his ultimate arrest was made more by luck than judgment. Two police officers saw a prostitute get into a car in Melbourne Avenue, Sheffield. When they ran a check on the vehicle's license plates, they found them to be false. When Peter Sutcliffe, the driver of the car, was arrested, it was learned that he had been interviewed several times in connection with the Ripper investigation. They quizzed him further, and on the following day, he confessed, claiming that God had ordered him to clean up the streets. Peter Sutcliffe was sentenced to life

Geographic Profiling in the Yorkshire Ripper Case

After five-and-a-half years without an arrest, Lawrence Byford began a review of the Yorkshire Ripper investigation. He formed an advisory group made up of senior officers and a Home Office forensic scientist. The group debated heatedly over where they believed the killer lived. George Oldfield, the chief investigating officer, believed he was from the Sunderland area, in the northeast of England, and some distance from the crime scenes. His theory was partly the result of anonymous letters and a tape that had been received from a man known as "Wearside Jack," who claimed to be the Ripper and spoke with a Geordie, or heavy northeastern, English accent. Others, however, thought that he was from the West Yorkshire area, where the majority of the attacks had taken place. The Byford team came to the conclusion that the killer was from West Yorkshire.

They put their conclusion to the test by looking at all the spatial and temporal data they had. First they calculated the location of the "center of gravity" of the killer's activity—a kind of spatial average for the attacks, the area on the map where the crimes centered. This was found to lie near Bradford. They then plotted the time of the offenses against the length of day, reasoning that the killer would not attack late at night, as he often had, if his journey home afterward was going to be a long one. That might arouse suspicion or, given the late hour, might increase the chances of him being noticed, as few people would be on the street at that time. Both tests supported the theory that the Ripper was local to Bradford, and it was recommended that "a special group of detectives be dedicated to inquiries in that area." However, it proved irrelevant when Sutcliffe was arrested following some opportune police work just weeks later.

Police search for evidence following the murder of Jacqueline Hill, who was killed close to her flat in Leeds, November 17, 1980.

imprisonment without opportunity for parole. Shortly afterward he was diagnosed as schizophrenic and sent to Broadmoor Hospital where he remains to this day.

Mapping the Crime

The scope of the geographical area—Bradford, Leeds, Manchester, Keighley, and Huddersfield—where Peter Sutcliffe committed his offenses created problems for investigators, who were unsure where to focus their attention. It is likely that he chose different locations to avoid capture or to avoid areas where girls might be more alert to the possibility of abduction and murder. A primitive attempt at geographic profiling, involving pins and lengths of string, told police that the killer lived in the Manningham or Shipley area of Bradford. Sutcliffe actually lived in Heaton, midway between Manningham and Shipley.

Case History: Peter Sutcliffe

▶ **October 30, 1975**   Sutcliffe kills prostitute Wilma McCann (28) in Leeds.

▶ **January 20, 1976**   Prostitute Emily Jackson (42) is found dead in Leeds.

▶ **February 5, 1977**   Irene Richardson (28) dies in Roundhay Park, Leeds.

▶ **April 23, 1977**   He kills Patricia Atkinson (32) in Bradford.

▶ **June 26, 1977**   He stabs and bludgeons Jayne MacDonald (16) to death. She is not a prostitute; the public takes notice.

▶ **October 1, 1977**   He murders prostitute Jean Jordan (21) in Manchester's Southern Cemetery.

▶ **January 21, 1978**   He kills Bradford prostitute Yvonne Pearson (22).

▶ **January 31, 1978**   Sutcliffe murders Helen Rytka (18) in Huddersfield.

▶ **May 16, 1978**   He kills Vera Millward (41) in the parking lot of Manchester Royal Infirmary.

▶ **April 4, 1979**   He murders clerk Josephine Whitaker (19) in Halifax.

▶ **September 2, 1979**   Barbara Leach (20) is killed close to her Bradford University lodgings.

▶ **August 18, 1980**   Sutcliffe kills Marguerite Walls (47) in Farsley.

▶ **November 17, 1980**   He murders Leeds University student Jacqueline Hill (20).

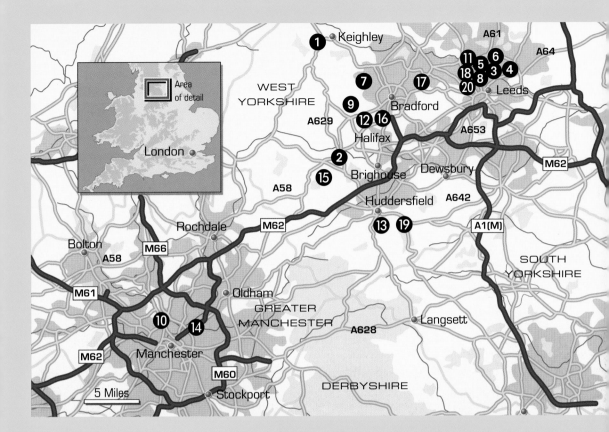

Locations of the Attacks

1 **Keighley**—Unsuccessful attack on Anna Rogulskyi, July 1975

2 **Halifax**—Unsuccessful attack on Olive Smelt, July 1975

3 **Chapeltown, Leeds**—Wilma McCann murdered, October 1975

4 **Roundhay Road, Leeds**—Emily Jackson murdered, January 1976

5 **Chapeltown, Leeds**—Marcella Claxton attacked, May 1976

6 **Roundhay Park, Leeds**—Irene Richardson murdered, February 1977

7 **Bradford**—Patricia Atkinson murdered, April 1977

8 **Scott Hall Avenue, Leeds**—Jayne McDonald murdered, June 1977

9 **Bradford**—Maureen Long attempted murder, July 1977

10 **Manchester**—Jean Jordan killed, October 1977

11 **Gipton Avenue, Leeds**—Marilyn Moore attempted murder, December 1977

12 **Bradford**—Yvonne Pearson killed, January 1978

13 **Huddersfield**—Helen Rytka killed, January 1978

14 **Manchester**—Vera Millward killed, May 1978

15 **Halifax**—Josephine Whitaker killed, April 1979

16 **Bradford**—Barbara Leach killed, September 1979

17 **Farsley**—Marguerite Walls killed, August 1980

18 **Headingley, Leeds**—Upadhya Bandara attempted murder, October 1980

19 **Huddersfield**—Theresa Sykes attempted murder, November 1980

20 **Headingley, Leeds**—Jaqueline Hill murdered, November 1980

Christopher Wilder:
The Beauty Queen Killer

By most people's standards, Christopher Wilder was a successful man. While living in Boynton Beach, Florida, he had made several million dollars from shrewd real estate dealings. He was a troubled man, however, and during an extraordinary three-month spree, lasting from February to April 1984, he killed at least eight women. Roaming across the United States, he killed in Florida, Texas, Oklahoma, Nevada, California, and New York, before eventually shooting himself during a struggle with police in New Hampshire. His interstate rampage resulted in changes in the way police approached murders occurring over a larger area and involving a wider range of methods than might be expected of most serial killers.

A Rough Start

Christopher Bernard Wilder was born in Australia in 1945, son of a U.S. naval officer and an Australian woman. He almost died at birth and then, at the age of two, almost drowned in a swimming pool. His bad luck persisted into his third year, when he suffered an attack of convulsions.

Dangerous Fantasies. At the age of 17, he pleaded guilty to participating in a gang rape on a Sydney beach. He was put on probation and ordered to undergo counseling and a course of electroshock treatments (now known as electroconvulsive therapy, or ECT). It was noticed that he felt an intense need to dominate women and even hold them captive. He also developed fantasies of subjecting women to electric shocks while having sex with them, and some authorities felt that the course of ECT may actually have intensified his sexual compulsions.

In 1968 Wilder married at the age of 23, but his wife stayed for only a week before leaving him.

In Trouble Again

In 1969 he immigrated to the United States. He moved to Boynton Beach, where he prospered during a construction boom, later getting into real estate and amassing a small fortune. He had all the trappings of a wealthy young man—a speedboat, sports cars, and a luxurious home with an indoor-outdoor swimming pool.

His unsavory urges were never far away, however. In 1971 he was arrested on various sexual misconduct charges after trying to persuade women to pose for photographs in the nude. Despite several convictions, Wilder was never jailed for any of these crimes and was slapped on the wrist with a fine. At one point, he was accused of forcing a high-school-age girl in a house he was renovating to have oral sex. Although two psychiatrists who examined him recommended that he receive treatment in a supervised, structured environment, when his case went to trial he was simply acquitted, with no provisions for any kind of treatment. Three years later, he committed rape.

Christopher Bernard Wilder in an undated photo released by the police in 1984.

Crimes Escalate

Using the name "David Pierce," Wilder approached two girls in a shopping mall, telling them he needed models for a photo shoot. One of the girls agreed to go with him, and he drugged and raped her in his truck. She went to the police, and he was arrested, but once again he got off lightly with no jail time, sentenced merely to probation and a course of treatment with a sex therapist.

More Trouble in Australia. Wilder returned to Australia to visit his parents in 1982, but while there he was charged with abducting and raping two 15-year-old girls. After his parents posted bail for him, he was allowed to return to the United States to await trial. But the trial was subject to frequent postponements. It was finally scheduled for April

1984, but by then at least eight young women were dead, and so was Christopher Wilder.

First Murders

His first murder victim was 20-year-old model Rosario Gonzalez, who was last seen on February 26, 1984, at the Miami Grand Prix, where Wilder was racing his Porsche 911.

Less than two weeks later, on March 5, Elizabeth Kenyon, a Miss Florida finalist and teacher of emotionally disturbed children, disappeared after driving out of the parking lot at the school where she worked.

Christopher Wilder slumped over the wheel of his car after shooting himself to death as police attempted to apprehend him on Friday, April 13, 1984, in Colebrook, New Hampshire. His boot and sock are shown lying on the ground beside the car after police used his foot for identification purposes.

Previously Acquainted. As the police were treating Beth Kenyon's disappearance as a simple missing persons case and not an abduction, her father hired a private investigator to look into her acquaintances. One of the friends he turned up was Christopher Wilder, who had even on one occasion proposed marriage to Beth, although at 17 years her senior, she turned him down, deciding he was probably too old.

It turned out that Wilder had also been an acquaintance of Rosario Gonzalez prior to her disappearance, but when police officers went to talk to Wilder about the two missing women, he had already fled. Neither of these two women has been found.

On the Move. On March 18, 1984, two hours north of his home in Boynton Beach, he used his old trick of promising a modeling career to lure pretty 21-year-old Terry Ferguson from a shopping mall in Satellite Beach. An hour later, he was phoning for a tow truck to get his car out of some sand near Canaveral Groves. He was alone with his car, and Terry Ferguson's body would be discovered nearby five days later.

Torture in a Motel Room. On March 20, in a Tallahassee shopping mall, Wilder approached an attractive 19-year-old co-ed from Florida State University, offering her a modeling assignment. When she hesitated in the mall's parking lot, he punched her in the stomach and threw her in the trunk of his car. He took her to a motel room, where he raped her and glued her eyes shut, using a hair dryer to dry the glue.

At one point, he produced an electrical contraption with a switch and two copper wires that he used to apply painful electric shocks to her feet. Later that night, she began to struggle with him, managing to get into the bathroom where she pounded on the wall and screamed for help. Panicking, Wilder quickly packed his suitcase and fled. He headed for Texas and his next victim.

Ten Most Wanted List

On March 21, 1984, in Beaumont, Texas, Wilder asked 24-year-old Terry Walden if she had ever thought of becoming a model. She declined his offer, but on March 23, she disappeared. He dumped her body in a canal and transferred the stolen license plates he was using to her Mercury Cougar. She was found on March 26, the same day that the body of 21-year-old Suzanne Logan was found in Oklahoma City. Abducted the previous day, Logan had been raped and tortured before being stabbed to death.

On March 29, Sheryl Bonaventura ate with Wilder in a Silverton, Colorado, diner, where she told friends there that they were driving to Las Vegas together. Sheryl was shot and stabbed in Utah, but her body would not be found until May. Wilder made it to Las Vegas, where on April 1, 17-year-old model Michelle Korfman disappeared. Her body would not be found until May 13. On April 3, the manhunt intensified as the FBI placed Wilder on its Ten Most Wanted list.

An End to Modeling Days

As 16-year-old Tina Marie Risico left a store north of Torrance, California, Wilder approached her, offering her $100 to model for a billboard he was shooting. After posing for some "test shots," Risico told him she wanted to go home, but Wilder turned nasty, pulling out a revolver and sticking the barrel in her mouth. He chillingly told her that her modeling days were over. For the next few days, Tina Marie would become Wilder's unwilling accomplice, assaulted and then intimidated into believing that the only way she and other potential victims would survive would be by following his orders.

Forced into Becoming an Accomplice. Wilder drove Tina Marie to El Centro, California, and raped her in a motel room. He did not kill her, however. It seemed as if he believed that she could be useful to him by helping him capture other victims.

With the police now aware that Wilder had abducted Tina Marie Risico, and the newspapers and television news full of pictures of him, he drove east, staying in Taos, New Mexico, on April 7.

Left for Dead. Wilder headed north for Gary, Indiana, where he sent his captive accomplice into a store after a young woman, Dawnette Wilt. Tina Marie introduced herself and told Dawnette that the manager would like to speak to her outside. Wilder was waiting for her with a gun. He forced her into the car, and at a hotel in Ohio, he used his electric torture machine on her. After a stop at Rochester, New York, where Dawnette was again raped and tortured, he stabbed her in some woods near Penn Yan, New York, and left her for dead. She was alive, however, and managed to stumble to the road, where she was found and rushed to a hospital. When questioned by investigators, she told them that Wilder had insisted that he would not be taken alive.

The Beginning of the End

Wilder's final victim, 33-year-old Beth Dodge, encountered Wilder as she was getting out of her gold Trans-Am at a shopping mall near Victor, New York. Wilder forced Tina Marie to persuade Beth to come over to his car, and he forced Beth to ride with him while Tina Marie drove the Trans-Am. At a gravel pit nearby, Wilder shot Beth Dodge in the back before driving the Trans-Am to Boston's Logan Airport.

There, on April 13, Wilder gave Tina Marie enough money to buy a ticket to Los Angeles. She would escape with her life, but even as she

A Killer on the Run

Some sources suggest that Christopher Wilder was a killer of the nomadic type, choosing to kill as he moved from place to place, like Ted Bundy. It is more likely, however, that he was simply a killer on the run and that his urge to kill surfaced whenever he saw an opportunity. Those opportunities occurred often and in different places—in Florida, Texas, Oklahoma, Nevada, California, and New York.

This notion—that Wilder was more a killer on the run than a "nomadic" killer whose *modus operandi* involved finding victims in new places—is bolstered by a fact that Wilder had already come to understand. This fact was that one way to beat a rap was to keep on the move and, ultimately, to leave the country. His experience with the Australian authorities had demonstrated this to him. Therefore, he had fled from Florida and his crimes in that state, and he was likely to have been trying to flee the United States, too. That would explain why he went as far away as California and why he wound up fairly close to the Mexican border when he traveled to Taos, New Mexico. For some unknown reason, he turned away from the border and headed north. It may be that he had decided that Canada was a better bet as a hiding place. In fact when he died in New Hampshire, he was only 10 minutes from the Canadian border.

boarded the plane she feared being shot in the back by Wilder. She later told friends and authorities that it seemed to her that he did not want her with him when he died. Wilder knew his time was up.

The End of the Line. It finally ended later that same day, April 13, after Wilder had abducted a young woman whose car had run out of gas. The woman managed to escape from the Trans-Am, and Wilder drove on to New Hampshire. There, at a gas station in Colebrook, he was noticed by two state troopers who thought he looked like the man on the FBI posters.

They approached his car and called out to him, at which point he jumped back into his car, scrambling around for his gun. One of the troopers, Leo Jellison, leaped on top of him, and as they struggled, Wilder fired two shots. One went through Wilder's heart and into Jellison. Wilder was killed instantly, and Jellison was seriously wounded, but lived. After 47 days, Christopher Wilder's murderous rampage was finally over.

Mapping the Crime

Christopher Wilder was one of the first transcontinental killers.
He was a nomad who killed three girls and abducted, tortured,
and raped another in Florida before heading off on a murderous
rampage across the United States, killing at least another five in
Texas, Oklahoma, Nevada, California and New York. Eventually
cornered by police in Colebrook, New Hampshire, he shot
himself dead rather than face arrest.

Case History: Christopher Wilder

▶ **February 26, 1984**   Model Rosario Gonzalez (20) is abducted from the Miami
Grand Prix and never seen again.

▶ **March 5, 1984**   Beauty pageant finalist Elizabeth Kenyon (23) is abducted
after leaving work and is never seen again.

▶ **March 18, 1984**   Theresa Ferguson (21) is lured away from a shopping mall
in Satellite Beach, Florida, and murdered, then dumped at
Canaveral Groves. Her body is discovered on March 23.

▶ **March 20, 1984**   An unknown student (19) from Florida State University is
abducted from a Tallahassee shopping mall. He drives her
to a motel in Bainbridge, Georgia, where she is tortured
and raped. She raises the alarm, and Wilder flees.

▶ **March 21, 1984**   Wilder approaches Terry Walden (24) in Beaumont, Texas.
She disappears two days later. Her body is dumped in a
canal, where it is found on March 26.

▶ **March 26, 1984**   The body of Suzanne Logan (21), who had last been seen
the day before in Oklahoma City, is found in Milford Lake.

▶ **March 29, 1984**   Wilder persuades Sheryl Bonaventura (18) to drive to Las
Vegas with him. She is murdered in Utah on March 31,
and her body is found on May 3.

▶ **April 1, 1984**   Michelle Korfman (17) disappears in Las Vegas. Her body
is found on May 13 north of Los Angeles, in the Angeles
National Forest.

▶ **April 12, 1984**   Beth Dodge (33) is shot in the back and dumped at a
gravel pit not far from the site of her abduction near
Victor, New York.

Locations of the Abductions and Murders

❶ Miami, Florida—Rosario Ganzales abducted, February 1984

❷ Miami, Florida—Elizabeth Kenyon abducted, March 1984

❸ Satellite Beach, Florida—Theresa Ferguson murdered, March 1984

❹ Bainbridge, Georgia—An unnamed student is abducted and raped, but escapes, March 1984

❺ Beaumont, Texas—Terry Walden is abducted and killed, March 1984

❻ Milford Lake, Kansas—Suzanne Logan's body discovered after her abduction in Oklahoma City, March 1984

❼ Grand Junction, Utah—Sheryl Bonaventura murdered in Utah, March 1984

❽ Las Vegas, Nevada—Michelle Korfman disappears in Las Vegas, April 1984

❾ Penn Yan, New York—Dawnette Sue Wilt is abandoned after being stabbed and left for dead

❿ Victor, New York—Beth Dodge is abducted and shot dead, April 1984

⓫ Colebrook, New Hampshire—Wilder kills himself after a struggle with state troopers, April 1984

Robert Black: The Schoolgirl Killer

The farther a killer travels to commit his crimes, the more difficult it becomes to find him. Very often apprehending a perpetrator depends on an alert police officer or a curious neighbor—or the police simply having the luck to catch him in the middle of committing a crime. In the case of Scottish pedophile and serial killer Robert Black, arrest was made even more difficult by his driving a van for a living, which may have allowed him the mobility to murder around 17 girls, 5 of them in France and the Netherlands, during a killing spree that lasted 21 years.

A police mugshot of Scottish serial killer and child molestor Robert Black.

Missing Schoolgirls

A series of young schoolgirls had gone missing across Britain in the 1980s, and the police had thrown a huge amount of money and resources at the investigation, including the compilation of a huge database. The database included the names of about 187,000 people and the details of almost a quarter of a million vehicles. Nearly 60,000 people were interviewed. Unfortunately, Robert Black's name was not among those listed.

A Loveless Life

It was a life without love. For a start, Robert Black's mother did not want him, and in 1947, at the age of six months, he was put in the care of a foster couple, Jack and Margaret Tulip, who lived in the small town of Kinlochleven, Scotland. Even there, he was unlucky, however. He recalls that he was often beaten with a leather belt, and his body was often covered with bruises. At school he was known as "Smelly Robby Tulip" on account of the body odor from which he suffered, and he is remembered as failing to mix well with kids his own age.

Early Interests. Instead, Black preferred to run with a younger crowd over which he could exercise some power. His situation was not improved when his foster father died when he was five or when his foster mother died six years later.

Even as a child, he developed a fascination with his sexual organs and an unnatural interest in his anal region. As a young boy, he also developed an interest in the genitals of other children.

An Unsettled Youth. When his foster mother died, he was sent to a children's home near Falkirk, Scotland. At the age of 12, he was involved in his first attempt at rape. He and a couple of other boys from the home took a younger girl into a field and sexually assaulted her. As punishment he was sent to the all-male Red House children's home, where he experienced a stricter regime. Unfortunately, however, a member of the staff subjected him to sexual abuse while he was there. At the age of 15, he left the home, and his social workers found him a job as a delivery boy.

More Early Crimes

Black began to see the advantages of being on the road. He has admitted to molesting 30 or 40 girls on his delivery rounds, although none of these incidents was reported.

A Slap on the Wrist. Later at the age of 17, he assaulted a 7-year-old girl in a park, choking her until she was unconscious and then masturbating over her and abandoning her in the park. He was convicted of "lewd and libidinous behavior." The charge was astonishingly mild considering that he nearly killed the little girl.

To allow him to make a fresh start, social-services authorities sent him to Grangemouth, the town in which Black had been born, where he worked in a building supply company. It was soon discovered that he was molesting the 9-year-old granddaughter of his landlady. The girl's family did not want to involve the police, but word got out, and Black lost his job. He returned to Kinlochleven but shortly after was convicted of assaulting a 7-year-old girl. In March 1967, he was sentenced to a young offenders' institution at Polmont.

Living a Secret Life in London. After his release, Black left Scotland, where he was beginning to become too well known, and settled in London, where he could remain relatively anonymous. During the 1970s, he managed to avoid any criminal convictions. Thanks in part to his discovery of child pornography, however, his obsession with young girls continued to grow.

By 1976 Black, aged 29, was still based in London, working as a delivery driver for a company called Poster Dispatch and Storage (PDS), delivering posters all over the country. It was work that suited him, as he did not have to talk to anyone and was his own boss. In the back of his van, he kept girls' clothing that he would put on to make himself become aroused. Touring the country, he could also scout for young girls.

The "Midland Triangle"

Susan Maxwell. Eleven-year-old Susan Maxwell lived in a farmhouse near Cornhill on Tweed on the English side of the border between Scotland and England. One summer afternoon in July 1982, she crossed the border to play tennis with a friend. After the game, when her mother went to pick her up, Susan failed to show up.

Two weeks later, after a massive police search, Susan's body was found in a ditch near a rest stop on the A518 road in central England near Uttoxeter, about 250 miles (400 km) from where she had been last seen. She had been sexually assaulted.

Caroline Hogg. A year later, on July 8, 1983, five-year-old Caroline Hogg went out to play before bedtime near her home in the Scottish seaside resort of Portobello, near Edinburgh on Scotland's east coast. Her mother had told her to be back in 5 minutes, but when 15 minutes went by, she sent Caroline's brother out to bring her home. He returned saying there was no sign of her. Panic set in, and Caroline's family called the police. Numerous witnesses were later found who reported seeing the little girl holding the hand of what they described as a "scruffy man" at the local fun fair where he had paid for her to go on a ride. They were last seen walking away from the fairground, still holding hands.

Caroline's body was found on July 18, at a rest stop at Twycross in Leicestershire, England, near the A444, 300 miles (483 km) from home and just 25 miles (40 km) from where Susan Maxwell had been found.

Sarah Harper. Three years later, on March 26, 1986, 10-year-old Sarah Harper went to a local shop to buy a loaf of bread and failed to return to her home in Leeds, England. Within an hour the police were called, and an intensive search was launched. A man walking his dog by the River Trent in Nottingham found her body on April 19. It was estimated that she had been dumped in the river at Junction 24 of the M1 motorway while she was still alive. The police described her injuries as "terrible."

The press and public were on high alert, horrified by the ages of the victims and the increased viciousness of their deaths. It was clear that the three killings were linked, and the media began to call the area in which the girls' bodies were found the "Midland Triangle."

A Failed Abduction and Arrest

Robert Black was ultimately caught by the vigilance of a neighbor of a little girl in the quiet village of Stow, just over the border into Scotland. As he worked in his garden, he saw her being bundled into a van, and he immediately alerted the girl's parents and called the police.

Black, having done a U-turn, was driving back through the village, heading south when the neighbor spotted him. Police ran onto the road

to try to stop him, and he swerved and brought the van to a halt. He was handcuffed and arrested, and his latest victim was found in the back of the vehicle. Black denied the killings that preceded his latest attempted abduction, but the unique pattern of his crimes and the sites where the bodies were dumped allowed detectives to build a good case against him.

Although his employer, PDS, did not keep daily records of journeys for very long, the payments they made to drivers were related to the length of the journeys they took. Black's earnings were high for the days on which each of the girls was abducted. Furthermore, the company credit card had records of gasoline purchases.

Officers plowed through reams of receipts in order to place Black near the scenes of the abductions. Black had filled his tank both before and after abducting Susan Maxwell, allowing police to map his route at the time in question. On the second of those fueling stops, he would have pulled into the gas station with Susan tied up in the back of the van.

Unsolved Murders. Travel afforded Black untold opportunity to indulge in his particular brand of horror. He was in France when three young girls were murdered, in Germany when another girl died. Some time he spent in Belfast, Northern Ireland, coincided with the unsolved murders of young girls there.

Conviction and Sentence

On May 19, 1994, he was sentenced to life imprisonment and told that he should serve at least 35 years. He will remain behind bars until at least 2029, when he will be 82.

HOLMES

Following the conviction of Peter Sutcliffe, also known as the Yorkshire Ripper, in 1981, the report on the case, entitled the "Byford Report," was severely critical of many elements of the investigation. Criticism included the management of the huge amount of data obtained from both police work, as well as tips and information provided by members of the public. The British police learned that they required better management systems, especially computers to collect information and crime analysts to scientifically analyze the data provided.

The computer system HOLMES (Home Office Large Major Enquiry System) was introduced in 1986 to enable law enforcement officers to improve the effectiveness of their investigations. As an administrative support system that helped senior officers manage the increasing complexities of investigating major crimes, HOLMES was put in place to process huge quantities of information.

When police figured out that the murders of the three little girls in the case for which Robert Black would eventually be arrested were linked, HOLMES was used in establishing a pattern in the actions of the killer.

Of course the HOLMES system was not of itself able to solve crimes, and one major flaw was its inability to link crimes. It still relied on an operator to set parameters upon which searches of its database could be made. Then, of course, that operator had to decide what the results of the search actually meant.

A new, improved version, HOLMES 2, was introduced in 1994 and made available in 2000. It is more flexible and provides quicker and more efficient access to information.

Footnote to the Terror: Another Charge in the New Millennium.

In 2010 Robert Black was charged with the killing of 9-year-old Jennifer Cardy, who disappeared while riding her bike to a friend's home in Balinderry, Northern Ireland, in August 1981. Her body was found six days later at a rest stop near Belfast, 22 miles from where she was abducted. Black's gasoline receipts show that he had been in that area at the time of Jennifer's abduction and murder. Legal experts have predicted that, with the huge amount of evidence and procedures to sift through, the case may not come to trial until at least the year 2020. In the words of one expert, "He is more likely to die in prison than go before a jury."

Mapping the Crime

The job with PDS was perfect for a predator like Robert Black. He was his own boss, able to deviate slightly from his route and search for young victims in the communities alongside the roads on which he traveled. He was free to dispose of their bodies hundreds of miles from where he had abducted them, adding complexity to the ensuing police investigation. Without the alertness of the man in Stow, when Black tried to abduct his last victim, it is doubtful if he would have been caught for a very long time, and the "Midland Triangle" would have become the last resting place of many more victims. The work of the police in mapping his route using receipts for purchases of gas was groundbreaking at a time when using computers in police investigations was in its infancy.

Case History: Robert Black

▶ **1959**
At the age of 12, Robert Black attempts his first rape while a resident of a children's home in Falkirk, Scotland.

▶ **1964**
Black is convicted of "lewd and libidinous" behavior after nearly choking a 7-year-old girl to death and sexually molesting her. He is merely issued a warning.

▶ **July 30, 1982**
Black abducts Susan Maxwell (11) near the border between England and Scotland and dumps her body 250 miles (400 km) away in central England.

▶ **July 8, 1983**
Black abducts Caroline Hogg (5) from Portobello, near Edinburgh. He dumps her body 25 miles (40 km) from where Susan Maxwell was found.

▶ **March 26, 1986**
Black abducts Sarah Harper (10) from Morley in Leeds, England. He dumps her body in the River Trent, near Nottingham.

▶ **January 2010**
Robert Black is charged with killing Jennifer Cardy (9), who disappeared while riding her bike to a friend's home in Balinderry, Northern Ireland, in August 1981. Legal experts predict that it could be at least another decade

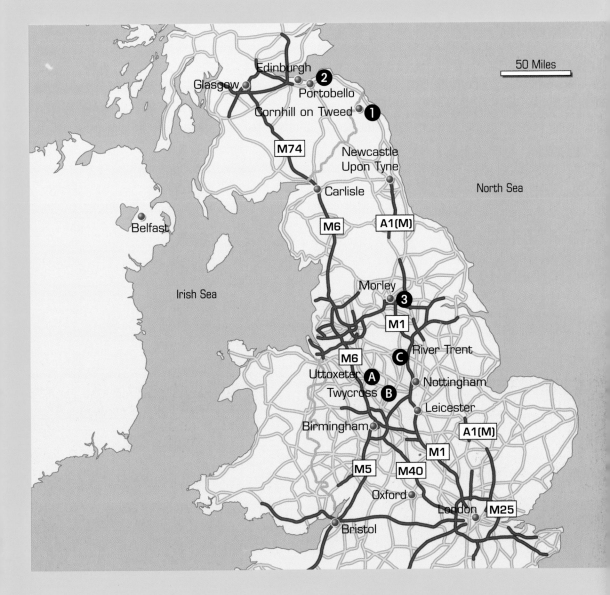

Locations of the Abductions and Murders

① **Cornhill on Tweed**—Susan Maxwell abducted; her body was found in a ditch near the A518 road near Uttoxeter **Ⓐ**, near Stoke-on-Trent

② **Portobello, Scotland**—Caroline Hogg abducted; her body found in a lay-by near to the A444 road, at Twycross **Ⓑ**, the Midlands

③ **Morley**—Sarah Harper abducted; her body found in the River Trent **Ⓒ**, near Nottingham

Edgar Pearce: The Mardi Gra Bomber

A series of explosive devices had been delivered to branches of Barclays Bank and Sainsbury's supermarkets and to individuals and businesses. The police were baffled. The packaging of the early bombs had featured a label based on an image from the movie *Reservoir Dogs*, and the police began to wonder if the bombs were the work of a group of avant-garde revolutionaries calling themselves the Situationists or of art saboteurs or anticonsumerism protesters. Or perhaps they had been constructed by disgruntled Barclays or Sainsbury's customers. The bombs failed to kill anyone, but for four years their maker, 61-year-old Edgar Pearce, managed to avoid detection by police, and no one knew where the next device might go off. He called himself the Mardi Gra Bomber, leaving analysts both before and after his capture to wonder if he had deliberately left off the "s" from the word Gras or whether, as with the bombs that failed to kill, he had simply made a mistake.

A portrait of the of the notorious Mardi Gra Bomber Edgar Pearce.

A Campaign of Terror

Edgar Pearce killed no one in his campaign of terror in the London area between December 1994 and April 1998, although one elderly woman died shortly after being traumatized when she took one of his devices home by mistake. Although the device had failed to explode, her family laid the blame for her death firmly on Pearce.

Humble Origins. Pearce was born sometime in 1937 or 1938 in the East End of London, the son of a tailor. Being a bright child, he was sent by his parents to a preparatory school in Oxford. It was expensive, however, and after three years his father was no longer able to keep up the payments. The young Edgar returned to his humble origins and attended school in Leyton. When he left, he studied advertising and worked in Birmingham before returning to London.

Anger, Frustration, Disappointment. In 1961 he married and 10 years later emigrated to South Africa, where his daughter Nicola was born. He was angered by South Africa's apartheid government and worried about the worsening political situation there, so he brought his wife and child back to London in 1976. He bought a restaurant in Hampshire, but by the early 1980s it was losing money, and he decided to sell it. It was going to be sold for £25,000, but the transaction fell through and he walked away with only £5,000. Pearce blamed the bank—Barclays—and a local attorney for his loss. The seeds of the Mardi Gra bombings were sown from his disappointment and frustration.

An image taken from a Metropolitan Police surveillance camera showing Edgar Pearce carrying a plastic bag containing a bomb.

A Bitter Recluse

Pearce was by this time drinking heavily and in 1984 was involved in a bad accident in which a cyclist knocked him down, seriously injuring him. He was in the hospital for a month and had to take painkillers for many years after. His drinking got worse, and his life became even emptier. It was not long before his wife had had enough. She left him, and he rented a house in West London.

He was now living on welfare and whatever cash he could get by illegally subletting rooms in the house he was living in. He became a recluse, rarely leaving the house and spending his days—and often his nights—watching television. His neighbors were wary of him and steered clear of him, especially after he threatened to poison their dogs after they had strayed onto his front yard. Meanwhile, he seethed with resentment at his failed deal.

"Fat Tuesday"

As the anger and resentment at the world welled up inside him, Pearce suddenly found his inspiration. One evening, he and his brother Ronald watched a television documentary about a former police sergeant in the United States, Rodney Witchelo, who had been jailed in 1990 after spiking jars of baby food with acid and broken razor blades in order to extort huge sums of money from the companies that made the products— Heinz and Pedigree.

Planting the Seeds of a Campaign of Terror. Before long, Pearce was going on shopping trips to the European continent. The supposed purpose of these trips was to bring back duty-free wine, but concealed in the bottoms of the cases he brought back with him were not bottles of wine, but explosives. He spent long hours in the shed at the back of his garden, but he was not gardening. He was creating the devices with which he would launch his campaign of terror and extortion.

Bomb-making equipment of all types was found during a police search of Pearce's home.

The Mardi Gra Experience Is Born. Pearce decided to name his campaign after the celebration known as Mardi Gras (literally "Fat Tuesday" in French, so-named because it is the last day before the period of fasting preceding Easter known as Lent). The significance of the term "Fat Tuesday" was that he planned to deliver his explosive devices on Tuesdays and the pay-off was going to be "fat." In his communiqués and calling cards, Pearce left off the "s" from "Mardi Gras" for some reason known only to him.

On Tuesday, December 6, 1994, six branches of Barclays each received a video cassette with a metal door, a shotgun cartridge, and a firing pin that Pearce had cobbled together from a nail and a couple of springs. Enclosed with the packages were labels picturing a scene from the Quentin Tarantino movie *Reservoir Dogs* and the legend "Welcome to the Mardi

The Geography of the Mardi Gra Bomber

Edgar Pearce's homemade bombs were delivered around various locations in London, and some in the areas surrounding the city, known as the Home Counties. When a geographical profiling program similar to the Dragnet program developed by David Canter (a London psychologist known for his pioneering work in criminal profiling) was laid on a map of London, it was clear that there were two distinct clusters of activity—one in West London and the other in Southeast London. Although Dragnet was not used in the investigation, investigators used something similar. They were able to establish that the western cluster was the most significant.

When it came to the eventual sting operation during which Pearce was finally arrested, police were aware that they obviously could not cover every single ATM in the capital—that would have required tens of thousands of officers. Using the geographic analysis, however, they were able to target their resources toward the area covered by the largest cluster, putting surveillance on ATMs in that area. Pearce was, indeed, arrested in Whitton, near Twickenham in West London, and he lived not far away in Chiswick. All of these towns are in boroughs in western sections of London.

It later transpired that the cluster in the southeast related to the address of Pearce's estranged wife, whom he often visited and in whose house he worked on some of his devices. Therefore, as the geobehavioral analysis suggested, he was working from two distinct bases—one in Southeast London and one in West London.

Gra Experience." Several people were slightly injured by the bombs, but police released no publicity about them. A demand for money arrived from Pearce at Barclays's head office in Northampton a couple of days later, but no response was made.

The Fury Grows. Pearce was furious and resolved to let the police and Barclays know he was serious. Realizing that the authorities would be keeping a watchful eye on packages arriving at Barclays branches, he sent packages with an improved firing mechanism to addresses around the country. There was no logic to the selection of his targets. He simply picked their names out of the phone book. It puzzled the police even more as they tried to make sense of it.

Personal

AUTHORS: Manuscripts wanted by publisher for U.K./U.S.A. Call Dorrance Publishing

IDEAS/INVENTIONS Wanted by large Intl.Co. Call ISC FREE on

MARDI GRA
We are ready to help and give value. Contact us on the verification number

One of the messages to the Mardi Gra Bomber placed by members of Scotland Yard's Anti-Terrorist Squad in the personal columns of various newspapers.

Getting the Public's Attention. Pearce even sent a device to his local pub, the Crown and Anchor. It exploded, and crowds gathered around the scene. Pearce has since claimed that he wanted to ensure that the parcels were getting through and not being intercepted by police. He also wanted to generate publicity. He succeeded. The crowds that gathered at the pub at the time of the blast were buzzing with excitement, and a few days later, as he sat quietly enjoying a drink in the corner, Pearce listened to the regulars speculate about who might have sent the bomb.

Targeting Ordinary People

Pearce continued to send increasingly sophisticated bombs to addresses in London, but he was frustrated by the lack of publicity for his campaign. The police had successfully engineered a news blackout.

Another Kind of Campaign. Pearce decided to launch his own publicity campaign, writing a letter to the *Daily Mail* saying the following:

> *Mardi Gra: A gripping story of cover up. Mardi Gra is the codename of a small group of Barclay Bank victims who are in the process of reversing the tide of fortune into their favor. After a year of activity, more than 25 devices of variable intensity have been deployed previously, our earlier devices were designed as frighteners to demonstrate political will, ability to strike, and access to a constant supply of explosive material. We are amazed that a bank or company appears to be able not to care who gets injured and get the police to keep quiet about it.*

Pearce went on to warn that he was going to start targeting ordinary people in the streets of the capital.

A New Corporate Target. Pearce switched to targeting the supermarket chain Sainsbury's, later telling police that it was because the global retailer Tesco had overtaken Sainsbury's as Britain's leading supermarket chain. With his twisted logic, he believed that, locked in a battle for retail supremacy with another chain, Sainsbury's would be reluctant to let people boycott their shops because of the threat of bombs. They would, therefore, for reasons related to keeping up their profits, meet his ransom demands.

He waited 19 months before carrying out his new plan, and then, on November 14, 1997, three devices were found near Sainsbury's branches in West London. The cassettes carried a sticker saying that if found and returned to a branch of the supermarket, the finder would be entitled to a £5 reward. Another 11 such devices were found in the following months, some exploding and injuring their finders.

Stung and Trapped

Pearce was finally trapped in a massive surveillance operation involving more than a thousand officers and covering hundreds of ATMs across the capital. As part of the sting operation, Sainsbury's had agreed to pay £20,000 into an account and had provided him with a credit card (obtained through a magazine promotion) and PIN number for that account. Negotiations had been carried out through the classified section of a newspaper. What he was unaware of, however, was that when he used the PIN, an alarm would go off at Scotland Yard.

Arrested. Pearce was arrested on April 28, 1998, as he drove away from an ATM in West London with £700 in his pocket, the first, he thought, of many such sums of money.

Convicted. On April 14, 1999, Edgar Pearce, the Mardi Gra Bomber, was convicted of 20 charges that included blackmail, causing an explosion, possessing firearms and wounding. He was sentenced to 21 years in prison.

> "MARDI GRAS. Why keep doing this if you will not talk? Your request is impossible, but I still want to help you somehow... We can then carry on with our lives. R."
>
> —A MESSAGE TO PEARCE FROM THE POLICE PLACED IN THE PERSONALS COLUMNS OF *THE DAILY TELEGRAPH* NEWSPAPER

Mapping the Crime

Police mapped the locations of the bombs and discovered that although devices had been posted to various locations in the Home Counties outside London, there was an interesting pattern to the locations in which bombs had been found in the capital. They had been left right across the city, but David Canter's Dragnet program provided a fascinating geographical profile that indicated that there were actually two centers of gravity, or focal points, within the pattern. One lay west of London. This was the area with the greatest concentration of devices. The other area was in the southeast, but there had been considerably fewer bombs in that area. This suggested that the perpetrator operated from two bases or that there may, in fact, have been two bombers, working either separately or in partnership.

Case History: Edgar Pearce

▶ **December 6, 1994**   Edgar Pearce sends explosive devices to each of six branches of Barclays Bank in North and West London. Two of them explode, injuring employees.

▶ **May–December 1995**   Pearce targets members of the public, sending devices to randomly selected addresses of individuals and businesses in London and surrounding counties. He also leaves several in telephone kiosks.

▶ **January 1996**   Pearce resumes his campaign with a bomb on a street in West London. Frustrated by the lack of publicity, he also writes to the *Daily Mail* newspaper.

▶ **November 1997**   Pearce targets Sainsbury's supermarkets with 11
   –March 1998   devices that come in video boxes containing the 1991 film *Grand Canyon*, promising finders a reward if they returned it to the nearest Sainsbury's branch.

▶ **April 28, 1998**   Pearce is arrested leaving an ATM with £700 after using a credit card provided by Sainsbury's. It had been given away as part of a computer magazine promotion, but only Pearce had the PIN that would make it work at

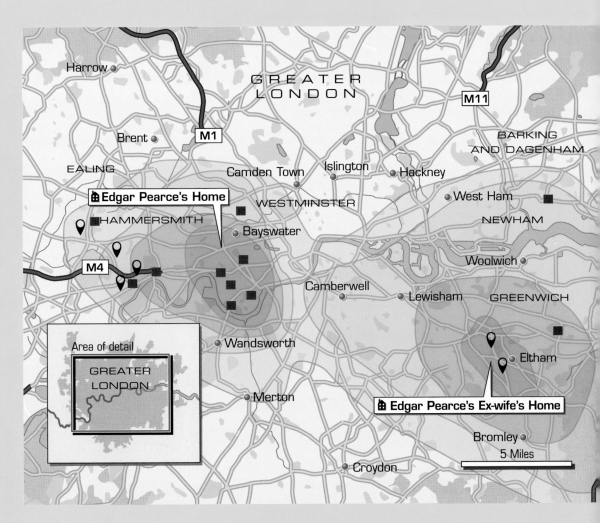

Locations of the Bombs

Locations of the Bombs

As it turned out, the bombs in the southeast were linked to the home of Pearce's ex-wife. As previously noted, geographic profiling not only helps to apprehend criminals but it also helps investigators to prioritize and efficiently use their resources. In this case, when it came to keeping surveillance on ATMs, police were able to focus their attention on machines in those two areas, especially the west.

📍 **Greater London**—Six explosive devices sent to branches of Barclays Bank, December 1994

⬛ **Greater London**—Eleven devices sent to Sainsbury's supermarkets, November 1997–March 1998

In a Lonely Place

Murderers need isolated places in which to perpetrate their dreadful crimes—remote locations away from society. The loneliness of a forest is ideal, especially a vast wilderness such as the Belanglo State Forest, where Ivan Milat brutally murdered backpackers. Robert Pickton used his isolated farmhouse at Port Coquitlam, which was miles away from anything. And Andrei Chikatilo, the "Butcher of Rostov" killed in the *lesopolosa*, a narrow strip of forested land created to prevent soil erosion.

- Andrei Chikatilo
- Gary Ridgway
- Ivan Milat
- Robert Pickton
- Steve Wright

Andrei Chikatilo was responsible for the murder of at least 56 people between 1978 and 1990.

Andrei Chikatilo: The Rostov Ripper

In the former Soviet Union (the nation made up of Russia, Ukraine, and other former states, called "republics," that are now independent nations), the authorities viewed serial killings as a Western phenomenon, a manifestation of Western decadence. So, when mutilated and sexually assaulted bodies began turning up with frightening regularity, the authorities were reluctant to admit that a serial killer was on the loose—and they were certainly not prepared to release any information to the media in case it was seen as displaying a weakness in the Soviet system. Consequently people were not given the opportunity to protect themselves or to provide information that might lead to the arrest of the murderer. As such Andrei Romanovych Chikatilo, the so-called "Rostov Ripper," was free to continue the murderous rampage that between 1978 and 1990 took the lives of at least 56 women, girls, and boys.

Andrei Chikatilo in his courtroom cage. His head was shaved as a standard prison precaution against lice infestation, but it had the effect of making Chikatilo look evil, especially when he shouted threats and insults, rolled his eyes, and pretended to be insane.

A Dawning Awareness of Horror

In the beginning, only a few senior officials entertained suspicions that the same man was responsible for the string of vicious murders in the Rostov district of southern Russia. On September 6, 1983, however, when the Soviet Public Prosecutor formally linked six of the murders, concluding that a serial killer was at work, authorities in the government and law enforcement began to concede that something had to be done.

A Profiler Enters the Investigation. A police task force, made up of Moscow detectives and headed by Major Mikhail Fetisov, was formed. Fetisov centered his investigations on the coal-mining town of Shakhty, where many of the victims had met their fate, and brought in a forensic analyst, the profiler Victor Burakov.

Vagrants, Runaways, and Prostitutes. The younger victims were often vagrants or runaways, approached at bus and train stations and enticed into a secluded area such as a forest with a promise of seeing some rare stamps, films, or coins. There he would kill them, usually stabbing them in a frenzied attack before eviscerating them, although on occasion he beat them to death or strangled them. In many cases, it appeared that he tried to gouge out their eyes with a knife.

A dirt path running through a wooded area of Aviator Park in Rostov, where the bodies of two of Andrei Chikatilo's victims were found.

His adult female victims were usually prostitutes, who were far more easily led to places away from prying eyes. He would try to have intercourse with them but often seems to have failed to stay physically aroused. This prompted him to fly into a murderous rage during which he would stab the victim, ultimately achieving orgasm as he did so.

"Killer X"

The brutality of the murders, coupled with their sexual nature, led detectives to initially believe that a mentally ill person, a pedophile, or a sex offender must have committed them. They checked the files of everyone in the area who fell into those categories. They also targeted known homosexuals, one of whom committed suicide in his cell after being interrogated. Another man, Aleksandr Kravchenko, a sex offender, confessed under torture and was hanged in 1984. Even after his death, however, the bodies continued to appear.

Profiler Burakov made efforts to analyze the motives of the unknown suspect, for whom he coined the name "Killer X." Investigators were particularly interested in why the killer paid such close attention to his victims' eyes. One reminded his colleagues of the old Russian superstition that the last image seen before death remains imprinted on the eyes of the deceased. Could Killer X merely have been superstitious?

A Profile Emerges. The profile that was eventually compiled described Killer X as a sexual deviant who believed himself to be particularly special—gifted or talented in some way. According to the profile, he wished to exercise control over his victims, and his mutilation of sexual organs was his way of demonstrating his power over women. He was undoubtedly heterosexual, even slicing off the genitals of his young male victims to make them appear female. His sexual gratification was undoubtedly derived from watching others die, and in his mind the stabbings represented sexual penetration.

Grotesque Souvenirs? Investigators noted that internal organs were often missing from the bodies. It was presumed that the killer was keeping them as trophies or possibly even eating them. He was estimated to be aged between 45 and 50, and investigators knew from boot prints found at the scenes that he had size 10 feet. Still, however, they got no closer to catching him.

A Frenzied Killer

It had all begun in December 1978, when the body of 9-year-old Lena Zakotnova was discovered in a sack in the Grushevka River, close to Shakhty. Lena had been strangled and sexually assaulted, and the lower part of her body had received numerous stab wounds. As he carried out his frenzied attack, the killer had climaxed sexually over her. Investigations revealed that Lena had been seen talking to a middle-aged man at a transit stop close to her school. She had walked off with the man and was never seen alive again.

Two years later, he struck again, murdering 17-year-old Larisa Tkachenko in September 1981. Larisa had been in the habit of exchanging sexual favors for a pack of cigarettes or a meal. The killer had bitten off one of her nipples and had used a stick to sexually assault her. Again he seemed to have failed to rape her, although semen was found on her body.

The following year, he became more prolific, killing seven times; in 1983, he killed eight times; and in 1984, he committed 15 murders.

The Wrong Blood Type

Andrei Chikatilo's name had emerged several times during the investigation, and he had, in fact, been interviewed nine times. He owned a rundown shack to which he took mainly homeless young women to engage in sexual acts that his wife was unwilling to perform at home. When a light in the shack was reported to have been seen on the night of the first murder, he was interviewed, but police merely surmised that he used the shack for sexual liaisons and eliminated him from their inquiries.

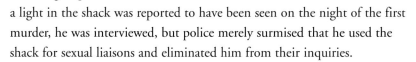

A Horrific Childhood. Chikatilo had been born in 1936 and endured a terrible childhood during which he experienced the horrors of a famine induced by government-forced seizures of crops for statewide distribution. Starvation was so widespread that there were reports of cannibalism in the region. Chikatilo experienced some of this horror when his mother told of an older brother who was kidnapped, never seen again, and thought to have been cannibalized by starving neighbors.

Photographs showing four of Andrei Chikatilo's victims. Although he was only convicted of 52 murders, Chikatilo confessed to murdering 56 people.

A Survival of Sorts. Chikatilo survived to become a teacher, but he lost his job when it was discovered that he had been sexually assaulting his pupils for years. In 1984 he had been picked up at Rostov station for acting suspiciously and was again seen a couple of weeks later accosting young people in the square outside the station. After he was seen receiving oral sex from a young woman, he was arrested. He told the police he was a businessman, but they were surprised by the contents of his briefcase—a jar of lubricant, a length of rope, and a long-bladed knife.

They were sure they had found "Killer X." His blood type was taken and compared with the blood type they had derived from semen found at the murder scenes. They were disappointed, however, to find that Chikatilo's blood was not a match for what the police had in evidence.

All they could do was convict him of stealing some linoleum that was found at his house, and for that he served a year in prison.

A Routine Check

In 1990 a massive surveillance operation was implemented in the Rostov area with 360 officers deployed throughout the Rostov railroad network. On November 6, an undercover officer saw Chikatilo emerging from woodland near Donleskhoz Station. He had just murdered a 22-year-old woman. The officer, who noticed that Chikatilo had grass and soil stains on his elbows and a small red smear on his cheek, stopped him to check his papers. When the officer returned to the police station, he filed a routine report. By now, however, the name "Chikatilo" was familiar to several of the investigators, and they decided to investigate further.

Making the Connections. When investigators checked into the records of Chikatilo's employers, they discovered that he had, in fact, been in several of the towns and cities on the dates that murders had been committed there. Looking even farther back, they uncovered his sexual assaults on pupils when he had been a teacher. He was arrested on November 20, 1990, and gradually began to confess to 36 of the killings, later confessing to even more that had not been linked to the case.

Psychiatrist Dr. Alexander Bukhanovsky looks through case files on Andrei Chikatilo. It was the first time in Soviet investigative history that a psychiatrist was consulted in a criminal case.

Resolving the Question of Blood Type. The question of Chikatilo's blood type resurfaced, but a Japanese scientist had recently discovered that in one case in a million the blood secreted into semen could be different from the actual blood group of the secretor. The authorities tested Chikatilo's semen and discovered that it did indeed match what they had found on the bodies of his victims.

Railroad and Bus Stations

Transportation hubs played a major role in the massive surveillance operations that led to the arrest of the man who came to be known as "Killer X" or "Citizen X." Rail and bus stations provided two elements of opportunity for a killer. First they are often an attraction to runaways and people at the bottom of society's social scale, such as prostitutes and drug addicts. As has been shown in the cases of many other killers, these groups of people provide easy prey for a predatory murderer; they are less likely to be missed, or, even if they are, their disappearances are likely to go unreported. Second, transportation hubs provide ease of access to centers of highly populated areas as well as a quick and easy means of escape.

During 1984 when the killer had claimed another 15 victims, a massive surveillance operation was mounted, and it almost paid dividends when authorities did in fact pick up Andrei Chikatilo, who had been behaving in a suspicious manner. The failure to match his blood type allowed him to escape suspicion of being the killer, however, even though he did spend time in prison for other offenses.

On his release, the geography of his killings changed when he found work as a traveling buyer for a train company. It was the ideal occupation for a killer, and he began to kill farther afield. Victims began turning up in Moscow, Leningrad, and places in Ukraine. Police computer systems in the Soviet Union were at the time incapable of doing the kind of work that was required to link murders and suspects with their movements.

Drooling and Raving

Andrei Chikatilo was judged to be sane, and he eventually appeared before an outraged Rostov court on April 14, 1992, protected from the public in a large iron cage. It was the first major event in Russia following the fall of communism and the break-up of the former Soviet Union. Throughout the proceedings, he drooled, raved incoherently, and rolled his eyes in pretence of insanity. With his shaved head and fierce expression, he presented a convincing portrait of a madman, but it was to no avail. The judge pronounced a sentence of death.

On February 15, 1994, Andrei Chikatilo was led to a soundproofed room, told to face the wall, and was executed with a bullet behind the right ear.

Mapping the Crime

Andrei Chikatilo often killed in close proximity to railway stations or bus terminals, because it was in these places that he was more likely to find runaways or dropouts that were vulnerable to his advances. Although he committed the majority of his murders in the Rostov area, near where he lived, his work later took him to the Moscow area, Leningrad, and Ukraine, where he also claimed victims.

Case History: Andrei Chikatilo

1978

▶ **December 22**   Yelena Zakotnova (9) is killed walking home from an ice-skating rink.

1981

▶ **September 3**   Larisa Tkachenko (17) is abducted while waiting for a bus.

1982

▶ **June 12**   Lyubov Biryuk (13) is abducted while on a shopping trip in Donskoi.

▶ **July 25**   Lyubov Volobuyeva (14) is killed near Krasnodar Airport.

▶ **August 13**   Oleg Pozhidayev (9), Chikatilo's first male victim, is killed in Adygea; his body is never found.

▶ **August 16**   Olga Kuprina (16) is killed in Kazachi Lagerya. Her body is found on October 27.

▶ **September 8**   Irina Karabelnikova (19) is met at the Shakhty station and killed nearby.

▶ **September 15**   Sergey Kuzmin (15), a runaway, is killed near the Shakhty station.

▶ **December 11**   Olga Stalmachenok (10) is abducted returning from piano lessons in Novoshakhtinsk.

1983

▶ **After June 18**   Laura Sarkisyan (15), an Armenian girl, disappears; her body is never found.

▶ **July 13**   Irina Dunenkova (13) is killed in Aviator Park, Rostov

▶ **July 24**	Lyudmila Kushuba (24) is killed near the Shakhty bus station; her body is found in March 1984.
▶ **August 9**	Igor Gudkov (7), from Bataisk, becomes the youngest victim.
▶ **September**	Valentina Chuchulina (22) is killed in woodland near Kirpichnaya.
▶ **Summer**	An unknown woman (18–25). Chikatilo claimed to have killed a prostitute around this time.
▶ **October 27**	Vera Shevkun (19) is killed near Shakhty.
▶ **December 27**	Sergey Markov (14) disappears coming home from work.

1984

▶ **January 9**	Natalya Shalapinina (17), coincidentally a close friend of a previous victim, is killed.
▶ **February 21**	Marta Ryabenko (45), killed in Aviator Park, Rostov, becomes Chikatilo's oldest victim.
▶ **March 24**	Dmitry Ptashnikov (10) is lured from her stamp store by Chikatilo, who poses as a fellow collector.
▶ **May 25**	Tatyana Petrosyan (32), a former girlfriend of Chikatilo, is killed with her daughter outside Shakhty.
▶ **May 25**	Svetlana Petrosyan (11), daughter of Tatyana Petrosyan, is killed with her mother.
▶ **June 22**	Yelena Bakulina (22) is killed in the Bagasenski area of Rostov.
▶ **July 10**	Dmitriy Illarionov (13) disappears in Rostov.
▶ **July 19**	Anna Lemesheva (19), a student, is last seen on her way to a dentist in Shakhty.
▶ **July 20**	Svetlana Tsana (20) is killed in Aviator Park, Rostov.
▶ **August 2**	Natalya Golosovskaya (16) is killed while visiting family in Novoshakhtinsk.
▶ **August 7**	Lyudmila Alekseyeva (17) is abducted at a bus stop in Rostov.
▶ **August 8-11**	An unknown woman (20–25) is murdered in Tashkent, where Chikatilo is visiting on business.
▶ **August 13**	Akmaral Seydaliyeva (12), a runaway, is killed in Tashkent.
▶ **August 28**	Alexander Chepel (11) is killed in Rostov.
▶ **September 6**	Irina Luchinskaya (24), a Rostov librarian, is killed in Aviator Park.

Case History (continued)

1985

▶ **July 31**   Natalya Pokhlistova (18) is lured from a train and killed in the Moscow area.

▶ **August 27**   Irina Gulyayeva (18) is killed near the Shakhty bus station.

1987

▶ **May 16**   Oleg Makarenkov (13) is killed while Chikatilo is on a business trip to Ukraine.

▶ **July 29**   Ivan Bilovetskiy (12) is killed in Ukraine.

▶ **September 15**   Yuri Tereshonok (16) is lured from the train in Leningrad.

1988

▶ **April 1–4**   An unknown woman (18–25) is killed near the Krasny Sulin railroad station.

▶ **May 15**   Alexey Voronko (9) is killed in Ukraine.

▶ **July 14**   Yevgeniy Muratov (15) is killed near Rostov.

1989

▶ **March 8**   Tatyana Ryzhova (16), a runaway, is killed in Chikatilo's daughter's apartment.

▶ **May 11**   Alexander Dyakonov (8) is killed in Rostov.

▶ **June 20**   Alexey Moiseyev (10) is killed east of Moscow.

▶ **August 19**   Helena Varga (19), a Hungarian student, is killed near Rostov.

▶ **August 28**   Alexey Khobotov (10) disappears outside a theater in Shakhty.

1990

▶ **January 14**   Andrei Kravchenko (11) is lured from a Shakhty movie theater.

▶ **March 7**   Yaroslav Makarov (10) is abducted from the Rostov railroad station and killed in the Rostov botanical gardens.

▶ **April 4**   Lyubov Zuyeva (31) is lured from a train near Shakhty.

▶ **July 28**   Viktor Petrov (13) is killed in the Rostov botanical gardens.

▶ **August 14**   Ivan Fomin (11) is killed on a beach at Novocherkassk.

▶ **October 17**   Vadim Gromov (16) disappears on a train journey to Taganrog.

▶ **October 30**   Viktor Tishchenko (16) is killed in Shakhty.

▶ **November 6**   Svetlana Korostik (22) is killed in woodland near the Donleskhoz station.

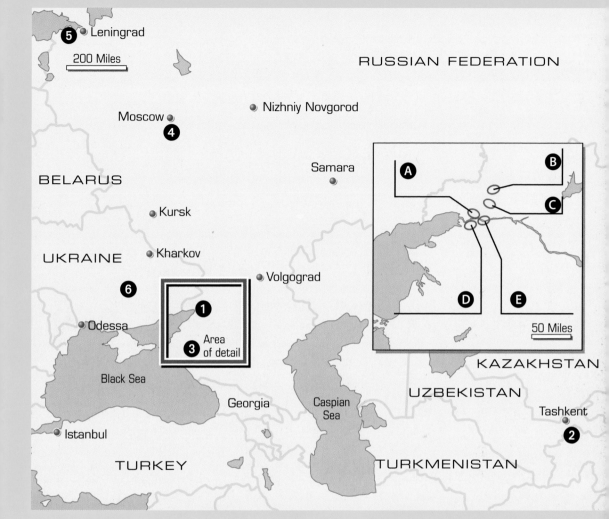

Locations of the Murders

1 Rostov on Don—At least 47 people were killed between December 1978 and November 1990

A B C Shakhty/Novoshakhtinsk/Novocherkassk area—15 people were murdered

D Aviator Park and surrounding woodland—20 people were murdered

E Rostov-on-Don—12 people murdered

2 Tashkent, Uzbekistan—An unknown woman and a boy, Akmaral Seydaliyeva, were killed, August 1984

3 Krasnodar—Lyubov Volubeyeva was killed, July 1982

4 Moscow—Natalya Pokhlistova was killed July 1985; Alexey Moiseyev was killed, June 1989

5 Leningrad—Yuri Tereshonok was killed while traveling by train, September 1987

6 Eastern Ukraine—Unknown woman and Alexey Voronko were killed, April–May 1988

Gary Ridgway: The Green River Killer

Most victims are attacked by people they know—a husband, a wife, a boyfriend, or an acquaintance. As soon as a murder is believed to have been committed by a stranger, however, the problems multiply for investigators. There is a grave danger of information overload, as in the case of the Green River Killer. In this case, at least 48 women—most of them prostitutes—were murdered between 1982 and 1998, and after an investigation lasting 10 years, police had compiled a list of 18,000 suspects. Ultimately, however, it was DNA collected from a 1987 murder that finally identified Gary Leon Ridgway as the Green River Killer.

Early Obsessions and Disturbances

It was a difficult childhood. He was born in 1949 in Salt Lake City, Utah, but was brought up in McMicken Heights, a community in the Seattle suburb of SeaTac, Washington. His domineering mother fought constantly with his father, and it affected the young Gary Ridgway badly. He was reportedly still wetting the bed at 14, and he has described how his mother used to wash his genitals, even when he was a teenager.

It is almost certain that this strange relationship had an impact on his later attitudes toward women. He was a poor student with a low IQ and an obsession with pornography. He also began to develop a violent streak, demonstrated when, at the age of 16, he stabbed a 6-year-old boy. The boy survived the attack but later described Ridgway walking away from him, laughing and saying, "I always wondered what it would be like to kill someone."

A Pair of Eyes beneath the Water

On August 15, 1982, a man was sailing a rubber raft on the Green River on the outskirts of Seattle when he saw what looked like a pair of eyes looking up at him from beneath the water.

The Green River along which the first victims of the Green River Killer were discovered.

The Body Count Begins. It was the body of a young female and next to it was another. When police officers arrived, they discovered another body on the grass beside the river. This woman had been strangled, and a pair of blue pants was knotted around her neck. The women in the water had also been strangled, and rocks had been inserted in their vaginas. One had been dead for more than a week, while the other had been in the water for only a few days.

Disturbing Discoveries. These discoveries were deeply disturbing, but there would be more—many, many more—in the days, weeks, and years to come. A few days earlier, Deborah Bonner's body had been found in the river, and another woman's corpse had been found floating in the river the previous month. When the police looked back even further, they found that the body of Leanne Wilcox had been discovered in January 1982 just a few miles from the Green River. They had a serial killer on their hands, and he had killed at least six times.

All Hands on Deck

A special task force was assembled, led by Major Richard Kraske of the Criminal Investigation Division and Detective Dave Reichert of the King County Major Crime Squad. (King County is home to the city of Seattle.) They brought on board criminal investigator Bob Keppel, who had worked on the Ted Bundy case eight years before, and FBI serial killer profiler John Douglas. The leads and tip-offs that began to flood in from an outraged public were so great that it was decided to enlist civilian volunteers to help manage it.

The murdered women had all been prostitutes, working in Seattle's main red-light area, a strip that stretched from South 139th Street to South 272nd Street. Women working there were interviewed and provided descriptions of a number of suspicious characters.

A Profile Emerges. Two more women disappeared in August and September, and a new type of suspect emerged from a profile compiled by John Douglas. According to this profile, the killer would be a confident but impulsive middle-aged man who would probably get a thrill out of returning to the murder scenes. He was undoubtedly local, knew the area, and had strong religious convictions. He would also have a deep interest in the ongoing investigation. An unemployed taxi driver who had volunteered to help on the management of information related to the case seemed to fit the profile and was pulled in for questioning. He was also put under surveillance during the winter of 1982.

Bodies Turning Up at an Alarming Rate. But women continued to vanish while this suspect was being watched, and bodies were turning up at an alarming rate. On September 26, the body of 17-year-old prostitute Gisele Lovvorn, missing for two months, was found near Seattle's Sea-Tac International Airport. Between the time of that discovery and the following April, 14 girls and young women, aged from 15 to 23, mostly prostitutes who worked the strip, vanished.

Something Dreadfully Wrong

On April 30, 1983, Marie Malvar's boyfriend saw her climbing into a dark-colored truck that drove off. Sensing that something was not right, he jumped into his car and followed them but sadly lost them at a traffic light. He never saw Marie again.

A week later, Marie's boyfriend spotted what he thought was the same truck and followed it to a house on South 48th Street. He called the police, who discovered that the owner of the house was a truck painter named Gary Ridgway. The police interviewed Ridgway, but he denied having ever met Marie Malvar. The cops believed him and dropped the matter, even though a similar truck had also been involved in the disappearance of another woman.

Nine girls and young women disappeared during the summer of 1983,

King County detectives search for evidence in the backyard of Gary Ridgway's home in Auburn, Washington, on December 3, 2001. Ridgway had been arrested four days earlier after DNA evidence linked him to the deaths of four of the Green River victims.

and bodies kept turning up. In June the remains of an unidentified 17- to 19-year-old female were found on Southwest Tualatin Road; in August, the bodies of Shawnda Summers and another unidentified woman were found close to the airport. A thorough search of the area around the airport in late October uncovered the skeleton of 22-year-old Kelly Ware. The body of Mary Meehan was found on November 13, surrounded by a bizarre array of items including a piece of clear plastic tube, three small bones, two yellow pencils, two small pieces of plastic, and, near her pubic hair, a large clump of hair. Before Christmas, another nine women disappeared and another three bodies were discovered.

Five Dumping Sites

The discovery of the skull of Kimi-Kai Pitsor in Auburn, near Mountain View Cemetery, also marked the discovery of the fifth such dumping ground used by the killer. Interestingly profiler John Douglas noted that most of the victims had been found near areas where waste was illegally dumped. The killer dumped the women's bodies in such places, he deduced, because he considered them to be no more than "human garbage."

Criticism of the investigation began to mount. A huge amount of money and resources were being put into the hunt, and it would eventually cost $20 million. Investigators even enlisted the help of another serial killer, Ted Bundy, to try to figure out the killer's rationale. Although John Douglas learned a great deal about the mind of a serial killer—and even extracted more confessions from Bundy concerning his own crimes—it brought investigators no closer to finding the culprit.

The Evidence Again Points to Ridgway

As bodies continued to be found, Gary Ridgway once again emerged as a suspect. He took a lie detector test, but he passed with flying colors and was released. However, his criminal record unveiled an interesting past. In 1980 he had been accused of trying to choke a prostitute near the airport but had never been charged. Investigators also discovered that in 1982 he had been stopped with a prostitute in his car. Her name was Keli McGuiness, and she had since been listed as missing. When they checked Ridgway's work records,

A bound and chained Gary Ridgway enters the courtroom of the King County Courthouse in Seattle during his trial.

HITS

The Homicide Investigation Tracking System known as HITS emerged from the deaths of the girls and young women in the Green River Killer case, most of them killed in the 1980s. It always seemed from information about the locations of the crimes that they were perpetrated by a local man, and, indeed, some 20 years after the murders, a local man, Gary Ridgway, was convicted of them. It was evident at the time, however, that there was a pressing need for a means of recording and analyzing murders in the northwestern part of the United States. HITS was the result.

There are numerous such systems being operated by police forces around the world, but what is different about HITS is that it links crimes with known perpetrators in the states of Washington and Oregon. It provides a wealth of information about the offenders on its database—personal details such as scars or tattoos, addresses of where they have lived, and information about whether they have lived close to the scenes of any unsolved crimes.

HITS has not only helped in the case against the Green River Killer, but also in the cases of John Allen Muhammad and Lee Boyd Malvo (the Beltway Snipers) and Spokane serial killer Robert Lee Yates.

they learned that he had been absent whenever a girl or young woman had gone missing. Still, however, there was insufficient evidence to charge him. The investigation had hit a brick wall, and by 1991 the task force consisted of just one man.

A Deadly Career

In April 2001, Dave Reichert, now the Sheriff of King County, reopened the Green River Killer case, hoping that new technology such as DNA matching might shed new light on the killings. Semen found on the body of an early victim was analyzed and found to match Gary Ridgway's. On November 30, 2001, Ridgway was arrested and initially charged with four counts of murder.

There was outrage when Ridgway made a plea bargain in order to avoid the death penalty, in which he confessed to 48 murders and committed to helping police find many of the bodies. In return, he received 48 life sentences without parole and an additional 480 years for tampering with evidence at the scene of a crime. Incarcerated at Washington State Penitentiary at Walla Walla, he has since claimed to have actually murdered around 90 women.

Mapping the Crime

Ridgway admitted to taking the lives of 48 women, 44 of whom have been identified. Many of their bodies were found in South King County, where Ridgway grew up, lived, and worked.

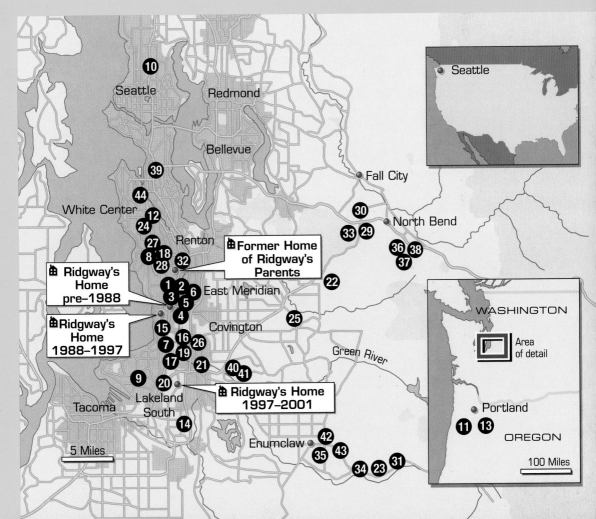

Case History: Gary Ridgway

MAP REF	DATE OF DISAPPEARANCE	NAME OF VICTIM	AGE
1	July 8, 1982	Wendy Lee Coffield	16
2	July 17, 1982	Gisele Ann Lovvorn	17
3	July 25, 1982	Debra Lynn Bonner	23
4	August 1, 1982	Marcia Fay Chapman	31
5	August 11, 1982	Cynthia Jean Hinds	17
6	August 12, 1982	Opal Charmaine Mills	16
7	August 29, 1982	Terry Rene Milligan	16
8	September 15, 1982	Mary Bridget Meehan	18
9	September 20, 1982	Debra Lorraine Estes	15
10	September 26, 1982	Linda Jane Rule	16
11	October 8, 1982	Denise Darcel Bush	23
12	October 9, 1982	Shawnda Leea Summers	16
13	October 20–22, 1982	Shirley Marie Sherrill	18
14	December 24, 1982	Colleen Renee Brockman	15
15	March 3, 1983	Alma Ann Smith	18
16	March 8–14, 1983	Delores LaVerne Williams	17
17	April 10, 1983	Gail Lynn Mathews	23
18	April 14, 1983	Andrea M. Childers	19
19	April 17, 1983	Sandra Kay Gabbert	17
20	April 17, 1983	Kimi-Kai Pitsor	16
21	April 30, 1983	Marie M. Malvar	18
22	May 3, 1983	Carol Ann Christensen	21

MAP REF	DATE OF DISAPPEARANCE	NAME OF VICTIM	AG
23	May 22, 1983	Martina Theresa Authorlee	18
24	May 23, 1983	Cheryl Lee Wims	18
25	May 31, 1983	Yvonne "Shelly" Antosh	19
26	May 31–June 13, 1983	Carrie Ann Rois	15
27	June 8, 1983	Constance Elizabeth Naon	19
28	July 18, 1983	Kelly Marie Ware	22
29	July 25, 1983	Tina Marie Thompson	21
30	August 18, 1983	April Dawn Buttram	16
31	September 5, 1983	Debbie May Abernathy	26
32	September 12, 1983	Tracy Ann Winston	19
33	September 28, 1983	Maureen Sue Feeney	19
34	October 11, 1983	Mary Sue Bello	25
35	October 26, 1983	Pammy Annette Avent	15
36	October 30, 1983	Delise Louise Plager	22
37	November 1, 1983	Kimberly L. Nelson	21
38	December 23, 1983	Lisa Yates	19
39	February 6, 1984	Mary Exzetta West	16
40	March 21, 1984	Cindy Anne Smith	17
41	October 17, 1986	Patricia Michelle Barczak	19
42	February 7, 1987	Roberta Joseph Hayes	21
43	March 5, 1990	Marta Reeves	36
44	January 1998	Patricia Yellowrobe	38

Ivan Milat: The Backpacker Killer

The Belanglo State Forest is situated south of the town of Berrima in the Southern Highlands of the Australian state of New South Wales. Open to hikers, it is about 2 miles (3 km) from the Hume Highway that connects Canberra and Sydney. In September 1992, Belanglo began to disgorge a number of bodies, young backpackers who had gone missing over recent years. Near the bodies, cigarette butts had been scattered and a fire had been lit. Perhaps the killer was comfortable there. Perhaps, as is most often the case with serial killers, he was operating in a place with which he was very familiar, in which case, these were not crimes committed spontaneously. They had been planned and committed for one reason only—pleasure.

A Grim Find

Saturday, September 19, 1992, was a gorgeous day, and a couple of orienteers were taking full advantage of the good weather to test their navigational skills in the Belanglo Forest. By early afternoon, they were deep in the forest, at a place known locally as Executioner's Drop. As they approached a large boulder, one of them was struck by a strange smell, as if something had died and started to decay. They looked more closely at the area around the boulder, and on the other side they found the source of the smell—a pile of human remains. Their discovery would spark the biggest murder investigation in Australian history.

Ivan Milat shown at home with a rifle.

Head Used for Target Practice

A second body turned up the next day, not far from the first. It was soon established that the bodies were of two British backpackers, Caroline Clarke and Joanne Walters, who had disappeared five months previously after heading out of Sydney's Kings Cross area to find work in the south.

The young women had been subjected to a vicious attack. The stab wounds on Joanne's body had been so deep that they had sliced into her spine and she also showed signs of having been strangled. Caroline had also suffered numerous stab wounds and had been shot in the head no fewer than 10 times. The forensic pathologist speculated that her head had been used for target practice.

The Forest Reveals Further Horror

The case had begun to fade from the headlines, until a local man out collecting firewood found a human skull on a fire trail deep in the forest. Police arrived and uncovered the bodies of two more backpackers, James Gibson and Deborah Everist, who had disappeared while hitchhiking in 1989. Again the wounds to their bodies were horrific; they had both been brutally stabbed countless times.

> "We could be looking for a group of brothers who spend their time in the forests shooting cans and wounding animals and generally 'showing off with each other'."
>
> —DR. ROD MILTON, POLICE PSYCHIATRIST

An Intense Investigation. Now with a major investigation on their hands, police formed a task force, known as Task Force Air, and an intense search of the entire forest was launched. Meanwhile, bullets and shell casings removed from the scene were found to have come from a Ruger repeating rifle, but it was a popular weapon and around 50,000 had been sold in Australia. Nevertheless, investigators set about examining weapons owned by people living locally.

Thousands of pieces of information were collated, including a statement by a man calling himself Alex Milat, who thought he had seen something suspicious in the forest the previous year—a couple of young women with what looked like gags tied around their heads driving past

Court officials visit the Belanglo State Forest, south of Sydney on November 1, 1994, during the trial of Ivan Milat.

him in two vehicles. Somehow he managed to convince the police that he had lost a scrap of paper on which he had written the number of the license plate of one of the vehicles, and his story was added to the growing mountain of leads and tip-offs.

More Time Passes; More Bodies Are Found. The meticulous search of the forest floor continued, and 26 days after the latest discovery, another body was found. Simone Schmidl was a young German woman who had last been seen in the town of Liverpool, west of Sydney in January 1991. She appeared to be alone and had been viciously stabbed like the others. She was partially dressed, but the pink jeans she was wearing matched a description of those worn by another missing German woman, Anja Habschied. She and her boyfriend, Gabor Neugebauer, had been missing since December 1991. Police spread their search of the immediate area and shortly after, the bodies of Anja and Gabor were found.

Horrific Details Emerge. The horror mounted when investigators concluded that Anja had been made to kneel with her head lowered and had been decapitated. The seven who had been found had each died in a different manner. They had been beaten, strangled, shot, stabbed, or decapitated. Male and female alike seemed to have been sexually assaulted in some way, and it was evident that the killer had spent an increasing amount of time with his victims as the killings progressed. They concluded that as well as being a vicious, heartless murderer, he was also calculating and arrogant.

A Vital Lead

As officers sifted through the countless pieces of information, one file looked as if it might warrant further investigation. In January 1990, a young Englishman, Paul Onions, had reported an incident on the Hume Highway. Like many youngsters, he had left Sydney in search of work picking fruit in the south and was hitchhiking just outside the town of Liverpool when a man approached him and offered him a ride.

A Scary Ride. The man, who introduced himself as Bill, seemed pleasant enough, but as the journey wore on, he became aggressive, making racist slurs. After a while, he stopped the car, saying that he wanted to get some tapes from the trunk of his car. As he did so, Onions noticed that there were already tapes in the front of the car, and he decided to get out. As he did so, the man ordered him gruffly to stay in the vehicle.

A moment later, Bill got back in, reached a hand under his seat, and to Onions's surprise, pulled out a gun. Onions wasted no time, however. He swiftly jumped out and, with the man shouting at him to come back, ran into the road and flagged down a passing van, pleading with the driver to let him in. Against her better judgment, the driver let Onions in and sped off, Bill shouting at them as they drove past.

A Delayed Reaction. Onions had reported the incident to the police, but he heard nothing further and returned home to England, and it just became a good story to tell his friends. In April 1994, however, he received a call from the New South Wales police and shortly after found himself back in Australia being shown photographs of suspects. He unhesitatingly identified one as the man who had tried to abduct him. His name was Ivan Milat.

More Than One Person Involved?

One theory making the rounds was that more than one person had been involved in the abductions and murders and that it might even have been brothers

On August 31, 2010, a police vehicle blocks access to an area of the Belanglo State Forest while investigators search for evidence following the discovery of the bones and skull of a young woman. Although suspicion immediately fell on Milat, forensic tests revealed that the remains had been there for less than 12 years.

working together. When this was discussed, the detective heading the inquiry realized that among the suspects was just such a family—the Milats.

Hard Evidence. The Milats owned property 25 miles (40 km) from Belanglo. When officers examined a vehicle that had formerly been owned by one of the Milat brothers, Ivan, the new owner showed them a bullet he had found in it when he had bought it. It was a .22, a match for the cartridge cases found at the Clarke and Walters crime scenes. They checked into Ivan Milat's work records and discovered that at the times of the murders, he had not been working.

At 6:30 A.M. on Sunday, May 22, 1994, police arrested Ivan Milat at his house at Eaglevale. Inside they found huge amounts of incriminating evidence including sleeping bags, camping gear, and clothes owned by the victims as well as parts of a Ruger firearm hidden in a loft space. They also found a long, curved cavalry sword.

Ivan Milat is led from court in Sydney on July 8, 1996. The previous day he had failed in an elaborate attempt with three other inmates to escape from Maitland Jail, New South Wales.

Guilty. On July 27, 1995, the enormous weight of evidence ensured that Milat was found guilty of the seven murders. He received seven life sentences as well as six years for his attack on Paul Onions.

In an interview after his sentencing, Ivan's brother Boris said, "The things I can tell you are much worse than what Ivan's meant to have done. Everywhere he's worked, people have disappeared.... If Ivan's done these murders," he said, "I reckon he's done a hell of a lot more." Asked how many, he replied, "About 28."

Dr. Rod Milton's Profile of the Killer

Often the introduction of a profiler to an investigation can push it in an entirely different direction, focus the thoughts of investigators, or quite simply give fresh momentum to the work of detectives. As the police were getting no closer to finding the killer, the leaders of the investigation called in a forensic scientist and police psychiatrist, Dr. Rod Milton. Dr. Milton had been instrumental in the recent arrest of the North Side serial killer, John Wayne Glover, who had murdered six elderly women in Sydney in 1989.

Dr. Milton was driven to Belanglo Forest, as he felt it was important for him to understand the crime scenes better. He needed to get a feel for the geography of the area, the manner in which the killer had approached his victims, and his reasons for leaving them the way he did.

Dr. Milton immediately concluded that the killer was familiar with the area and that rather than being opportunistic crimes, the murders were, in fact, premeditated. He also identified control as one of the signature elements of the killer's behavior and motivation. The single stab wound to Caroline Clarke's body after death and the way in which he laid out her body—arms above her head—both signified a desire to demonstrate control. The absence of Joanne Walters's underwear suggested that he took trophies. Dr. Milton chillingly informed investigating officers that the motive for the murders was likely to have been pleasure.

He described the killer as in his mid-30s and likely to be living in a semirural location; he would be employed in a semiskilled job or possibly worked outdoors; he would be in an unstable relationship with a woman, and he would have a record of violence.

When Ivan Milat's name surfaced, detectives discovered that he did indeed work outdoors, on road gangs with his brother Richard on the Hume Highway, for a company called Readymix. They learned that Ivan owned a property in the vicinity of the Belanglo Forest and that he had already been in trouble, accused in 1971 of abducting two women and raping one of them. The charges had later been dropped, but the nature of those charges supported the investigators' conviction that Milat could have been at the earliest stages in his eventual life as a perpetrator of horrific crimes.

Ivan Milat is serving his sentence in the maximum-security wing of the prison in Goulburn, New South Wales, Australia. He has intimated that he will take every opportunity to escape.

Mapping the Crime

Ivan Milat must have believed his victims would never be found in the 3,800 hectares of the thickly wooded Belanglo State Forest. Milat's targets were backpackers and travelers, and in that sense they were similar to the poor victims of West, Ridgway, and Pickton. After Milat's victims disappeared, not only did it take some time to establish that they were missing, their movements were almost impossible to establish quickly. Most of them were last seen around Sidney's main hostel and hotel district, Kings Cross. Milat was able to reach Kings Cross within a short time from his home in 22 Cinnabar Street, Eagle Vale. And the same road connected him to the isolated Belanglo State Forest, some 50 miles to the south. When he led his backpacker victims into the forest, having almost certainly picked them up as they hitchhiked along the main road to and from Sydney, he was confident that he would be undisturbed.

Case History: Ivan Milat

▶ **September 19, 1992**   Caroline Clarke (missing since May 1992).
Shot 10 times in the head.

▶ **September 19, 1992**   Joanne Walters (missing since May 1992).
Stabbed 9 times.

▶ **October 1993**   Deborah Everist (missing since 1989).
Stabbed to death.

▶ **October 1993**   James Gibson (missing since 1989).
Stabbed to death.

▶ **November 1, 1993**   Simone Schmidl (missing since January 20, 1991).
Died of numerous stab wounds to the upper torso.

▶ **November 4, 1993**   Gabor Neugebauer (missing since Christmas 1991).
Stabbed to death.

▶ **November 4, 1993**   Anja Habschied (missing since Christmas 1991).

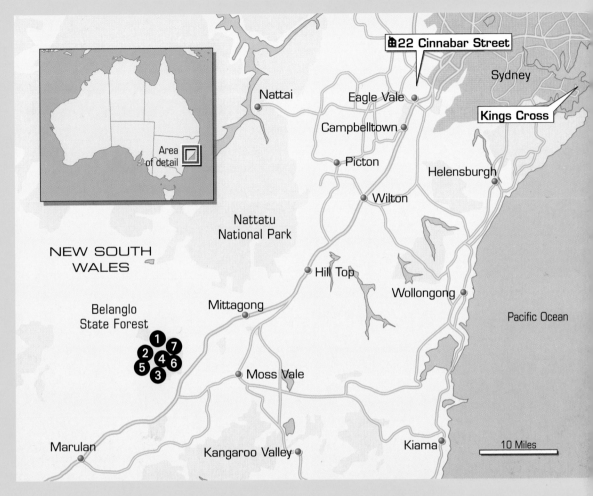

Locations of the Bodies

Belanglo State Forest

❶ —Caroline Clarke, last seen in the Kings Cross district of Sydney May 1992; discovered September 1992

❷ —Joanne Walters, last seen in the Kings Cross district of Sydney May 1992; discovered September 1992

❸ —Deborah Everist, last seen in Frankston, Victoria, in 1989; discovered October 1993

❹ —James Gibson, last seen in Frankston, Victoria, in 1989; discovered October 1993

❺ —Simone Schmidl, missing since January 20, 1991; discovered November 1993

❻ —Gabor Neugebauer, last seen in the Kings Cross district of Sydney December 1991; discovered November 1993

❼ —Anja Habschied, last seen in the Kings Cross district of Sydney December 1991; discovered November 1993

Robert Pickton: The Pig Farmer Killer

It was the case that led to the resignation of Canadian geographic profiling pioneer Dr. Kim Rossmo from the Vancouver Police Department. There had been a large number of unsolved disappearances of local women in Vancouver since 1971. They were women from all levels of society, but 16 were found to have come from the Low Track area, Vancouver's red light district. The question was asked: Could there be a serial killer on the rampage in the city? Dr. Rossmo certainly believed there was, noting a high concentration of disappearances in the Downtown Eastside, but his superiors publicly dismissed this theory. While not completely rejecting the notion of a serial killer, they claimed that, in all likelihood, the women had probably left Vancouver of their own free will. Dr. Rossmo stuck to his theory, was demoted for his refusal to let it go, and left the force.

A screen grab showing Robert Pickton, the Pig Farm Killer.

Canada's "Poorest Postal Code"

The Downtown Eastside area of Vancouver, British Columbia, is Canada's "poorest postal code," according to one newspaper. It is a squalid tract of urban wasteland, 10 blocks of seedy hotels, bars, and pawnshops. Its streets are littered with garbage, syringes, and condoms. The inhabitants of the city call it Low Track, and it is a name that has suited it very well.

Dangerous Ground. Drugs are a big business in Low Track. Heroin and crack cocaine are easily available, and many female addicts support their habits by working the streets at night as prostitutes. It is a desperate place to end up in, and by 1997 a quarter of its residents had tested HIV-positive.

In the early 1980s, the denizens of Low Track began to notice a strange and disturbing phenomenon. Prostitutes were disappearing. By the early 1990s, 14 had vanished.

Vancouver's Missing Women

It is often difficult to establish whether a girl or woman working the streets has actually disappeared. Many are runaways and move around a lot. The very nature of what they do to make money can make them evasive and difficult to pin down.

A Sad Reality. If a prostitute is not in her usual spot, it is hard to know if she has been abducted or has just moved away. The sad reality is that in such a neighborhood, there may be few people around who care anyway.

It was in this way that a number of women disappeared, and some were not reported as missing for months or even years after, while others were never reported at all.

Early Cases. Among the early cases, 23-year-old Rebecca Guno was reported missing just three days after she was last seen on June 22, 1983, but it was three years before 43-year-old Sherry Rail's January 1984 disappearance was reported.

Thirty-three-year-old Elaine Auerbach had told friends and associates that she was moving to Seattle in March 1986, but she failed to turn up and was reported missing the following month. It took 8 months, however, to report 23-year-old Teressa Ann Williams missing in March 1989 and 14 months to tell police that psychiatric patient Ingrid Soet had been gone from the streets since August 1989.

A Hiatus in the Disappearances. Three years went by before the next victims of the unknown abductor went missing. Twenty-four-year-old Tanya Holyk vanished in October 1996, and 22-year-old Olivia Williams was reported missing on July 1997, having been last seen 7 months earlier. Twenty-year-old Stephanie Lane was last seen at the Patricia Hotel on Low Track's Hastings Street, and Janet Henry disappeared on June 28,

> "Mr. Pickton's conduct was murderous and repeatedly so. I cannot know the details, but I know this: What happened to them was senseless and despicable."
>
> —JUSTICE JAMES WILLIAMS, ON PASSING SENTENCE ON ROBERT PICKTON

1997. She had already encountered one maniac, having almost been killed by Canadian serial killer Clifford Olson 10 years earlier.

Although three women vanished in August 1997, the fact was not made known to police until a year later. Another woman who went missing in September would not be reported until April the following year.

The Police Finally Take Notice. It would take the disappearances of another half dozen girls and women to finally persuade police to take interest. One girl was just 15 and another left a diary in which she had detailed the horrors of her life, writing at one point, "I think my hate is going to be my destination, my executioner."

The Search Begins

It was a difficult investigation, not the least of which because of internal disagreements about what sort of cases the police were dealing with. There had been no bodies and, therefore, no crime scenes, dump sites, or forensic evidence. The missing women's associates were, by their very nature, reluctant to talk to detectives.

A number of suspects were identified and cases farther afield were considered, with the thought that a serial killer from another area or even from the United States had transported his mayhem to Vancouver.

A poster showing 48 missing women displayed outside the courthouse where Robert Pickton was being tried. The poster was used by police when interrogating Pickton and was entered into evidence in the trial.

The Count Continues. Meanwhile, the statistics grew. More women vanished toward the end of 1998. But it was not all bad news. One woman who had disappeared in 1978 and had finally been reported missing in 1996 telephoned police in 1999 after seeing her name on a list of missing persons. Five out of 54 missing women turned up, but the rest stayed missing.

The Piggy Palace Good Times Society

Thirty-seven-year-old Bill Hiscox worked at P&B Salvage in Surrey, southeast of Vancouver, the owners of which were two pig-farming brothers, Robert—known as "Willie"—and David Pickton.

A Creepy Place. Their Port Coquitlam farm—a "creepy-looking place," according to Hiscox—was located where the Fraser and Pitt Rivers meet, on the north shore.

Hiscox contacted police after reading about Vancouver's missing women. He told them about events held at the farm in support of a charity the brothers had founded, the Piggy Palace Good Times Society. The events were drunken affairs, and the entertainment consisted of a regular supply of Downtown Eastside prostitutes.

Slipping out of Their Grasp. The Pickton brothers were no strangers to the law, David having been convicted of sexual assault in 1992 and Robert having been charged with the attempted murder of a prostitute in 1997. The charges were dismissed the following year. Unfortunately, after having had Pickton in their grasp and letting him go, at least another 11 women died. Hiscox also told police that there were purses, IDs, and other items in Robert Pickton's trailer and that he was a regular among the women working in Low Track. The Picktons became "persons of interest" and the farm was searched several times, but nothing was found and no surveillance was mounted on them.

Fed to the Pigs?

As the investigation grew, so too did the speed at which women vanished. Between November 2000 and November 2001, 10 women were reported missing. Finally an announcement was made on February 7, 2002, that members of a joint Royal Canadian Mounted Police-Vancouver Police

A Royal Canadian Mounted Police caravan (upper left) sits in the yard of the Pickton farm at Port Coquitlam on February 7, 2002, while police investigate the house (bottom) and the surrounding 28 acres as part of their investigation into the disappearances of up to 50 women.

Police investigators gather evidence during a search at the pig farm in Port Coquitlam.

Department (RCMP-VPD) task force set up to investigate the disappearances were searching the Pickton farm and adjacent property. Meanwhile, Robert Pickton was safely in custody, having been charged with possessing illegal firearms. He was eventually released on bail, but on February 22, he was arrested again and charged with two counts of first-degree murder.

A Horrific Twist. A month later, three more murder charges were added. The search of the Pickton pig farm went on for another 18 months, amid horrific reports that Robert Pickton had fed his victims to his pigs or that human flesh was ground up and mixed with pork produced by the farm. This pork was said to have never been sold commercially but was given to friends and people visiting the farm. Nonetheless, health officials could not vouch with absolute certainty that no human remains had been mixed in with pork that found its way to the marketplace. Despite assurances that the proper cooking of the pork itself would likely also destroy any diseases carried by humans, the public was understandably outraged.

On January 30, 2006, after a lengthy police investigation that cost $70 million, Robert Pickton pleaded not guilty to 27 charges of first-degree murder in the Supreme Court of British Columbia. During his trial, which opened on January 22, 2007, it was revealed, however, that he had actually confessed to 49 murders to an undercover police officer who had been posing as a cellmate.

The Verdict and Sentence. Pickton's trial was marked by disputes in the credibility of some of the prosecution witnesses and therefore in their testimony. The lack of evidence that would have convinced prosecutors to file charges against Robert Pickton's brother David was also notable.

Robert Pickton was eventually convicted of the second-degree murders of six women and sentenced to life in prison—the maximum allowed in

Kim Rossmo and the Robert Pickton Investigation

It was community groups in Vancouver that first noticed the pattern of missing women in Vancouver's Downtown Eastside neighborhood, but it was also a pattern that detective Kim Rossmo had noticed. Senior officers in the Vancouver Police Department's Major Crime Section maintained that there was a good chance the missing women had simply moved to another area, and a junior officer was assigned from Missing Persons to try to find them.

These women were mostly on welfare, however, and when people on welfare move to another location, one of the first things they do is visit the nearest welfare office to change their address in order to keep receiving their welfare checks. Rossmo had noticed that these women had not done so. They had, quite simply, vanished—and this immediately suggested foul play to him.

When Rossmo presented his analysis and concluded that the disappearances of all these women could not be mere coincidence, the officer in charge of the Major Crime investigation brushed it aside with the claim that there had just not been sufficient time for the women to be found. In time Rossmo's cluster would flatten out as the missing women began showing up, he said. However, research into missing persons nationally demonstrated that people generally only go missing for two days before turning up. Rossmo asked Major Crime a number of questions that he felt needed to be addressed: Why this was happening now and not before? Why in Vancouver and nowhere else? Why had no bodies turned up? And why was it only women who seemed to be disappearing?

Major Crime came up with various theories that seemed designed less to answer Rossmo's questions than to dodge them. These included the suggestion that these were "pimp murders" and therefore essentially isolated; that they were drug murders; or that they were all due to drug overdoses. Bizarrely, Major Crime authorities also suggested that the women may have died of natural causes but hospitals were failing to maintain proper records. Finally, the Major Crime Section argued that, having no bodies, there was nothing they could do. Rossmo has compared this conclusion to "a fire department saying they cannot respond because they only see smoke, not fire."

Canada. Because of the heinousness of Pickton's crimes, the judge ordered that his life sentence carry no possibility of parole for 25 years, which is also the maximum allowed for first-degree murder convictions. It is unlikely that Pickton will ever leave prison.

Mapping the Crime

The women that Robert Pickton murdered were members of the invisible underbelly of society—runaways, dropouts, drug addicts, and prostitutes, and it was a characteristic of their lifestyles that they were transient. When they vanished from the corner they normally worked, no one thought much of it. For Pickton, it was all very convenient, since Downtown Eastside could be reached in a short time on the highway from Port Coquitlam.

Case History: Robert Pickton

MURDERS FOR WHICH PICKTON WAS CONVICTED:

▶ **August 1997** — Marnie Lee Frey is last seen. She is reported missing on September 4, 1998.

▶ **1999** — Georgina Faith Papin is last seen some time during this year.

▶ **February 1999** — Brenda Ann Wolfe (32) disappears. She is reported missing in April 2000.

▶ **June 2001** — Andrea Joesbury (22) is last seen.

▶ **August 2001** — Sereena Abotsway (29) disappears.

▶ **November 23, 2001** — Mona Lee Wilson (26) is last seen. She is reported missing on November 30, 2001.

UNSOLVED MURDERS AND DISAPPEARANCES FOR WHICH PICKTON WAS NOT CONVICTED:

▶ **December 1995** — Diana Melnick is last seen.

▶ **1996** — Cara Louise Ellis, also known as Nicky Trimble (25), is last seen in this year.

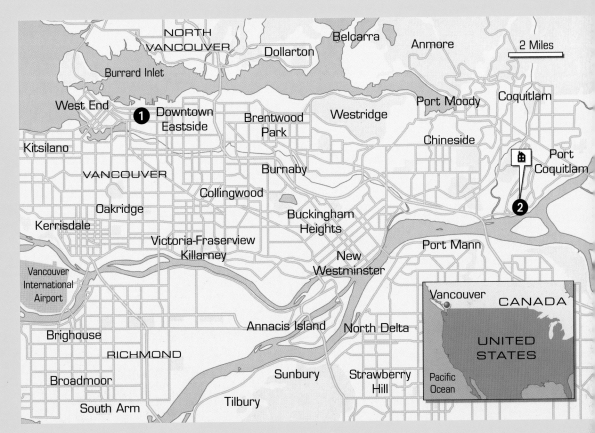

Locations of the Abductions and Murders

① Downtown Eastside—Virtually all of Pickton's victims were picked up in this area between 1995 and 2001

② Port Coquitlam—The location of Pickton's farm, where he killed and dismembered at least 6 women, and possibly as many as 49

▶ **November 20, 1998**   Angela Rebecca Jardine is last seen at Oppenheimer Park at a rally in the Downtown Eastside.

▶ **1999**   Jennifer Lynn Furminger is last seen.

▶ **December 1999**   Tiffany Drew is last seen.

▶ **December 1999**   Wendy Crawford last seen.

▶ **January 1999**   Jacqueline Michelle McDonell (23) is last seen.

▶ **December 2000**   Debra Lynne Jones is last seen.

▶ **March 2001**   Patricia Rose Johnson is last seen.

▶ **April 17, 2001**   Heather Kathleen Bottomley (25) is last seen and reported missing the same day.

▶ **April 2001**   Heather Chinnock (30) is last seen.

▶ **October 19, 2001**   Dianne Rosemary Rock (34) is last seen. She is reported

Steve Wright: The Suffolk Strangler

When prostitutes began to disappear and turn up dead a few weeks later in the vicinity of the English east coast town of Ipswich, in the county of Suffolk, police launched the biggest investigation the country had ever seen, involving 600 officers from almost every police force in England. Five separate incident rooms were established at the Suffolk Police headquarters at Martlesham Heath, near Felixstowe, Suffolk. Ultimately, however, it was meticulous forensic science work that brought Steve Wright, the "Suffolk Strangler," to justice, but not before five women had lost their lives between October 30 and December 10, 2006.

Red Light Disappearances

Late on November 1, 2006, Kerry Nicol, a cleaner from Ipswich, Suffolk, called Suffolk Police to report that her 19-year-old daughter, Tania, had not returned home after going out the previous evening. Police launched a missing person investigation that quickly revealed that, unknown to Mrs. Nicol, her daughter, a user of heroin since the age of 16, had become a prostitute a few weeks earlier.

A policeman stands guard outside of Steve Wright's Victorian era home. The windows have been boarded up to prevent illegal entry.

More Women Missing. On November 15, another prostitute was reported missing. Twenty-five-year-old Gemma Adams, who was also a heroin addict, had last been seen on West End Road in Ipswich. Seventeen days later, her body was found in a river at Hintlesham. She was naked but had not been sexually assaulted.

A third woman, Annette Nicholls, a 29-year-old mother of one and also a heroin addict, was reported missing on December 8, and that same day, the body of Tania Nicol was found by police frogmen in a river close to Copdock Mill near Ipswich. She had not been subjected to a sexual assault, but her cause of death was impossible to establish due to her lengthy immersion in water.

Stay Home, Stay Alive

Police were baffled, and a sense of panic permeated Ipswich's red-light district. Women, if they were out at all, stayed in groups and tried their best to watch out for each other. They had no idea where or when the killer would strike next. The story of the murders was all over the newspapers and television news. A local Ipswich businessman offered a reward of £50,000 for information leading to the killer's arrest, while the tabloid Sunday newspaper, the *News of the World*, offered £250,000.

More Details Than Can be Managed. The response from the public was impressive. The authorities received about 3,000 calls a day on a hotline from people who believed they had information. So great was the weight of detail that was being produced that local police established a system called Miriweb that linked into a network of other British police forces' systems.

It was a massive job. The investigation was very fast moving, and police had to be ready to respond to daily developments. Meanwhile, police searched 176 separate sites in the Ipswich area and carried out around 1,500 door-to-door inquiries.

When the body of another young woman, 24-year-old Anneli Alderton (who was, like the others, also a heroin user), was discovered on December 10 in the woods in front of Amberfield School near the village of Nacton, just outside Ipswich, the investigation found itself with more information to digest and analyze. Anneli had not been reported missing but had last been seen getting off of a train in the town of Manningtree at 6:15 P.M. on December 3. When found, she was naked and had been asphyxiated. The killer had laid her out in a specific pose, in the shape of a cross. Around 11,000 hours of footage taken from railroad surveillance cameras was scrutinized for any clue, no matter how small.

Another Dreadful Day

December 12, 2006, proved to be another dreadful day. Annette Nicholls's body was found, four days after her disappearance, near the Suffolk village of Levington, a few miles southeast of Ipswich. Naked, like the others, she had also not been sexually assaulted. Her killer had also laid her out in the

Steve Wright, also known as the Suffolk Strangler, was found guilty of the murder of five young women in the Ipswich area of eastern England.

shape of the cross, however. It was again uncertain how she had died, but police believed her breathing had somehow been hampered.

That same day, the body of Paula Clennell, who would prove to be the killer's last victim, was discovered, again close to the village of Levington. She had been strangled, was naked like the others, and had not been sexually assaulted. Just days prior to her own death, she had, ironically, given a television interview about the murders to Anglia Television News. She told the reporter that all the women were terrified of climbing into a stranger's car, but that they had to; they needed the money. The women who worked the streets were warned by police to stay home.

A Red Herring

Naturally, police were finding suspects, and almost all of them were swiftly eliminated. One man, however, had contacted officers not long after Tania Nicol had gone missing. Tom Stephens took an inordinate interest in the case and was in touch with police on several occasions in November. On November 9 and 10, 2006, he was placed under police surveillance, so concerned were they about him. Then, on December 18, he was arrested and questioned, but no charges were brought, and he was released.

The Trial of the Century

Eventually it was indisputable DNA evidence that brought about the arrest of an Ipswich truck driver, Steve Wright. In 2001 he had started a relationship with a Felixstowe woman, and when she started to work nights, he became frustrated by their lack of sex. He had used prostitutes since his days at sea as a merchant sailor and became a regular visitor to the city's red light district, near which he had rented a flat.

Media interest in Steve Wright's trial was extraordinary, even for Britain, where sensational cases routinely receive nationwide media attention. Wright spent three days in the witness box denying any involvement with the murders and providing elaborate excuses for the DNA and fiber evidence.

The forensic evidence was overwhelming, however, and on February 21, 2008, he was found guilty of all five murders. He was sentenced to life

Operation Sumac: Unprecedented Forensic Support

Operation Sumac, as the huge police task force that was created was codenamed, involved not only officers on the street. Of the 270 scientists employed at the Forensic Science Service in Huntingdon, Cambridgeshire, 250 were called on to work full-time on the case. During the course of the investigation, they spent more than 6,000 hours examining more than 100 swabs for body fluids and DNA, and thousands of minute clothing fibers were meticulously analyzed. It was soon clear that the women had been killed elsewhere, before being dumped where they were eventually found.

It was analysis of DNA that provided the richest reward. A Specialist Advisor, Judith Cunnison, had been appointed to make sure that there was a swift forensic response to the fast-moving and constantly changing circumstances of the investigation. Twenty-four-hour support was being provided in eight different scientific disciplines.

It was because of this unprecedented support that a match to material on a swab was found on the National DNA database. The same DNA had been found on the bodies of Paula Clennell, Anneli Alderton, and Annette Nicholls. The name that emerged from the DNA database was that of Steve Wright, an Ipswich truck driver. Wright's DNA was on the database due to a 1992 conviction for stealing money from a pub he was running.

A search of Wright's car and house provided further material that would eventually help convict him. Fibers from clothing found at the house matched those found on the victims. And fibers that matched the carpet of his car were found in Tania Nicol's hair.

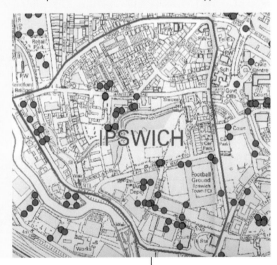

This police map shows the location of CCTV cameras in the area of Ipswich where the various women disappeared.

in prison with the stipulation by the trial judge that because of the element of premeditation and planning, in this case life should mean life.

Steve Wright is currently serving his sentence in HM Prison Long Lartin in Worcestershire, England.

Mapping the Crime

Steve Wright was a man who enjoyed sex with prostitutes. This was made convenient for him by the fact that the home he was renting was located close to Ipswich's red light district. It was relatively easy for him, therefore, not only to engage the services of prostitutes but also to find and abduct victims. He was familiar with the area, and he had easy access to a safe place if he needed to escape quickly. He disposed of the bodies of his victims on the outskirts of Ipswich, not far from main arterial roads.

Case History: Steve Wright

▶ **October 30, 2006**   Tania Nicol (19) fails to return home.

▶ **November 15, 2006**   Gemma Adams (25) is last seen on West End Road, Ipswich.

▶ **December 2, 2006**   The body of Gemma Adams is found in a river at the village of Hintlesham; she is naked but has not been sexually assaulted.

▶ **December 3, 2006**   Anneli Alderton (24) is last seen getting off a train at Manningtree. She is not reported missing.

▶ **December 8, 2006**   Annette Nicholls (29) is reported missing. The body of Tania Nicol (19) is found in a river near Copdock Mill. Like Gemma Adams, she is naked but has not been sexually assaulted.

▶ **December 10, 2006**   The body of Anneli Alderton is found in woodland in front of Amberfield School near the village of Nacton, just outside Ipswich. She is naked, has died of asphyxiation, and is laid out in the shape of a cross.

▶ **December 12, 2006**   The body of Annette Nicholls is found near the village of Levington. She is naked and, like the others, has not been sexually assaulted. It is uncertain how she died, but she is laid out in the shape of a cross. The body of Paula Clennell (24) is found, again near Levington, naked, and she has not been sexually assaulted.

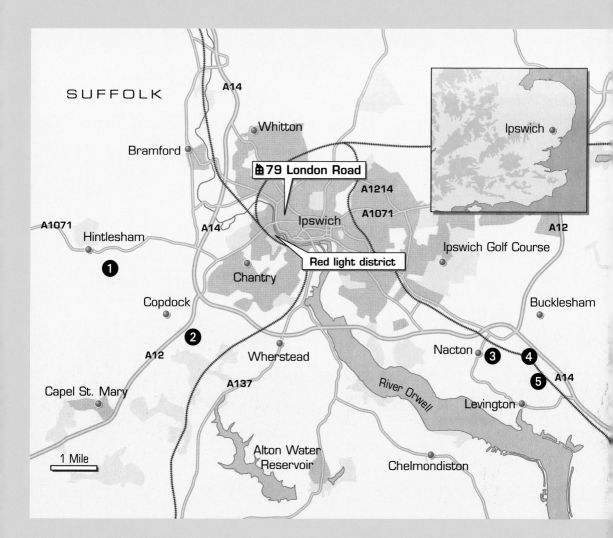

Locations of the Bodies

1. **Hintlesham, Suffolk**—The body of Gemma Adams is discovered in a nearby river, December 2006

2. **Copdock Mill, Suffolk**—The body of Tania Nicol is discovered in a nearby river, December 2006

3. **Nacton, Suffolk**—The body of Anneli Alderton is found in woodland in front of Amberfield School, December 2006

4. **Levington, Suffolk**—The body of Annette Nicholls is discovered near the village, December 2006

5. **Levington, Suffolk**—The body of Paula Clennell is also discovered outside of Levington, December 2006

Additional Reading

BOOKS

Brantingham, P.J. and Brantingham, P.L. *Environmental Criminology*. Sage, 1981.

Brantingham, P. J., & Brantingham, P. L. *Patterns in Crime*. Macmillan, 1984.

Canter, David. *Criminal Shadows: Inside the Mind of the Serial Killer*. HarperCollins, 1995.

Canter, David. *Mapping Murder: The Secrets of Geographical Profiling*. Virgin Books, 2007.

Canter, David. *Mapping Murder: Walking in Killers' Footsteps*. Virgin Books, 2005.

Canter, David and Donna Youngs. *Principles of Geographic Offender Profiling*. Ashgate, 2008.

Canter, David and Donna Youngs. *Applications of Geographical Offender Profiling*. Ashgate, 2008.

Chainey, Spencer and Ratcliffe, Jerry. *GIS and Crime Mapping*. Wiley-Blackwell, 2005.

Cyrian, Oliver; Wilson, Colin and Wilson, Damon. *The Encyclopedia of True Crime*. Sevenoaks, 2005.

Douglas, John and Olshaker, Mark. *Mindhunter: Inside the FBI's Elite Serial Crime Unit*. Arrow, 2006.

Innes, Brian. *Profile of a Criminal Mind*. Reader's Digest Association, 2003.

Kerr, Gordon. *World Serial Killers*. Futura, 2010.

Kerr, Gordon; Black, Ray; Welch, Ian and Castleden, Rodney. *Killers in Cold Blood*. Futura, 2007.

Lane, Brian and Gregg, Wilfred. *The Encyclopedia of Serial Killers*. Berkley, 1995.

McNab, Chris. *Timeline of Murder: Serial Killers*. Amber Books, 2010.

Ressler, Robert. *Whoever Fights Monsters*. St. Martins Griffin, 1992.

Rossmo, Dr. Kim. *Geographic Profiling*. CRC Press, 1999.

Wang, Fahui. *Geographic Information Systems and Crime Analysis*. IGI Publishing, 2004.

Wilson, Colin. *A Plague of Murder: The Rise and Rise of Serial Killing in the Modern Age*. Robinson Publishing, 1995.

Wilson, Colin and Seaman, Donald. *The Serial Killers: A Study in the Psychology of Violence*. Virgin, 2007.

WEBSITES

www.all-about-forensic-psychology.com

Application of Computer Mapping to Police Operations. McEwen, J. Thomas and Taxman Faye S. http://www.popcenter.org/library/crimeprevention/volume_04/12-McEwenTaxman.pdf

Crime Library. http://www.trutv.com/library/crime/index.html

www.criminalprofiling.ch

Geographic Profiling: The Debate Continues. Bennell, Craig; Snook, Brent and Taylor, Paul. http://www.psych.lancs.ac.uk/people/uploads/PaulTaylor200 70919T214403.pdf

Place, Space, and Police Investigations: Hunting Serial Violent Criminals. Rossmo, Dr. Kim. http://www.popcenter.org/library/crimeprevention/volume_04/10-Rossmo.pdf

www.txstate.edu/gii/geographicprofiling.html

True Crime Library. http://www.truecrimelibrary.com

Index

Photo Credits

Alamy: Front cover bottom, and back cover (Renegadephoto.net), 31 (Thomas Hallstein), 48 (Mirrorpix), 63 (David White), 65 (Mirrorpix), 77 (Brenda Kean), 180 & 181 (Mirrorpix), 192 (Mirrorpix)
Corbis: 9 (Marc Asnin), 11 (Dave Ellis), 52, 78 (George Frey/EPA), 86 (Reuters), 87 (Ralf-Finn Hestoft), 89 (EPA), 101 &102 (Reuters), 104 (Yoan Valat/EPA),113 (Didier Bauewergerts/Sygma), 126 (Reuters), 150 (Ron Sachs/CNP), 151 (Brendan McDermid/Reuters), 155 (Lawrence Jackson/CNP), 210 (Sygma/Epix), 220 (Matthew McVay), 223 (Elaine Thompson/Reuters), 231 (Miles Godfrey/EPA), 232 (Megan Lewis/Reuters), 236 (Reuters),

238 (Andy Clark/Reuters), 240 (Andy Clark/Reuters)
Corbis/Bettmann: 6, 16–21 all, 36, 38, 42, 44, 68–72 all, 118, 121, 123, 168, 171, 172, 177
Getty Images: 13 (Tracy Woodward), 45, 47, 105 (AFP), 119 (New York Daily News), 122 (New York Daily News), 153 (Fairfax Circuit Court), 161 (Peter Stackpole/Time & Life Pictures), 163 & 164 (New York Daily News), 178 (Popperfoto), 211–214 all (Terry Smith/Time & Life Pictures)
Press Association: 14 (Lennox McLendon), 25 (Canadian Press), 55, 56, 76, 93 (Canadian Press), 100 (ABACA), 108, 112 (ABACA), 116, 127 (Duncan Livingston), 129 (Russ Carnack), 152, 154 (Chris Gardner),

158 (Topham), 176, 185, 186 (Terry Rose), 196 (John Giles), 200, 201, 204, 208, 222 (Cheryl Hatch), 230 (Rick Rycroft), 239 (ABACA), 247 (Suffolk Police)
Photoshot: 142, 179
Rex Features: 33 (The Sun), 37, 60 (South West News Service), 61, 64, 85, 94–95 (Keystone USA), 111 (Sipa), 135 (Alex Woods), 138 (Photo News Service), 139 (News Group), 143 (Paul Lomartire), 145 (Sipa), 146 (Doug Engel), 160 (CSU Archives/Everett Collection), 195 (J. Duxbury/Manchester Daily Mail), 228 (Austral Int.), 244 (Jason Bye), 245 (Albanpix)
TopFoto: 53, 134, 137, 202 (National Pictures)